Approaches to
Teaching Shakespeare's
King Lear

Edited by

Robert H. Ray

The Modern Language Association of America
New York   1986

Copyright © 1986 by The Modern Language Association of America

Library of Congress Cataloging-in-Publication Data

Approaches to teaching Shakespeare's King Lear.
  (Approaches to teaching world literature)
  Bibliography: p.
  Includes index.
  1. Shakespeare, William, 1564–1616. King Lear.
2. Shakespeare, William, 1564–1616—Study and teaching
(Higher)   3. Lear, King, in fiction, drama, poetry, etc.
I. Ray, Robert H., 1940–   II. Series.
PR2819.A95   1986   822.3'3   86-12734
ISBN 0-87352-497-7
ISBN 0-87352-498-5 (pbk.)

Cover illustration of the paperback edition: medieval tile design (Carol Belanger
Grafton, ed., *Old English Tile Designs* [New York: Dover, 1985] 65).

Second printing, 1990

Published by The Modern Language Association of America
10 Astor Place, New York, New York 10003

CONTENTS

PREFACE TO THE SERIES

In *The Art of Teaching* Gilbert Highet wrote, "Bad teaching wastes a great deal of effort, and spoils many lives which might have been full of energy and happiness." All too many teachers have failed in their work, Highet argued, simply "because they have not thought about it." We hope that the Approaches to Teaching World Literature series, sponsored by the Modern Language Association's Committee on Teaching and Related Professional Activities, will not only improve the craft—as well as the art—of teaching but also encourage serious and continuing discussion of the aims and methods of teaching literature.

The principal objective of the series is to collect within each volume different points of view on teaching a specific literary work, a literary tradition, or a writer widely taught at the undergraduate level. The preparation of each volume begins with a wide-ranging survey of instructors, thus enabling us to include in the volume the philosophies and approaches, thoughts and methods of scores of experienced teachers. The result is a sourcebook of material, information, and ideas on teaching the subject of the volume to undergraduates.

The series is intended to serve nonspecialists as well as specialists, inexperienced as well as experienced teachers, graduate students who wish to learn effective ways of teaching as well as senior professors who wish to compare their own approaches with the approaches of colleagues in other schools. Of course, no volume in the series can ever substitute for erudition, intelligence, creativity, and sensitivity in teaching. We hope merely that each book will point readers in useful directions; at most each will offer only a first step in the long journey to successful teaching.

Joseph Gibaldi
Series Editor

PREFACE TO THE VOLUME

The world's finest dramatist appropriately enters the Modern Language Association's Approaches to Teaching World Literature series in a volume on what may be his greatest play and is probably the one most often taught in college. The volume, like all others in the series, primarily concerns itself with teaching undergraduates. It should be most useful for beginning teachers of *King Lear* and for nonspecialists who teach the play in various undergraduate literature courses. Though experienced Shakespeareans probably will encounter much that seems elementary, they may also find much of interest, including some new ideas about teaching the play; the second part of the volume particularly should offer matters of significance to specialists and nonspecialists alike. It is also hoped that many teachers will recommend the book, or portions of it, to graduate students, along with other research and pedagogical tools.

The volume follows the format established for the series. Part 1, "Materials," deals with such questions as editions, student readings, books and articles most helpful as resources for the teacher of the play (reference, background, source, theatrical, critical, and linguistic works), and aids to teaching (illustrations, slides, films, videotapes, and recordings). The suggestions in this part derive mainly from information supplied by respondents to a survey conducted by the MLA. This section makes no attempt to be exhaustive in treating the materials available on *King Lear*; rather, the intent is to be selective and to discuss those materials most mentioned, used, and valued for the practical purpose of helping one to teach the play.

The series format dictates the essential content, style, and tone of the "Materials" section. This section is not a subjectively evaluative review essay. Rather, its subdivisions are guides, aids for reference on particular topics, and are more reportorial and descriptive than prescriptive and critical. For more subjective evaluations of materials, the reader may consult the reviews of articles and books that regularly appear in such journals and annuals as *Shakespeare Quarterly* and *Shakespeare Survey*. In addition, the limitations of space in the present volume dictate mere listings and brief annotations in the "Materials" section rather than the lengthy reviews permissible for single items in quarterlies and annuals. For topics discussed and evaluated more fully in contributors' essays later in the volume, however, appropriate cross-references are provided.

Part 2, "Approaches," presents sixteen essays that describe a variety of approaches in teaching *King Lear*. Contributions were invited from those who participated in the survey, and invitations were issued on the basis of responses to the questionnaire. A range of classroom emphases, techniques, problems, and solutions are thus represented and shared with other teachers. An appendix of survey participants, a list of works cited, and an index conclude the book. All works quoted or mentioned appear with full bibliographical information in the list of works cited.

For generous assistance I am indebted to many persons and groups. First, I wish to thank the participants in the Modern Language Association survey for responding to the questionnaire; without these responses the volume would not be possible. The members of the MLA Committee on Teaching and Related Professional Activities are to be commended for their sponsorship of this series. Joseph Gibaldi, general editor of the series, provided astute suggestions and judgments throughout the project. The encouragement, advice, and insights of Maurice Hunt and Carole Slade are also greatly appreciated. I am grateful to various groups and individuals at my own institution, Baylor University, for providing essential time and funding. I particularly wish to thank James Barcus, chair of the department of English, for his full support, and William G. Toland, a dean willing to grant needed released time for faculty projects. For research sabbaticals and grants for this work, I am heavily indebted to the Faculty Development Committee and the University Research Committee. For their most efficient help in managing correspondence and typing, I thank the office staff of the department of English, Mary Margaret Stewart and Nancy Floyd.

The greatest acknowledgment for deep and continuing support must be reserved for my parents, wife, and daughters: Ben and Allene, Lynette, and Robin and Donna.

RHR

Part One

MATERIALS

Robert H. Ray

Editions

Introduction

This section assesses editions of *King Lear* now being used in courses, as reported by participants in the survey that preceded preparation of this volume. Attention is given to the relative popularity of editions, as well as to strengths and weaknesses in such areas as completeness of text, accuracy of text, commentary, introductions, notes, and physical format. Both favorable and unfavorable comments by respondents are included. This information should aid instructors in selecting editions most suitable for their particular situations and purposes.

Three categories of texts are covered here—complete, one-volume editions of the works of Shakespeare, editions of *King Lear* alone, and anthologies that contain *King Lear* among other plays or among other works of literature. These categories determine the organization of the following discussion. For full bibliographical information on editions discussed, refer to the list of works cited, where editions are listed by editor.

Complete Editions of Shakespeare

By far the most widely used edition of Shakespeare's works is *The Riverside Shakespeare* (G. Blakemore Evans, textual ed.). Supplying introductions and explanatory notes are Herschel Baker (histories), Frank Kermode (tragedies), and Hallett Smith (romances and poems). For the comedies, Anne Barton wrote the introductions, and the notes were begun by Lloyd E. Berry and completed by G. Blakemore Evans and Marie Edel. This edition contains the complete works of Shakespeare, including *The Two Noble Kinsmen* and the portions of *Sir Thomas More* ascribed to Shakespeare. Other major sections in the volume are a general introduction by Harry Levin; "Shakespeare's Text," "Chronology and Sources," "Records, Documents, and Allusions," and "Annals, 1552–1616" by G. Blakemore Evans; and "Shakespeare's Plays in Performance: From 1660 to the Present" by Charles Shattuck. The plays are printed in a double-column format with notes and glosses at the bottom of each column. After each play Evans includes a note on the text and a list of textual variants. A selected bibliography appears near the end of the volume. A generous number of portraits and contemporary illustrations are provided throughout the work.

The most frequently mentioned reason for using this edition is its textual strength. Most respondents view the text as carefully edited with a "strong bibliographical orientation" and "textual authority," and they give high praise to Evans's essay "Shakespeare's Text," with its "clearly articulated principles of analytic and descriptive bibliography." The notes on texts following each play are illuminating. For example, Evans comments on the complicated and confusing textual problems of *King Lear* and explains some of the major cruxes. The basis for his edition of the play is the First Folio, but he does incorporate some lines and readings from quarto editions. One teacher remarks that the bracketing of questionable readings within the text is somewhat distracting but that this text is still the best available for undergraduate study. Despite the generally favorable view of the text and the editorial policy behind it, several instructors indicate dissatisfaction with what one terms the "inconsistent printing of original and modernized spellings." The random archaisms left in the text seem "odd" to one respondent, and another advises the editor to "either modernize or print old spellings."

The introductory and appended sections of this edition are frequently applauded by teachers who use them. Levin's introduction provides an excellent overview. The appended "Records, Documents, and Allusions" is also highly praised as useful for perceiving Shakespeare and his works in a contemporary context. One teacher notes that two valuable and relatively unique features are the essay by Shattuck, which discusses the changing styles of Shakespearean performance, and the annals by Evans, a year-by-year synopsis of major literary and political events from 1552 to 1616.

Other features of the edition are commended. Since the line numbers correspond to those in Marvin Spevack's *Harvard Concordance to Shakespeare*, this edition facilitates research into verbal patterns in Shakespeare. The introductions to the individual plays also are generally well received. Even though some teachers feel the introductions are not uniform in quality, others value the diversity of approaches represented. Many comment particularly on the excellence of Kermode's introduction to *King Lear*, indicating that it is one of the best in the volume; one survey respondent calls it "remarkably inclusive for its length."

There are disagreements concerning other facets of the *Riverside*. Although the explanatory notes seek a happy medium in number and fullness, teachers who wish to save class time prefer more notes, whereas those who wish to provide their own explanatory information in class prefer fewer. Perhaps the majority opinion is best summarized by one respondent's comment that the notes do not overwhelm undergraduate students and are "adequate." One disadvantage to the system of footnoting in this edition is that the text provides no indication that a word, phrase, or line is explained in the notes below: line number and gloss simply appear at the bottom of the page. Also, a frequent criticism of this volume as a teaching text is very practical: many feel it simply is too cumbersome, "too heavy for students to carry comfortably." Despite the disadvantages and limitations of the *Riverside*, its strengths seem to carry the day with many Shakespeare instructors. As one says, "In general the text provides more inclusive coverage than any other single volume of the collected plays."

The edition that currently presents the strongest challenge to Evans's is David Bevington's *The Complete Works of Shakespeare*. This edition contains the same works as Evans's, except *The Two Noble Kinsmen* and the *Sir Thomas More* fragments. The volume begins with a general introduction containing "Life in Shakespeare's England," "The Drama before Shakespeare," "London Theatres and Dramatic Companies," "Shakespeare's Life and Work," "Shakespeare's Language: His Development as Poet and Dramatist," "Editions and Editors of Shakespeare," and "Shakespeare Criticism." Portraits, photographs, and illustrations appear at intervals through the introduction. Four appendixes are entitled "Canon, Dates, and Early Texts," "Sources," "Shakespeare in Performance," and "Doubtful and Lost Plays." After the appendixes come royal genealogical charts; maps of London, England, and western France; and a bibliography for further reading and research. Bevington places his textual notes near the end of the volume rather than after each play. He also includes a glossary of Shakespearean words. The plays are printed in a double-column format with explanatory notes at the bottom of each column.

The advocates of Bevington's edition emphasize its superior readability and usability as a teaching text. Its type is larger and more easily read than the ones used in other complete editions of Shakespeare. Bevington also prints speech prefixes in full and thus avoids confusion among variously abbreviated names of characters. Moreover, teachers note the easier, more rapid reading possible in an edition that numbers only those lines with ideas explained in the notes.

Several respondents praise the quality of those explanatory notes and of the introductions to the individual plays. They say that Bevington's glosses are concise and accurate and provide more than conventional views, that the introductions are "clear" and "illuminating."

Other features of Bevington's edition are admired. These comments of teachers who use it are typical: "well-edited," "sound editions of plays," "copious and reliable introductory material," "useful material on the theater of Shakespeare's day." One instructor notes that this edition has the most up-to-date bibliography and that the bibliography seems very well selected for individual plays. In general, the number of teachers already using this latest edition of Bevington's is impressive, and its adherents point out many advantages and few disadvantages in its use.

Another edition still preferred by many is *William Shakespeare: The Complete Works* (Alfred Harbage, gen. ed.). This volume does not contain *The Two Noble Kinsmen* or the extracts from *Sir Thomas More*. The plays have individual editors, though some of the scholars edit more than one play; *King Lear* is edited by Harbage. The volume contains few illustrations: it is primarily made up of the works themselves. Its general introduction contains the following sections: "The Intellectual and Political Background" by Ernest A. Strathmann, "Shakespeare's Life" by Frank W. Wadsworth, "The Canon" by Alfred Harbage, "Shakespeare's Theatre" by Bernard Beckerman, "Shakespeare's Technique" by Alfred Harbage, "The Original Texts" by Cyrus Hoy, and "Editions and Current Variant Readings" by Alfred Harbage. The plays are printed in a double-column format with notes and glosses at the bottom of the inner column on each page.

Users note many strong features. Its size makes it easier to carry than any other complete edition. Like Bevington's, this text is admired for the system of numbering lines that need a gloss or note and for printing characters' names in full. One teacher likes the "minimal use of post-Shakespearean stage directions." The introductions to the individual plays receive high praise for their "sophisticated commentary" and for focusing on interpretation. Harbage's introduction to *King Lear* is particularly lauded for its excellence: in fact, one teacher says, "No introduction matches Harbage's for eloquence and penetration." The glosses and notes are generally assessed as "brief" but "adequate."

The major reservation expressed about this edition concerns textual weaknesses—specifically that the editing is uneven, its quality varying from play to play and from editor to editor. The apparent assumption in this criticism is that the authority of the texts and editions behind some of the plays needs to be examined more carefully. As a consequence, one might urge that certain plays in this edition be reedited, especially in the light of modern discoveries on quarto and folio texts.

A few teachers prefer to use another older one-volume edition, *The Complete Signet Classic Shakespeare* (Sylvan Barnet, gen. ed.). In contrast to the three editions previously discussed, this one does not categorize and arrange plays by type (comedy, tragedy, etc.); instead, it presents them chronologically (including *The Two Noble Kinsmen* but not the *Sir Thomas More* fragments). The poems follow the plays. Separate editors are assigned to the plays; Russell Fraser edits *King Lear*. A double-column format, with notes and glosses at the bottom of each column, is employed. A small superscript circle is placed directly after each word or phrase explained in the notes. Speech prefixes are in full. Barnet provides a general introduction to the volume, discussing such matters as the life of Shakespeare, the theater and actors, intellectual background, the major types of Shakespearean drama, and Shakespeare's English. A limited number of illustrations appear in the introduction. A selective bibliography entitled "Suggested References" appears at the end of the volume. One teacher commends the general introductory material, but another expresses dissatisfaction with the introduction to *King Lear*, feeling that it is verbose and directed more toward literary critics than undergraduates.

For the future, teachers of Shakespeare anticipate the publication of *The Complete Oxford Shakespeare,* an edition that particularly addresses the issues of old and modern spellings and the textual problems of *King Lear.* (See the essay by Michael Warren in part 2 of this volume for more information.)

Single Editions

Many teachers in a variety of courses (particularly in those using a survey anthology of British literature that does not contain *King Lear*) select a single edition of the play. One of the most widely used is that edited by Kenneth Muir for the Arden Shakespeare series. One teacher who uses the *Riverside* in a Shakespeare course requires, in addition, the Arden *King Lear* for class use and says, "I think majors ought to confront at least once a fully edited text." Teachers using this edition (available in paperback) stress its fullness and comprehensiveness. Muir's introduction discusses the text, date, sources, history of the play from 1605 to 1950, the play itself, and recent criticism. The "copious notes" and "elaborate scholarly annotations" are highly regarded by many instructors, some of whom emphasize the edition's value both for students and as a reference tool for teachers. Textual and explanatory notes appear on the pages with the text. Several respondents to the survey feel that the Arden edition particularly helps in explaining Shakespeare's sources. Muir's comments in his introduction are helpful, but also of great aid is the reprinting (in seven appendixes) of relevant material from *King Leir, The Mirror for Magistrates,* Holinshed, Spenser, Sidney, Florio, and Harsnett.

Of the few reservations expressed about this edition, the major one is that it might not be the most appropriate for undergraduates: several teachers specifically recommend its use on the graduate level and in seminars but not below the advanced undergraduate level. Instructors also point out that the binding easily cracks: as one says, after praising the content of the volume, "it is falling apart."

For undergraduates, probably the most widely used single edition of *King Lear* is that edited by Russell Fraser in 1963 for the Signet Classic Shakespeare series. Some teachers like its lack of full scholarly and critical apparatus. One respondent comments, "The annotation is brief enough not to distract from the main job of reading the text." Most instructors using this volume remark that it is quite attractive in price, compared to similar editions ("one of the best inexpensive paperback editions"). The cost apparently explains why it is still more widely used than more recent, up-to-date, and textually sophisticated single editions (such as Hunter's, discussed below). A few teachers acknowledge that the text of the play is "weaker" than in other editions; one suggests that a second Signet edition is now needed; and another warns that the quality of paper has deteriorated in recent printings.

The most favorable comments about the Signet single edition concern its inclusion of excerpts from source materials and critical commentaries. Selections from Holinshed, Sidney, and *King Leir* are appended. Teachers particularly value the classroom usefulness of critical excerpts from Samuel Johnson, A. C. Bradley, Harley Granville-Barker, and Harry Levin.

Three other single editions available in paperback are mentioned by teachers who use them. The Pelican text, edited by Alfred Harbage, is respected for its introduction to the play. Those who use G. K. Hunter's New Penguin Shakespeare edition commend it highly. Hunter provides an introduction, suggestions for further reading, an account of the text, and a section entitled "Words for Music in *King Lear*." One unique feature of this edition is the absence of glosses or notes on the pages of the text. All commentary is printed immediately following the play in a section of 128 pages, divided according to acts and scenes. Despite his edition's inconvenient arrangement, Hunter's superior textual knowledge, scholarly accuracy, and critical incisiveness make the New Penguin a most intellectually satisfying single edition. His introduction and comments are full of clarifications for both the student and the teacher. Finally, Louis B. Wright and Virginia A. Lamar are the editors of *King Lear* in the Folger Library General Reader's Shakespeare. One teacher suggests that this edition is useful for students reading the play for the first time, since the glosses are on pages facing the text and brief synopses of the play's overt action appear before each scene. Also, spelling and punctuation are modernized, and a general introduction is included.

An important single edition projected for the future is that of the Oxford English Texts edition. (See the essay by Michael Warren in part 2.)

Anthologies

For a course (or a part of a course) that covers a limited number of Shakespeare's plays, a particularly useful anthology is *Shakespeare in Performance: An Introduction through Six Major Plays*, edited by John Russell Brown. Along with *King Lear*, this paperback contains *Romeo and Juliet*, *Henry IV, Part 1*, *Twelfth Night*, *Othello*, and *The Tempest*. Glosses and explanatory notes are in the margins of the pages of text. Many photographs of productions, scenes, and actors are also provided. As one would expect, this edition is particularly tailored to a study through the theatrical approach. One teacher who uses this method of teaching *King Lear* prefers Brown's anthology because of its help in blocking, staging, and acting out the play. The editor's copious commentary on positioning, movements, cues, pauses, tones, and facial expressions are illuminating to both teachers and students who wish to envision the play from the perspective of performance.

The anthology apparently most used in English literature survey courses is the two-volume *Norton Anthology of English Literature* (M. H. Abrams, gen. ed.). Whether Shakespeare specialists or not, many teach *King Lear* from the text in the first volume of the *Norton Anthology,* which also contains *Henry IV, Part 1* and selections from Shakespeare's poetry. The inclusion of *King Lear* in this popular anthology probably means that it is the most frequently taught Shakespearean play, at least in the United States. The sixteenth-century section is edited by Hallett Smith, who provides a two-page introduction to the play; his glosses and explanatory notes appear as footnotes.

Teachers generally feel that the *Norton Anthology* is the best of its type and particularly agree with the selection of *King Lear* as one of its major works. Some feel, however, that the "cramped text in a thick volume" makes it difficult for students to read and take notes. Most instructors consider both the introduction to *King Lear* and the explanatory notes as "acceptable" or "adequate." One respondent, however, feels that the introduction is "simple" and the notes "mediocre." But this same teacher thinks the edition acceptable if supplemented by some critical works. Another instructor would like the volume to provide students with more help in understanding Shakespeare's language. Another criticism is that the Norton edition should more carefully consider the new knowledge concerning original texts of *King Lear.* Respondents are satisfied with the anthology as a whole and recognize that any such work will vary in the quality of its parts. The convenience of a textbook that includes *King Lear* among so many other major works of English literature and the economical price are attractive features that offset its disadvantages.

Required and Recommended Student Readings

Many teachers indicate that the introductory and appended materials in the editions selected for their courses are sufficient for extra student readings. But others believe that one or two additional books, either recommended or required, aid student understanding and assist the teacher in the classroom.

Some books frequently suggested to students fall into the category of background of the age, especially intellectual background. Theodore Spencer's *Shakespeare and the Nature of Man* is frequently recommended for its treatment of ideas in Shakespeare's time that are particularly relevant to *King Lear*. Similarly, several teachers suggest C. S. Lewis's *Discarded Image: An Introduction to Medieval and Renaissance Literature*. Many students are interested in Lewis's work generally and are receptive to reading him further. John Erskine Hankins's *Backgrounds of Shakespeare's Thought*, a more recent treatment of the philosophical background, relates the concepts of microcosm and macrocosm, multiple souls, humors, natural hierarchy, and fallen nature to Shakespeare's works. The book probably most recommended and required for intellectual background is E. M. W. Tillyard's *Elizabethan World Picture*. Tillyard clearly explains in this concise volume some major philosophical concepts of the universe and humanity in sixteenth-century eyes. The short sections are accessible to student readers, and the work is handy as a compact reference to concepts frequently encountered in Shakespeare. Tillyard allows students to understand historically both Lear's assumption that nature is ordered and coherent and the metaphysical problem of nature in the play. Nonspecialists should be aware, however, that recent studies have questioned some of the traditional, and perhaps overly simplistic, views of Tillyard. (See the discussion of background works in "The Instructor's Library" below.)

Another type of work frequently recommended is the "reader's companion." Some teachers still suggest F. E. Halliday's *A Shakespeare Companion*, a dictionary of Shakespearean matters (plots, characters, acquaintances, contemporaries, editors, scholars, etc.). It is convenient as a reference work for students. Much more frequently recommended now, however, is *A New Companion to Shakespeare Studies*, edited by Kenneth Muir and S. Schoenbaum. Unlike Halliday's work, the *New Companion* is primarily a collection of essays by distinguished scholars and critics on Shakespeare's life, reading, language, rhetoric, and the like. Essays also cover such topics as the playhouses and stage, actors and staging, the historical and social background, the intellectual background, and textual problems. A few essays comment on Shakespeare's poetry and plays in logical groups, and two essays survey Shakespeare criticism since Dryden.

One general book on Shakespeare and his works that teachers commend as particularly appropriate for undergraduates is Roland M. Frye's *Shakespeare: The Art of the Dramatist*. Frye surveys Shakespeare's life and work, types of plays, structure, style, and characterization. One teacher recommends the book to students specifically because of its "concise introductions to types of plays."

Some instructors require or recommend books that are essentially made up of separate critical and interpretive essays on individual plays. Teachers feel, as one respondent says, that "students need perspectives on plays other than the views of the instructor and textbook." Some of the books frequently recommended are collections of essays by single authors. Still recommended by some teachers, for example, is Mark Van Doren's *Shakespeare*, which one respondent calls "an excellent point of departure" for students. Also suggested is D. A. Traversi's *Approach to Shakespeare*, which one teacher considers "an excellent general reading of *King Lear*." Still frequently recommended, as well, is Harold Goddard's *Meaning of Shakespeare*. Despite some of its idiosyncratic readings, Goddard's work is interesting and stimulates students' thinking about the plays; they may see it as representative of the highly "optimistic" interpretation of the play's ending.

Other recommended books of essays are anthologies of criticism by different authors. Often suggested is *Shakespeare: Modern Essays in Criticism*, edited by Leonard F. Dean, containing a chapter of John F. Danby's *Shakespeare's Doctrine of Nature: A Study of* King Lear ("The Fool and Handy Dandy") and J. Stampfer's essay "The Catharsis of *King Lear*." Also commended is the collection edited by Alvin B. Kernan, entitled *Modern Shakespearean Criticism: Essays on Style, Dramaturgy, and the Major Plays*. This volume reprints a portion of Jan Kott's *Shakespeare Our Contemporary* entitled "*King Lear* or *Endgame*." (See "The Instructor's Library" for further discussion of these three works.)

The preceding books were most often cited by teachers in the MLA survey as helpful for students to read. Teachers of *King Lear* require or recommend that students read or consult many other major scholarly and critical books and articles. The next section includes studies that are also valuable for students in certain courses.

The Instructor's Library

Introduction

Any literature instructor knows that competence to teach Shakespeare requires close and wide reading, to say nothing of the value of seeing performances. Certainly no one book, or even several, can provide simple solutions for teaching *King Lear*. The attempt here is to provide, from the seemingly endless stream of Shakespeare scholarship and criticism, a selection of the works regarded by experienced teachers of *King Lear* as most helpful, and even "essential," especially from a pedagogical standpoint. Concentration is on essential reference, background, source, theatrical, textual, critical, and linguistic works.

Exigencies of space require emphasis on works published in book form, including, of course, important essays and articles that have appeared in book-length collections. Many important journal articles have not yet been incorporated into collections of criticism. Several of the most important and pertinent ones to the teaching of *King Lear* are included here, and several are mentioned in the essays in the second part of the volume; many, however, necessarily have been omitted. The reader, therefore, is encouraged to pursue bibliographies and reviews of criticism to find the major journal articles devoted to *King Lear* and other relevant Shakespearean topics.

Nonspecialists should become familiar with the major annuals and periodicals, to keep abreast of books, articles, performances, and other Shakespearean items of interest. An important annual publication is *Shakespeare Survey*, which, in addition to publishing important essays on Shakespeare, reviews relevant criticism, scholarship, and theatrical performances of the previous year. Another annual, *Shakespeare Studies*, prints essays and book reviews. *Shakespeare Quarterly* publishes critical and scholarly essays and notes, as well as theater and book reviews. Through 1981, one of this quarterly's four issues was "Shakespeare: Annotated World Bibliography," the major annual guide to Shakespearean studies for the previous year. Since 1981, however, the bibliography is published as a fifth issue. Other journals, such as *PMLA*, frequently publish articles on Shakespeare. The annual *MLA International Bibliography*, of course, lists books and articles on Shakespeare, with an extensive section each year on *King Lear*. The *Shakespeare Newsletter*, now published four times a year, is the most effective means of keeping current on Shakespearean discoveries, publications of books, and other events of interest to Shakespeareans. One respondent in the MLA survey indicates the usefulness of its reports on conferences and its book reviews and advertisements; items published range from the humorous to the serious. Finally, the *Shakespeare on Film Newsletter* appears twice a year, presenting information on and reviews of both film and videotape productions of Shakespeare's plays.

The aim in the succeeding pages of this section is to organize, in a way convenient for the teacher who needs help on Shakespeare and *King Lear*, the works most profitably consulted. Extended descriptive and evaluative summaries generally are not attempted, not only because space is limited but also because such full descriptions are already available in some of the bibliographies indicated below (such as Larry Champion's King Lear: *An Annotated Bibliography* and David M. Bergeron's *Shakespeare: A Study and Research Guide*). This section, then, seeks to offer a guide to the most useful materials. When justified by respondents' frequent mention (and extensive discussion), however, more space is devoted to the description of works uniquely helpful in teaching *King Lear*.

Reference Works

Modern scholars and editors continue to provide Shakespeare studies with essential tools for research and teaching. Such works as facsimile and variorum editions, descriptive bibliographies, compendiums of facts and documents of Shakespeare's life and works, dictionaries, concordances, and reader's guides enhance the understanding and teaching of *King Lear*.

Several instructors consider Charlton Hinman's *The First Folio of Shakespeare: The Norton Facsimile* a valuable reference tool, especially in the light of the recent textual controversies regarding *King Lear* (see Warren's essay in this volume). Several teachers use the 1880 New Variorum edition of *King Lear* by Horace Howard Furness as a reference for checking the views of earlier scholars and critics.

Bibliographical search in Shakespeare begins, for all practical purposes, with *A Shakespeare Bibliography* (1930) and its *Supplement for the Years 1930-1935*, both by Walther Ebisch, in collaboration with Levin L. Schücking. Gordon Ross Smith continued these efforts in *A Classified Shakespeare Bibliography, 1936-1958*. The annual bibliographies published by *Shakespeare Quarterly*, the *MLA International Bibliography*, and the *Annual Bibliography of English Language and Literature* (published by the Modern Humanities Research Association) must be consulted for thorough coverage of Shakespearean topics since 1958. One respondent particularly endorses the bibliography produced by *Shakespeare Quarterly*, saying that its full annotations give an overview of critical tendencies.

Other bibliographies on a smaller, selective scale may serve the needs of many teachers of Shakespeare. All are currently available in paperback form. Ronald Berman's *Reader's Guide to Shakespeare's Plays: A Discursive*

Bibliography is useful for general reference and as a good place to begin acquaintance with some major books and articles on individual plays. Berman groups works under the following divisions: text, editions, sources, criticism, staging, and bibliography. The selection and annotation of works on *King Lear* are generally descriptive and sensible. One respondent in the survey noted that the bibliography, revised in 1973, is "now a bit dated." Other teachers prefer *Shakespeare: Select Bibliographical Guides*, edited by Stanley Wells, also published in 1973. Several recommend this volume for an overview of scholarship and criticism on *King Lear*; Kenneth Muir writes the section on *Lear*. Wells includes other discursive bibliographical essays on plays, groups of plays, poems, and topics such as text and theater. David M. Bergeron's *Shakespeare: A Study and Research Guide* is also regarded as an effective beginning in Shakespeare criticism. Bergeron, in fact, directs his book to the "student or general reader beginning a serious study of Shakespeare's works" (Preface). After surveying Shakespeare criticism chronologically and by type, Bergeron turns to the larger matter of guiding one to the available resources. In contrast to some other bibliographies, Bergeron devotes his space almost exclusively to books, allowing somewhat fuller descriptions of the selected books than would otherwise be possible; he also includes a final section on preparing a research paper on a Shakespearean topic. A more inclusive (but unannotated) bibliography is available in *A Selective Bibliography of Shakespeare: Editions, Textual Studies, Commentary* by James G. McManaway and Jeanne Addison Roberts. Also referred to by several teachers as useful is David Bevington's *Shakespeare* in the Goldentree series of bibliographies.

The preceding bibliographies serve scholars, critics, and teachers interested in any play by Shakespeare. But for those interested primarily in *King Lear*, special mention must be made of Larry S. Champion's recent two-volume King Lear: *An Annotated Bibliography*, in the Garland series of Shakespeare bibliographies, which has been enthusiastically welcomed by teachers of the play. Although the work is rather expensive for private ownership, university libraries should acquire it. Books and articles published between 1940 and approximately 1979 are comprehensively covered, with some exceptional earlier works also included. Volume 1 lists and annotates criticism chronologically. Volume 2 does the same in separate sections for studies comprehending sources; dating; text; bibliographies; editions; stage history; and adaptations, influence, and synopses. For a teacher wishing an overview of and a guide to criticism of *King Lear* within the period covered, the work is excellent. Champion's annotations are objective and descriptive. The possibilities for stimulating and guiding student research on the play are significantly increased by such a reference tool.

Biographical and documentary research has created several truly significant reference works in the twentieth century. Even though later scholarship has added bits of information, *William Shakespeare: A Study of Facts
and Problems* by E. K. Chambers has not been surpassed in comprehensiveness. It is at once a biography and a reference tool, with an impressive
collection of records on Shakespeare's life, stage, and theater company. A
valuable contribution in the same vein is S. Schoenbaum's *William Shakespeare: A Documentary Life*, which ties large facsimiles of major documents to a factual narrative of Shakespeare's life. In *William Shakespeare:
Records and Images*, a later, supplementary work of similar size and format,
Schoenbaum reproduces additional documents such as signatures (both
authentic and spurious), portraits (both genuine and doubtful), and legal
records. Teachers indicate that they not only read and reread these books
but also frequently refer students to them. Another of Schoenbaum's works
frequently employed for purposes of reference is the entertaining *Shakespeare's Lives*, in which he surveys the Shakespearean myths and legends
accumulated over the centuries, as well as the scholarly and critical
perspectives of various groups from the seventeenth to the twentieth
century.

Linguistic aids begin with the *Oxford English Dictionary*: teachers in the
survey mention consulting it and directing students to it more often than
they do any other reference work. The difficulty of words and phrases in
King Lear indeed calls for such a tool. Available also are Alexander
Schmidt's *Shakespeare-Lexicon* and C. T. Onions's *Shakespeare Glossary*.
Several teachers report receiving from Eric Partridge's *Shakespeare's
Bawdy* specialized information to supplement the explanatory notes in
editions that overlook many bawdy words and phrases.

Many instructors consult works that help one recognize sayings and
allusions significant in Shakespeare and his contemporaries. Such a reference tool is Morris Palmer Tilley's *Dictionary of the Proverbs in England
in the Sixteenth and Seventeenth Centuries*. A valuable supplement to Tilley
is R. W. Dent's *Shakespeare's Proverbial Language: An Index*, which revises
and expands Tilley's "Shakespeare Index," considering discoveries made
since the publication of Tilley's work. It is, in fact, for one interested only in
Shakespeare's works, a self-contained, up-to-date tool that essentially su-
persedes Tilley. Extremely important for understanding Shakespeare's
knowledge and use of the Bible is a facsimile of a version frequently used
by Shakespeare himself, *The Geneva Bible: A Facsimile of the 1560 Edition*
(with an introduction by Lloyd E. Berry). The Protestant translators wrote
a marginal gloss that also is important to Shakespeare's perception of biblical interpretation by contemporaries. Biblical echoes in *King Lear* may be
compared to their sources in this version.

One of the tools most employed by teachers is Marvin Spevack's *Har-

vard Concordance to Shakespeare. For tracing recurring words, phrases, and images, it is indispensable. One instructor mentions bringing it to class when teaching *King Lear* and pursuing particular words in the play. Spevack lists all words that appear in Shakespeare, quotes all lines in which they occur, and provides act, scene, and line references to *The Riverside Shakespeare* (ed. Evans).

Two other works that may be classified as handbooks or guides to Shakespeare are considered of great help to an instructor. *The Reader's Encyclopedia of Shakespeare*, edited by Oscar James Campbell and Edward G. Quinn, employs alphabetical entries with convenient summaries of source material, dating, stage history, and criticism. One instructor feels that it gives a "fine overview of scholarly and critical matters pertaining to *King Lear*." More recent is the respected *Guide to Shakespeare* by David M. Zesmer. Early chapters concern Shakespeare in the Elizabethan context and the matters of text, chronology, and sources. The remaining chapters cover Shakespeare's works; *King Lear* is grouped with *Othello* and *Macbeth*.

Background Studies

Several books reveal Shakespeare in the context of his time and place. Muir and Schoenbaum's *New Companion to Shakespeare Studies* (discussed above as recommended to students) contains chapters on the historical, social, and intellectual background that respondents applaud as excellent for a teacher of *King Lear*. The contemporary descriptions in *Life in Shakespeare's England: A Book of Elizabethan Prose*, edited by John Dover Wilson, give an immediate sense of the times. General historical, political, and social accounts are found in S. T. Bindoff's *Tudor England*, G. R. Elton's *England under the Tudors*, and A. L. Rowse's *The England of Elizabeth: The Structure of Society*. A book emphasizing political and social structure, philosophical assumptions, and literature of the Elizabethan and Jacobean age is B. L. Joseph's *Shakespeare's Eden: The Commonwealth of England 1558–1629*, which contains many references to the play, including a discussion (28–32) particularly relevant to teachers of *King Lear*: an application of social history to some comments and events in the play, illuminating, for example, the implications in "bandy looks" of I.iv. One of the most elaborate works is Lacey Baldwin Smith's *Elizabethan World*, especially in its reprinted form as *The Horizon Book of the Elizabethan World*. This latter version contains beautiful illustrations, as well as an interesting text. G. P. V. Akrigg's *Jacobean Pageant: Or, The Court of King James I* provides a good account of Jacobean England; one respondent comments that it is particularly appropriate background for *King Lear*, because it conveys a sense of the "prevailing corruption" of the time.

More specific and fuller discussions of the social, economic, and cultural conditions and assumptions of Shakespeare's time appear in several works, including Muriel St. Clare Byrne's *Elizabethan Life in Town and Country*, Louis B. Wright's *Middle-Class Culture in Elizabethan England*, and Lawrence Stone's *The Family, Sex and Marriage in England, 1500–1800*. Stone's *Crisis of the Aristocracy: 1558–1641*, a book particularly valuable for instructors of *King Lear*, portrays a realistic view of courtly life and answers such questions as why a king would have one hundred men in his following.

One respondent in the MLA survey comments, "A teacher of *King Lear* should be able to talk about the social snobbery of Elizabethans of all classes and their hostility toward such social climbers as Oswald." Several of the books just noted aid in that task. In addition, two books by Ruth Kelso help one to understand courtliness and chivalry in general: *The Doctrine of the English Gentleman in the Sixteenth Century* and *Doctrine for the Lady of the Renaissance*.

The philosophical background is discussed in several well-respected works. Hardin Craig's *Enchanted Glass: The Elizabethan Mind in Literature* treats Renaissance cosmology, hierarchy, and intellect. A more elaborate and demanding investigation of the concepts of hierarchy and nature is found in Arthur O. Lovejoy's now-classic *The Great Chain of Being: A Study of the History of an Idea*. The value of Theodore Spencer's *Shakespeare and the Nature of Man* and E. M. W. Tillyard's *Elizabethan World Picture* for student reading already has been noted, but even more respondents in the survey recommend them for the teacher's background than for the student's. One instructor says, "Tillyard's study is essential for all Shakespeare teachers." Two books that help explain the skeptical tradition emerging at the time *King Lear* was written are Hiram Haydn's *Counter-Renaissance* and Sukanta Chaudhuri's *Infirm Glory: Shakespeare and the Renaissance Image of Man*.

The traditional historical and philosophical views of Craig, Lovejoy, and Tillyard have been modified and corrected by several scholars and critics of the last twenty-five years. Ernest William Talbert's *Problem of Order: Elizabethan Political Commonplaces and an Example of Shakespeare's Art* endorses the Elizabethan world picture but reminds us that we also must consider the more specific pictures of various states, including that of Elizabethan England. Henry Ansgar Kelly's *Divine Providence in the England of Shakespeare's Histories*, although not directly concerned with *King Lear*, greatly changes our traditional concepts of what providential direction meant to Shakespeare's audience. Instead of emphasizing comfortable answers from an ordered cosmos, Joel B. Altman (*The Tudor Play of Mind: Rhetorical Inquiry and the Development of Elizabethan Drama*) finds questioning and debate central in sixteenth-century literature, including Shakespeare's works. In *Renaissance Self-Fashioning: From More to Shakespeare* Stephen Greenblatt examines the reaction of the individual to certain cultural phenomena (especially specific forms of authority) in order to fashion the "self" of both the writer and his characters. An article by Louis Adrian Montrose proposes that the theater was a means of recognizing and accepting social conflict: the stage purposefully reflected the social world. The effect of a ruler's public nature on the theater is explored by Jonathan Goldberg, briefly in a 1981 essay in *Research Opportunities in Renaissance Drama* and more fully in his *James I and the Politics of Literature: Jonson, Shakespeare, Donne, and Their Contemporaries.* Goldberg notes the ruler's essential lack of privacy and how dramatists reflect this role in art. Like kings, dramatists concern themselves with the relation between inner and external being, and they represent (or, in Goldberg's terms, "re-present") private, royal lives in public form.

The instructor of *King Lear* also needs some understanding of the traditions of folly and the Renaissance fool or jester. Enid Welsford's seminal *The Fool: His Social and Literary History* not only reports comprehensively on the tradition itself but also illuminates the role of the Fool in the play and particularly the notion of wise foolishness. The place to pursue this matter further is Robert Hillis Goldsmith's *Wise Fools in Shakespeare.* Also important is an article in which Carolyn S. French provides theological background on wise men and fools.

Some scholarly studies focus on Shakespeare in the context of other medieval and Renaissance artistic, dramatic, and literary traditions. Medieval values in Shakespeare and his indebtedness to early dramatic forms are a part of Willard Farnham's *Medieval Heritage of Elizabethan Tragedy.* Of value, too, is Farnham's *Shakespearean Grotesque: Its Genesis and Transformations.* M. C. Bradbrook's *Themes and Conventions of Elizabethan Tragedy* and Madeleine Doran's *Endeavors of Art: A Study of Form in Elizabethan Drama* allow us to see *King Lear* in the context of earlier tragedy. Shakespeare as seen from the perspective of the values held by Elizabethan and Jacobean audiences is the focus of both Alfred Harbage's *As They Liked It: An Essay on Shakespeare and Morality* and Robert Ornstein's *Moral Vision of Jacobean Tragedy.* Ornstein's discussion of *King Lear* is helpful in relating the play to Machiavellian concepts.

A study of Shakespeare's learning, poetics, and theology in relation to *King Lear* is best begun with Virgil K. Whitaker's *Shakespeare's Use of Learning: An Inquiry into the Growth of His Mind and Art* and continued with Russell A. Fraser's *Shakespeare's Poetics in Relation to* King Lear. Fraser surveys Shakespeare's use of such concepts as providence, fortune, reason, will, and redemption and relates them to emblems and iconography. Several plates illustrating important emblems are included in the volume, and Fraser shows how Shakespeare's poetics in *King Lear* are based on such symbols and metaphors common to the Renaissance mind. The importance of both religion and biblical knowledge to Shakespeare and his age is emphasized in Peter Milward's *Shakespeare's Religious Background* and *Biblical Themes in Shakespeare: Centring on* King Lear. For what one respondent calls "the contrary view" of Shakespeare's use of Christianity and for opposition to a Christian reading of *King Lear*, the teacher might wish to read Roland Mushat Frye's *Shakespeare and Christian Doctrine.*

Source Studies

Teachers responding to the MLA survey overwhelmingly recommend one major work in order to study the sources of *King Lear*: volume 7 of Geoffrey Bullough's *Narrative and Dramatic Sources of Shakespeare* (267-420). Bullough prints the major known sources for the play, some designated as definite sources and others as probable and possible ones. He also provides an extensive introduction commenting on the sources and Shakespeare's means of adapting them for his dramatic purposes. One instructor says, "Bullough's collection of the materials of source-criticism is best because fullest." Another notes that Bullough leaves little to be said. Several teachers indicate that they assign to students some of Bullough's material, especially major passages of *The True Chronicle Historie of King Leir*, so that the students can appreciate the remarkable improvements made by Shakespeare. One instructor points out that some of the sources may have provoked the skepticism in Shakespeare's play.

Kenneth Muir studies the sources for *King Lear* in "Samuel Harsnett and *King Lear*," *Shakespeare's Sources: Comedies and Tragedies*, and *The Sources of Shakespeare's Plays.* (For further studies of sources and for ways to use them in teaching the play, see the essay by Vincent F. Petronella in part 2.)

Theatrical Studies

Scholarship and criticism concerned with such matters as the types and construction of theaters and stages in Shakespeare's time, actors and acting, audiences, and stage representation and performance are vital in teaching Shakespeare. Lively discussions and scholarly disagreements about these matters permeate the study of Shakespeare today, and one cannot answer students' questions or teach the play without some basic knowledge of these topics.

To see the continuity and development of stages and staging from the Middle Ages through Shakespeare, one best begins with Glynne Wickham's three-volume *Early English Stages, 1300–1660*, which treats the medieval stage traditions inherited by Shakespeare. A more explicit study of the stage in Shakespeare's time is E. K. Chambers's four-volume *The Elizabethan Stage*. Chambers collects detailed material on the various kinds of theaters, theater companies, modes of presentation, actors, and other figures associated with the drama of the time. Various conjectural renderings of the structure of the Globe Playhouse have demanded attention in the twentieth century and are still the subjects of heated debates. John Cranford Adams's *The Globe Playhouse: Its Design and Equipment* and Irwin Smith's *Shakespeare's Globe Playhouse: A Modern Reconstruction in Text and Scale Drawings* represent what has become known as the older or traditional view, which is now challenged on many points. C. Walter Hodges in *The Globe Restored: A Study of the Elizabethan Theatre* points out unresolved problems about the construction and argues for a simpler playhouse and stage. Richard Hosley's essays over many years constitute a major corrective to the older views. Of greatest value for teachers is his easily accessible "The Playhouses and the Stage," in which he concisely presents the major types of theaters and stages of the time, with appropriate sketches, and alerts one to the controversial areas of the discovery space, the upper station, and the music room; in the process, he emphatically discredits the existence of an inner stage. For the indoor playhouse used by Shakespeare's company, the teacher may wish to consult Irwin Smith's *Shakespeare's Blackfriars Playhouse: Its History and Its Design*.

Useful studies of acting in Shakespeare's time and since are Bertram L. Joseph's *Elizabethan Acting* and *Acting Shakespeare*. Arthur Colby Sprague's *Shakespeare and the Actors: The Stage Business in His Plays (1660–1905)* is helpful on both stage history and acting.

A small book that is valuable for answering student questions about the types of people attending plays, the prices of admission, and the size of crowds is Alfred Harbage's *Shakespeare's Audience*. Harbage's work should be supplemented, however, by Ann Jennalie Cook's *Privileged Playgoers of Shakespeare's London, 1576–1642* and Michael Hattaway's *Elizabethan Popular Theatre: Plays in Performance*. Andrew Gurr's *Shakespearean Stage, 1574–1642* also examines the audience but, in addition, covers matters of companies, actors, theaters, and stages. Similar concerns appear in Bernard Beckerman's earlier *Shakespeare at the Globe, 1599–1609*, but Beckerman strictly limits himself to production at the Globe during Shakespeare's career there. Beckerman generally is a follower of Hodges, as far as construction is concerned. For further study of historical staging, of how *King Lear* and other plays would have been presented at the Globe and elsewhere, T. J. King's *Shakespearean Staging, 1599–1642* fills in details. An older work still regarded as important in the study of staging is Harley Granville-Barker's essay on the play in his *Prefaces to Shakespeare*.

One respondent comments on its "insights into stage production," and another says that it is very good on the staging of certain scenes in *King Lear*. Several teachers also recommend familiarity with Charles Lamb's 1811 essay "On the Tragedies of Shakspeare, Considered with Reference to Their Fitness for Stage Representation," which provides an awareness of Lamb's antistage prejudice and his famous comments on *King Lear*. One teacher makes the following interesting observations about Lamb's work:

> Curiously, this essay, which purports to tell men of the theatre that *Lear* is unsuitable for the theatre, has had more influence on actual productions than any other. I give a course on the history of Shakespearean criticism and therefore feel entitled to say that this is the best essay ever written on the play.

One of the most significant developments in Shakespeare scholarship, criticism, and teaching in the past two decades is the reinvigorated emphasis on Shakespeare's plays as plays and, consequently, on the theatrical, or performance, approach to them. The potential effects on the classroom study of *King Lear* are significant. Influential in this general movement is John Russell Brown's *Shakespeare's Plays in Performance*. One teacher calls it a "lively entry to the topic of performance." Also seminal in this approach to Shakespeare is J. L. Styan's *Shakespeare's Stagecraft*, which one respondent says is "indispensable for an understanding of Shakespeare's dramatic skills." Another contribution in this area is Styan's *Shakespeare Revolution: Criticism and Performance in the Twentieth Century*. (Styan illustrates the performance approach in teaching *King Lear* in part 2 of the present volume.)

Among other studies concerned with related theatrical matters, Marvin Rosenberg's *The Masks of* King Lear was frequently mentioned. Theatrical history of the play is one of Rosenberg's interests. A respondent says that the book "gives a good sense of how *Lear* has been altered in production and what problems such alteration causes, thereby helping us to know Shakespeare's play better by contrast." William H. Matchett's essay "Some Dramatic Techniques in *King Lear*" appears in the volume *Shakespeare: The Theatrical Dimension*. Dramatic technique and structure also are emphasized in James E. Hirsh's *Structure of Shakespearean Scenes*, in which portions are devoted to *King Lear*. (Hirsh illustrates a way of teaching the play through dramatic structure in part 2 of the present volume.)

Textual Studies

Advances in analytical bibliography in the twentieth century have been great indeed, and their effects on the study of Shakespeare must be faced by teachers. This is nowhere truer than in the case of *King Lear*, currently the subject of a textual controversy. To many instructors, such examination of the intricacies of original texts remains a mystery. But other respondents to the MLA survey indicate key studies that offer immediate help to teachers, particularly for matters pertinent to the texts of *King Lear*.

Several works of varying length provide the novice in bibliographical study a good start. Frequently mentioned by instructors as the first one for the teacher of any Shakespearean play is G. Blakemore Evans's essay "Shakespeare's Text" in *The Riverside Shakespeare* (discussed above in the section on editions). For fuller understanding of the printing process behind Renaissance texts, the serious beginner in the general field of analytical bibliography should study carefully Philip Gaskell's *New Introduction to Bibliography*. W. W. Greg focuses more explicitly on Shakespeare's works in *The Editorial Problem in Shakespeare: A Survey of the Foundations of the Text*. Also of great value is Fredson Bowers's *On Editing Shakespeare*. To pursue the matter of the First Folio texts, the teacher, after having acquired some background in analytical bibliography, may wish to examine Charlton Hinman's technical, two-volume *The Printing and Proof-Reading of the First Folio of Shakespeare*, one of the most influential contributions in the history of textual studies. Hinman also gives helpful explanations (easily understood by the student and nonspecialist teacher) in his facsimile edition *The First Folio of Shakespeare: The Norton Facsimile*, which is the best place for a teacher to examine one of the two major versions of *King Lear* in existence. For the other major version, the best reproduction is found in the recent work, edited by Michael J. B. Allen and Kenneth Muir, entitled *Shakespeare's Plays in Quarto: A Facsimile Edition of Copies Primarily from the Henry E. Huntington Library*.

Several respondents in the survey feel that some available editions and studies from 1949 to 1960 still illuminate the text of *King Lear*, despite new knowledge and recent arguments. For textual questions, these teachers consult *Shakespeare's* King Lear: *A Critical Edition*, edited by George Ian Duthie; *King Lear* in the Arden series, edited by Kenneth Muir; Alice Walker's *Textual Problems of the First Folio*; and *King Lear* in the Cambridge Shakespeare series, editied by George Ian Duthie and John Dover Wilson.

The current controversy over the two *Lears*, or the first quarto and First Folio versions, is best approached with a reading of Michael J. Warren's "Quarto and Folio *King Lear* and the Interpretation of Albany and Edgar." Similarly important is Gary Taylor's 1980 essay "The War in *King Lear*." Also in 1980 appeared two important books valuable for any teacher of the play but perhaps best understood by those with some textual background: P.W.K. Stone's *Textual History of* King Lear and Steven Urkowitz's *Shake-*

speare's Revision of King Lear. Stone argues that the quarto *Lear* is a pirated version made from a report of performances and that the Folio derives from it. Urkowitz, however, contends that Shakespeare himself revised the play to achieve different theatrical effects and characterizations. One instructor comments that Urkowitz "sensitizes the teacher to the textual problems and also is brilliantly responsive to the dramaturgy." Also recommended is Peter W. M. Blayney's *The Texts of* King Lear *and Their Origins*: volume 1, *Nicholas Okes and the First Quarto*, was published in 1982, and volume 2 is forthcoming. Blayney's work is a thorough study of the actual process of printing the texts. A collection of essays entitled *The Division of the Kingdoms: Shakespeare's Two Versions of* King Lear, edited by Gary Taylor and Michael Warren, is more easily read and more directly relevant to a teacher of the play than are some of the technical studies cited above. (For further information on the textual puzzles and controversy, see Michael Warren's essay in part 2. Warren explains the textual problem and adapts it to a teaching of the play.)

Critical and Linguistic Studies

Some editions, such as Bevington's, survey criticism of Shakespeare from his time to the present. For the period from 1623 to 1801, however, the best survey (with excerpts reproduced) is the six-volume *Shakespeare: The Critical Heritage*, edited by Brian Vickers. Also highly commended as older, classic criticism are Samuel Johnson's preface and notes to his 1765 edition of Shakespeare. One teacher indicates that Johnson's comments on *King Lear* stimulate students to consider alternative endings and the idea of poetic justice.

Three collections of critical excerpts and essays on *King Lear* are particularly noteworthy. The one most often suggested by respondents is *Twentieth Century Interpretations of* King Lear, edited by Janet Adelman, which contains convenient excerpts from such critics as Bradley, Knight, Danby, and Mack. Stephen Booth's "On the Greatness of *King Lear*" is an original contribution to the volume. The excerpts and essays total sixteen. In addition, Adelman writes an introduction that is excellent in itself, especially on Edgar's role in the play. *Some Facets of* King Lear: *Essays in Prismatic Criticism*, edited by Rosalie L. Colie and F. T. Flahiff, contains twelve essays, only one of which had already appeared in print. Among these essays are Sheldon P. Zitner's "*King Lear* and Its Language" and Bridget Gellert Lyons's "The Subplot as Simplification in *King Lear*." Lawrence Danson is editor of *On* King Lear, a collection of essays viewing *King Lear* as history, theater, and poetry, among other perspectives. Eight essays, including " 'Nothing Almost Sees Miracles': Tragic Knowledge in *King Lear*" by Thomas P. Roche, Jr., make up the volume.

The MLA survey reveals that ten critical books concerning *King Lear*, in whole or in part, are most mentioned as helpful in understanding and teaching the play. All have been published in the present century (from 1904 to 1974). The earliest is that modern classic of Shakespeare criticism, A. C. Bradley's *Shakespearean Tragedy*. Instructors cite Bradley for the "traditional view of ideas and characters" and say that his work "continues to be helpful." For many, however, the place to begin in modern criticism of *King Lear* is G. Wilson Knight's *Wheel of Fire: Interpretations of Shakespearean Tragedy*, first published in 1930. One teacher recommends it for its treatment of "religion and naturalism" in the play, and another notes that Knight "makes *King Lear* into the poem it must be." Knight's influential views on the poetry and imagery of Shakespeare are felt greatly in Robert Bechtold Heilman's *This Great Stage: Image and Structure in* King Lear, which one teacher calls "probably the best book on *King Lear*." Other accolades are "still best for imagery" and "clarifies major issues." The philosophical perspective on the play appears in John F. Danby's *Shakespeare's Doctrine of Nature: A Study of* King Lear. As one instructor says, "Danby notes the tug between malevolence and benevolence in Shakespeare's world view." The study delineates the two definitions of *nature* in the play and the contest between them. Edmund is seen as the new man, the precursor of the new age. Danby also aids in understanding the Fool.

Another of the most frequently mentioned books is Jan Kott's *Shakespeare Our Contemporary*, a controversial volume from its publication in 1961 to the present. It is variously described by respondents as "nihilistic," "absurdist," and "existential." Other representative comments are "read it for abrasive value," "a politicized approach," and "a myopic misreading of *King Lear*." An answer and a corrective to Kott's work is Maynard Mack's King Lear *in Our Time*, which one teacher calls "the best little book on *King Lear*," full of information that can be used in class to direct students to major issues of interpretation. Another notes that it helps one relate the play to a modern audience. Appearing in 1966, a year after Mack's book, is the study more teachers called "essential" than any other: William R. Elton's King Lear *and the Gods*, praised for its elucidation of intellectual background and religious issues and its explanations of the significance of particular phrases. Another respected work in the same decade is Paul A. Jorgensen's *Lear's Self-Discovery*, which emphasizes knowledge, self-knowledge, and the tragedy as a learning experience.

The final two of the ten most noted books appeared in the 1970s. Marvin Rosenberg's *The Masks of* King Lear has been discussed above for its importance as a theatrical study. As one instructor notes, however, "This book is a brilliant combination of theatrical history and criticism: it gives the interpretative spectrum for every moment in the play." Another finds Rosenberg's book "the most useful one on the play because it is so full of information about possible interpretations." Its thorough scene-by-scene commentary and its criticism of Danby's two definitions of *nature* are also valued by some teachers. S. L. Goldberg's *Essay on* King Lear is a tightly constructed study that covers the minor characters better than most other books do.

Several other books are useful for studying special facets of the play. Some teachers prefer to focus on the plot of *King Lear*. Lily B. Campbell's *Shakespeare's Tragic Heroes: Slaves of Passion* emphasizes character and emotion, but one teacher finds the chapter on *Lear* an effective way to analyze its plot. Campbell's pattern of pride, anger, revenge, shame, and reconciliation provides the method. For the purpose and meaning of the double plot in *Lear*, Richard Levin's *Multiple Plot in English Renaissance Drama* is excellent. A useful essay on Shakespeare's reason for combining the two plots is Bridget Gellert Lyons's "The Subplot as Simplification in *King Lear*."

Other teachers are interested in character study, most of which begins with Bradley's work cited above. However, Richard B. Sewall's *Vision of Tragedy* expands character into larger contexts and treats Lear along with Job and other tragic characters. One respondent comments, "Sewall's work helps a teacher understand and explain to students how one sympathizes with a rash, egotistical, pompous old man as a tragic figure." An excellent article on one character is Leo Kirschbaum's "Albany," which one teacher calls "the best study in character development that I have come across." A fine essay treating Edgar's deception of Gloucester is Alvin Kernan's "Formalism and Realism in Elizabethan Drama: The Miracles in *King Lear*." The problem of whether Edgar's deception of his father by a false vision and miracle is morally legitimate frequently concerns teachers and students. Further help in dealing with it is found in Philip Edwards's "Shakespeare and the Healing Power of Deceit." Teachers also refer to Michael Goldman's *Shakespeare and the Energies of Drama* for his discussion of Edgar.

Much of the twentieth century's contribution to Shakespeare criticism depends on seeing the plays as poems with important motifs or patterns of imagery. The importance of Knight and Heilman in this movement has been noted above. Caroline F. E. Spurgeon's *Shakespeare's Imagery and What It Tells Us* is useful in listing and cataloging images. Her work has been developed further in such studies as W. H. Clemen's *Development of Shakespeare's Imagery* and Donald A. Stauffer's *Shakespeare's World of Images: The Development of His Moral Ideas*. Imagery is also crucial to the interpretation of *King Lear* in Sigurd Burckhardt's *Shakespearean Meanings*. One of the play's most important patterns of imagery is the subject of Paul

J. Alpers's "*King Lear* and the Theory of the 'Sight Pattern.'" In addition to verbal imagery, the importance of stage imagery appears in Maurice Charney's "'We Put Fresh Garments on Him': Nakedness and Clothes in *King Lear.*" The stripping of clothing points to moral progression.

One critical approach easily and effectively adapted to the classroom is that of Lear's self-knowledge. The importance of Jorgensen's book has already been mentioned. Also frequently cited as helpful for its discussion of *Lear* is Irving Ribner's *Patterns in Shakespearian Tragedy.* Ribner traces a pattern of self-knowledge, penance, and expiation that leads to regeneration. Similarly valuable on the self-knowledge theme is Manfred Weidhorn's "Lear's Schoolmasters." Related to self-knowledge is a character's role-playing as a means of identity. This critical approach to *King Lear* appears most notably in Thomas F. Van Laan's "Acting as Action in *King Lear*" and *Role-Playing in Shakespeare.*

A recent critical approach to Shakespeare fuses the psychoanalytic with the familial. *King Lear* from the perspective of marriage, family, and the father-daughter relationship has been an important part of this critical movement. Marianne Novy's "Patriarchy, Mutuality, and Forgiveness in *King Lear*" focuses on the tragic violation of father-daughter mutuality in a patriarchal society and explores the play from the perspective of feminist criticism. C. L. Barber's "The Family in Shakespeare's Development: Tragedy and Sacredness" is a psychoanalytic study of how, in the tragedies, Shakespeare places the masculine identity crisis in a filial context and, in turn, how he relates this context to Christian rites of passage and ceremony. Lynda E. Boose in "The Father and the Bride in Shakespeare" illustrates how Shakespeare, in many plays, evokes the altar tableau of the marriage ceremony and depicts the tragic consequences of either the father's or the daughter's refusal to submit to such a ritual severance. (In part 2 of the present volume, Boose translates her views into a technique for teaching *King Lear.*)

Certainly a critical crux of *King Lear* is its metaphysical vision, usually described by critics as one of "optimism" or "pessimism." The problem of interpreting the end of the play is a vital part of this crux. It is not surprising that many books and articles argue positions that frequently are diametrically opposed. Respondents in the survey indicate which works seem most pertinent to the debate, and those are reported here. The individual teacher, of course, must make the ultimate decision on whether to stand with one school of critics or to present both sides to students.

A study of works that tend toward a generally optimistic view, especially of the ending, should begin with A. C. Bradley's *Shakespearean Tragedy,* which finds a note of spiritual regeneration in Lear's experience. G. Wilson Knight in *The Wheel of Fire* sees some of the less solemn aspects of the play in the light of grotesque humor. He also regards Lear's suffering as a purging that leads to peace, humility, and love. Harold Goddard's reading of the play in *The Meaning of Shakespeare* develops the purgative emphasis even further and argues that Lear's final vision of Cordelia is an optimistic one that transcends physical death. Geoffrey Bush's *Shakespeare and the Natural Condition* emphasizes the failure of Renaissance "natural philosophy" to support humanity's ultimate emotions, spirit, and faith and sees a redemption from "distress" occurring in the play. In *On the Design of Shakespearian Tragedy*, Harold S. Wilson emphasizes the "imaginative, poetic pattern" of the play and sees Lear as a great representative of human love at the end. A Christian approach to *Lear* is found in Roy W. Battenhouse's *Shakespearean Tragedy: Its Art and Its Christian Premises*. Battenhouse notes the many biblical echoes and allusions in the play and also interprets the deaths of both Gloucester and Lear affirmatively: Gloucester dies smiling, after gaining insights into life; Lear dies not deceived in thinking Cordelia lives, but with an insight suggesting faith. Hugh L. Hennedy in "*King Lear*: Recognizing the Ending" also interprets the deaths of Gloucester and Lear optimistically, stressing the series of miracles and recognitions in the play and the fact that Lear envisions Cordelia living spiritually. Joseph Wittreich's recent "*Image of that horror*": *History, Prophecy, and Apocalypse in* King Lear discusses the play in its Christian and apocalyptic contexts but sees it as neither overly optimistic or pessimistic. Wittreich emphasizes the inevitability of its ending, one prepared for by the bleakness of the world of the play, but one that can teach humanity possibilities for reformation.

Certain books and articles written from 1949 to 1979 best represent the harsher metaphysical view. John F. Danby's *Shakespeare's Doctrine of Nature* points out the malevolence that balances the benevolence in Shakespeare's vision in the play. For an existential reading, Jan Kott's *Shakespeare Our Contemporary* should be consulted. Perhaps the negative view of the *Lear* universe is most effectively delineated in William R. Elton's King Lear *and the Gods*. An earlier voice arguing against interpreting Lear's regeneration as Christian is Sylvan Barnet's in "Some Limitations of a Christian Approach to Shakespeare." The harshness of the universe portrayed in the play is also noted by L. C. Knights in *Some Shakespearean Themes*, even though love moderates this harshness. J. Stampfer in "The Catharsis of *King Lear*" regards the end of the play as the greatest problem in its interpretation and argues that Lear dies unreconciled in a universe without reason. Nicholas Brooke endorses the same generally nihilistic view in "The Ending of *King Lear*," a study that praises Shakespeare for his ideal presentation of negation. Another work that describes a morally absurd universe in *Lear* is Harold Skulsky's "*King Lear* and the Meaning of Chaos." Other studies that teachers mention as helpful in examining the metaphysical view and the ending of the play are Robert H. West's *Shake-*

speare and the Outer Mystery, Phyllis Rackin's "Delusion as Resolution in *King Lear*," and René E. Fortin's "Hermeneutical Circularity and Christian Interpretations of *King Lear*." (For more on the problem of the ending and for a method of using it in the classroom, see the essay by David L. Kranz in part 2 below.)

Other twentieth-century books and articles were less frequently mentioned by respondents in the survey, but certain teachers find them valuable for solving a variety of critical problems. A few teachers cite Barbara Everett's "New *King Lear*" as valuable for its challenge to Danby's views. Northrop Frye's *Anatomy of Criticism: Four Essays* is praised as the best introduction to archetypal criticism, which the teacher may, in turn, apply to *King Lear*. Rosalie L. Colie's *Shakespeare's Living Art* is useful in helping one "come to terms with the complexity of tones in the play," as one respondent says. Other studies (published from 1933 to 1978) are Elmer Edgar Stoll's *Art and Artifice in Shakespeare: A Study in Dramatic Contrast and Illusion*, George R. Kernodle's "Symphonic Form of *King Lear*," Willard Farnham's *Shakespeare's Tragic Frontier: The World of His Final Tragedies*, William Rosen's *Shakespeare and the Craft of Tragedy*, John Holloway's *Story of the Night: Studies in Shakespeare's Major Tragedies*, Norman N. Holland's *Psychoanalysis and Shakespeare*, Stanley Cavell's "Avoidance of Love: A Reading of *King Lear*," Preston Thomas Roberts's "Redemption of King Lear," Richard Fly's *Shakespeare's Mediated World*, and Edward Pechter's "On the Blinding of Gloucester."

After the *OED* and other such reference tools mentioned above, linguistic studies and aids proceed with *Shakespeare's Pronunciation* by Helge Kökeritz. Another helpful work by Kökeritz is *Shakespeare's Names: A Pronouncing Dictionary*. A classic work that studies Shakespeare in relation to rhetoric in his time is Miriam Joseph's *Shakespeare's Use of the Arts of Language*. Hilda M. Hulme's *Explorations in Shakespeare's Language* examines the meanings of words in context and concerns itself with such matters as proverbs, bawdy language, Latinate diction, spelling habits, and pronunciation. Respondents also mention M. M. Mahood's *Shakespeare's Wordplay*, G. L. Brook's *Language of Shakespeare*, and S. S. Hussey's *Literary Language of Shakespeare*. A useful essay on the varieties of language in the play is Sheldon P. Zitner's "*King Lear* and Its Language."

Aids to Teaching

Teachers do not agree on the extent to which such teaching aids as illustrations, slides, recordings, tapes, and films should be used in a college classroom. Some feel that these materials are more appropriate on the secondary level and indicate that they use practically no visual or audio resources in teaching *King Lear*. Others, however, note that such aids are a vital part of their approach to Shakespeare and to this particular play. Aids may range from the simplest kind that require minimal planning and expense to those that are more expensive and demanding to acquire and employ.

Some teachers say that presenting in class such illustrative tools as a quarto and the First Folio (available in facsimile) is illuminating to students of Shakespeare. This is especially true in illustrating the two versions of *King Lear*. Also easily available and frequently used are extant illustrations of such theaters as the Swan, with which the teacher can discuss the structure of a typical playhouse, possible variations of it, and the specifics in staging *King Lear*. Conjectural renderings of the Globe and photographs of models are frequently passed around or projected in the classroom, if not available in the edition or textbook being used. Some teachers report making, or having students make, models of the Globe to display in class. One respondent purchased the model sold by the Folger Shakespeare Library, Washington, DC, and he finds it quite helpful in "bringing to life" the staging of *King Lear* as the play is being read and discussed. Teachers might be well advised, however, to alter any model based on Adams's conception of the Globe to accord with some of the more recent discoveries by such scholars as Hodges and Hosley (see discussion above in "Theatrical Studies"). Other respondents mention purchasing a paper or cut-and-paste model sold in Stratford: one comments that it serves classroom purposes as well as any other available.

A good number of instructors prepare their own slides of relevant sites in England to use in discussing both Shakespeare's life and *King Lear*. Others purchase slides that are helpful in teaching background on Shakespeare's life and theater. Some specifically praise the Folger Library Slide Sets on costumes, Shakespeare's life, and the Globe (see list of works cited for further information on these and other aids mentioned in the rest of this section). One teacher says that these slides are quite good and come with full explanatory notes; another notes that they help a teacher illustrate the minimal number of props needed for *King Lear* and discuss the staging of the first scene. Other slides found useful are those in *Shakespeare: New Productions (1975–80)* by KaiDib Films.

Two recordings of the play are frequently mentioned by teachers who use them in class. The four-record *King Lear* by the Marlowe Society and Professional Players (directed by George Rylands) appeared in 1961. The Shakespeare Recording Society produced a four-record *King Lear* in 1965 (directed by Howard Sackler); Paul Scofield plays the part of Lear. This latter recording is the one most frequently used by teachers in the MLA survey. One respondent uses selected scenes in class to stimulate alternative readings posed by students. Playing the last scene on this record may produce a striking, emotional silence in the classroom, but one that leads to earnest discussion of the ending.

Several films and video productions of *King Lear* are available, and many teachers report using them. (Information on rental or purchase of these is found in the film and video section of the list of works cited.) The film chosen more than any other is that of 1971, photographed in Jutland and directed by Peter Brook, with Paul Scofield and Irene Worth acting. The film is in black and white. One respondent says, "The black-and-white photography, barren landscapes, and ancient stone buildings are principal means by which Brook emphasizes those qualities of the tragedy that are most difficult to represent in the classroom." Another teacher comments, "The starkness and bleakness of the film effectively dramatize the theme of 'nothingness,' and the acting is quite good." Others praise the film with such comments as "captures the starkness and monolithic primitivism of *King Lear*," "an excellent critical stimulus," and "conveys the nihilism of the play better than any other film or stage production I've ever seen." There are dissenting voices, however. One teacher says that it is an "extreme version of the nihilistic interpretation of the play and a demonstration of extreme license with Shakespeare's text to favor this interpretation." Another criticizes how the "visual presence of one hundred knights creating mayhem diverts our sympathy from Lear to Goneril" and how "the blinding of Gloucester is spoiled by the omission of the splendid protest by Cornwall's servant."

The other film of *King Lear* frequently used by teachers is the version directed by Grigori Kozintsev, with Yuri Jarvet and Elza Radzins acting. It is a 1971 black-and-white USSR film in Russian, with English subtitles. The most frequent criticisms of this film are that the print and sound are of poor quality and that the subtitles are difficult to read. But, despite these flaws, teachers praise it for the positive view it presents, in contrast to the Brook version. Several say that it provides a critical stimulus and sparks discussion among students. Kozintsev also wrote King Lear: *The Space of Tragedy,* a book that comments on the film and the making of it. (For further details and evaluation of these two films, the reader should consult the essays by Kenneth S. Rothwell and Hugh M. Richmond in part 2 below.)

Two recent video productions of *King Lear* promise to be useful for the classroom. Jonathan Miller directed the 1982 production for BBC-TV/Time-Life, Inc. Michael Hordern plays King Lear. Despite its availability for the classroom and some obvious virtues in performances, the teacher might have some reservations about facets of this 1982 version: Kenneth Rothwell reviews both its strengths and weaknesses in his contribution below. Steven Urkowitz has reviewed the BBC production in *Shakespeare on Film Newsletter* ("*King Lear* without Tears"). Granada Television's 1983 production, directed by Michael Elliott, presents Laurence Olivier as Lear. Critics praise the Granada production highly, particularly because of Olivier's performance: for further details and evaluation, the reader again should consult Rothwell's essay. This 1983 version has also been reviewed by Steven Urkowitz ("Lord Olivier's *King Lear*") and by Marion Perret.

Also valuable for teachers are commentaries on films and guides to films and other media versions of *King Lear* and Shakespeare's works in general. Roger Manvell's *Shakespeare and the Film*, a guide to films of Shakespeare's works, contains a good discussion of Brook's staging, in contrast to Kozintsev's. Another useful book is the collection edited by Charles W. Eckert entitled *Focus on Shakespearean Films*. A highly respected, perceptive commentary on *King Lear* films, as well as others, is *Shakespeare on Film* by Jack J. Jorgens. Barry M. Parker's *Folger Shakespeare Filmography* is a directory of feature films based on Shakespeare's works. For a current guide and commentary on films and videotapes of Shakespeare's plays, one should read the *Shakespeare on Film Newsletter* (edited by Kenneth S. Rothwell, Univ. of Vermont, and Bernice W. Kliman, Nassau Community Coll.). Since December 1976, it has published two numbers a year. Excellent for developing fresh material and aids in teaching Shakespeare is Andrew M. McLean's *Shakespeare: Annotated Bibliographies and Media Guide for Teachers*. McLean covers feature films, television, filmstrips, slides, tapes, and records. He cites several reviews of the Brook and Kozintsev films. A directory of producers, distributors, and rental sources concludes his volume.

Part Two

APPROACHES

INTRODUCTION

Each of the following sixteen essays, written by selected participants in the MLA survey, illustrates a particular approach to teaching *King Lear*. The intent is to present a variety of approaches as guides for practical use at all levels of undergraduate instruction. The authors write about their particular emphases, techniques, and activities in teaching the play.

Most of the contributors are Shakespeare specialists who regularly teach courses on Shakespeare, but several also teach *King Lear* in other types of courses, such as a survey of British literature. Most have written books or articles in the field. They have taught, thought about, and experimented with *King Lear* more than the nonspecialist and, therefore, have much to offer both nonspecialists and specialists.

Many of the essayists' approaches are designed to help solve some problems in teaching *King Lear*. A portion of the MLA questionnaire asked respondents what they perceived as the major problems in teaching the play and also asked for suggested solutions. The numerous responses uncovered many common difficulties teachers have in discussing and presenting this play in the classroom. Most often mentioned is the inability of young students to empathize with an old man and to comprehend fully the obligations of youth to age. The pessimistic vision of the play as a whole and its relation to the interpretation of the ending is the next most frequently mentioned problem.

Teachers find it difficult to have students come to terms with the bleakness of the play and to see some of the affirmative elements that may moderate the pessimism: as one teacher says, "We all get so depressed!" After these two dominant problems, others noted in the questionnaires are as follows (generally from most to least frequently mentioned): conveying the universality of the play, teaching the two concepts of nature, managing the complex imagery, interesting the students in the action of the play through its staging, presenting the archetypal characters, and explaining kingship in the Renaissance. A practical problem also mentioned by several instructors is the lack of class time to convey fully the richness of the play. Although some of these difficulties have been noted above in "Materials" (with certain books and articles that help solve them), many of them, along with stimulating solutions, are addressed by the essays.

The approaches begin with two essays (by Vincent F. Petronella and Kenneth S. Rothwell) that present overviews of the play from a variety of critical perspectives and classroom techniques. More specialized emphases and approaches follow in the succeeding essays.

Several of the approaches place primary focus on theme and character. Lynda E. Boose discusses the play through marriage and family relationships. Linked to Boose's essay by a common concern with the family is Ann E. Imbrie's development of an archetypal treatment. Ann Paton then presents the continuity of theatrical, religious, and cultural traditions in several literary works preceding and linked to *King Lear*. Frances Teague illustrates the integral relation of a major theme (perception) with a motif of imagery (sight) in the play. In the process, she suggests how to teach the play by a classroom focus on this or other lines of its imagery.

Three essays approach *King Lear* in its dramatic and philosophical contexts. James E. Hirsh illustrates how the play's unique dramatic structure reveals both Shakespeare's genius and the essence of *King Lear*. Maurice Hunt then shows how a teacher can employ student-constructed "maps" to convey this antiformalist structure and theme of the play, especially in a survey course covering several dramas of a more traditional, formalist nature. Bruce W. Young discusses the philosophical assumptions common to *King Lear* and Hooker's *Of the Laws of Ecclesiastical Polity*.

The role of the written text and its oral and visual performance figure in the next series of approaches. Michael Warren's essay concerns finding a proper text, in light of the two early versions of the play. J. L. Styan and John B. Harcourt focus on dramatic performance and production, thus emphasizing the experiences of actors and audience as methods for teaching the play.

The last four essays present perhaps the most highly specialized approaches, either in terms of teaching techniques employed or courses taught or facets of the play under examination. Jean Klene's pedagogical technique uses slides in conjunction with student-composed "investigations." Hugh M.

Richmond shows how *King Lear* may be taught in a film course on Shakespeare. David L. Kranz illustrates how a technique of student debates can be used to highlight the pervasive problem of the ending of the play and the related controversy of its pessimistic or optimistic metaphysical vision. As a conclusion, J. W. Robinson discusses his development of a unique course that covers only *King Lear,* implying ways that other instructors could teach a similar class.

The essays represent a cross section of teaching techniques and critical interpretations. Some instructors employ primarily lecture, others mainly discussion, and still others a combination. Many use performance methods, visual and audio media, and various creative assignments. Several authors' interpretations resemble those of other contributors, but like critics of the play, many of these teachers reveal divergent interpretations and emphases. The burden still falls on the individual readers of these essays to establish the best interpretations and approaches for themselves. One survey respondent says, "The greatest problem in teaching *King Lear* is its multiplicity of meaning, the fact that of so many interpretations it can be said 'And that's true too.'" Thus, even though these essays can provide no simple and final answers, they may make matters a bit easier for the trek on the heath. They are so offered to colleagues by these dedicated teacher-authors.

RHR

GENERAL OVERVIEWS

An Eclectic Critical Approach: Sources, Language, Imagery, Character, and Themes

Vincent F. Petronella

Because *King Lear*, as well as the amount of commentary on it, is massive, teaching the play requires selectivity. Consequently, I focus attention in class on three or four longer portions of each act and touch on briefer moments for continuity, spending about six class meetings on the play. My critical approach is eclectic. I consider the play in terms of sources, language, imagery, character, themes, and the interrelations of these elements. After considering sources, I proceed in sequence through the play. In actual practice, I combine the consideration of language, imagery, character, and themes, referring to sources when necessary. In this paper, however, I shall treat the five categories separately in order to facilitate discussion of their important features.

Teachers of *King Lear*, who usually do not have enough time for a detailed in-class account of sources, may wish to organize an overview of sources to demonstrate how Shakespeare's imagination works and hence should be familiar with the following informed discussions: W. W. Greg's "The Date of *King Lear* and Shakespeare's Use of Earlier Versions of the Story," Volume 7 of Geoffrey Bullough's *Narrative and Dramatic Sources of Shakespeare*, Kenneth Muir's *Sources of Shakespeare's Plays*, Joseph Satin's *Shakespeare and His Sources*, Wilfrid Perrett's *Story of King Lear from*

Geoffrey of Monmouth to Shakespeare, G. K. Hunter's "Shakespeare's Reading," John J. M. Tobin's "Apuleius and the Bradleian Tragedies," Muir's Arden Shakespeare edition of *King Lear*, and G. Blakemore Evans's "Chronology and Sources" in his *Riverside Shakespeare*, which serves as the edition for all quotations from *King Lear* in this paper. Armed with the information in these studies, the teacher becomes aware of the wide array of sources and analogues for *King Lear*, should select some of the most important sources to emphasize in class, and may assign some of the sources themselves and the relevant discussions of them to students.

Four of the most important sources of *King Lear* (1605) are the anonymous play *The True Chronicle Historie of King Leir and His Three Daughters*, published in 1605 but thought to have been performed as early as 1593; Sir Philip Sidney's *Arcadia* (1590); Spenser's *Faerie Queene*, 2 (1590); and Samuel Harsnett's *Declaration of Egregious Popish Impostures* (1603). Respectively, these works supplied the overall movement of the play, the subplot, the death of Cordelia by hanging, and the diction and lore of Poor Tom's bizarre world. These are, then, the key sources for the play, and teachers should be aware of what Shakespeare draws from them and how he shapes the derived material for his dramatic purposes.

The longest of the sources, the old *Leir* play, opens with the King of Brittayne grieving for the recent loss of his wife and, because of this grief, deciding to divide his kingdom and to abdicate. Leir plans the love test in order to trick Cordella into becoming the wife of the King of Brittany. On hand are two advisers, one good (Perillus) and one bad (Skalliger), who represent in the fashion of a morality play good and bad angels that compete for the king's approval. After the love test, which Cordella fails because she chooses to speak plainly and not to indulge in the kind of flattery offered by Gonorill and Ragan, the Leir family starts to disintegrate. Cordella eventually marries the King of Gallia and later assists her father to regain health following the mistreatment he suffers at the hands of Gonorill and Ragan. Once the evil sisters and their husbands, the Kings of Cornwall and Cambria, are defeated, Cordella restores her father to the throne of Brittayne. Before leaving for Gallia, Cordella and her husband remain for a time in Brittayne at the request of Leir.

What takes place over the course of eight scenes in *Leir* is condensed in the opening scene of *King Lear*. The concentration of events is dense with ideas that undergo development during the remainder of Shakespeare's play. Although much of what occurs in *King Lear* does not derive from the *Leir* play, the older play provided the general format, including basic character relationships and the sequence of events in the main plot; in addition, it provided some themes and diction. What Shakespeare added to the *Leir* material is the character of the Fool, Lear's insanity and extreme age, the banished Kent (in contrast with the unbanished Perillus), the story of Gloucester and his sons, the death of Cordelia, and the raging storm. Shakespeare's imagination, then, blended original ideas with derived ones.

To exemplify this blend, the teacher should consider how in *Leir* Cordella disappoints her father during the love test with these words: "I cannot paynt my duty forth in words," to which Leir responds, "Why how now, Minion, are you growne so proud? / Doth our deare love make you thus peremptory?" (Bullough 344). Generally this is the exchange in *King Lear*, but that in the source falls short of the devastating effect of Cordelia's repeated "Nothing" and her follow-up to that stark, unpainted word:

> Unhappy that I am, I cannot heave
> My heart into my mouth. I love your Majesty
> According to my bond, no more nor less. (I.i.91–93)

As if wanting to remind us of this agonizing moment in Cordelia's early dramatic appearance, Shakespeare includes two key words from the above passage in the beautiful verbal portrait of Cordelia spoken by the Gentleman in IV.iii: " . . . she heav'd the name of 'father' / Pantingly forth, as if it press'd her heart" (25–26). *Heave* represents hard-hitting diction; in the first scene it almost suggests regurgitation. *Heart*, by contrast, evokes the softness and warmth of the cordial Cordelia. Both words serve to characterize her, for she is a mixture of softness and strength. She is tender in her love for her father and tough in employing military force to rescue him. The teacher may choose to assign the preceding exchange for students to compare in *Leir* and *King Lear* or may simply point out in lecture or discussion how Shakespeare has used his source and to what effect.

When Spenser, in *The Faerie Queene*, refers to Cordelia's response during the love test, he uses language like that of the *Leir* play: "[Her] simple answere, wanting colours faire / To paint it forth, him to displeasance moov'd" (2.10.28), but Spenser's version of the story differs in important ways: it uses the "Shakespearean" spelling for Cordelia's name and speaks of her death by hanging. These features Shakespeare incorporated into his play along with several details from Sidney's *Arcadia* (see Bullough): (1) the manner of Lear's suffering and death (Sidney: "[The Paphlagonian king's] hart broken with unkindnes and affliction, stretched so farre beyond his limits with this excesse of comfort" [Bullough 407]; Shakespeare: "I tax [i.e., "accuse"] not you, you elements, with unkindness" and "he hates him / That would upon the rack of this tough world / Stretch him out longer" [III. ii.16, V.iii.314–16]); (2) the deception practiced by Edmund against Gloucester (from the story of Plangus); (3) the matter of suicide, justice, and innocent victims (from a verse dialogue between Plangus and Basilius); and (4) the storm. This last detail may also have been suggested by some incidents in the *Leir* play: Gonorill's soliloquy denigrating her father in order to remove blame from herself for having mistreated him (" . . . after him Ile send such thunderclaps / Of slaunder, scandall, and invented tales" [Bullough 361]) and the flash of lightning and the repeated sound of thunder in the messenger scene (Bullough 377–79). The storm in *King Lear* may also derive from Spenser's brief but vivid description of the tempestuous times of Rivallo, a descendant of "Leyr," recalled in *The Faerie Queene* (2.10.34): "In [Rivallo's] sad time [cf. the phrase at the close of *King Lear*] blood did from heaven raine." But it is Harsnett who speaks most frequently of violent storms blowing "downe steeples, trees, maypoles"; of "the huge thunder cracke of adiuration" along with "lightning from heaven" and "shelter against what wind or weather so ever" (Muir, *King Lear* 239–41). In addition, Harsnett provided Shakespeare with an array of diabolical names ("Frateretto," "Fliberdigibbet," "Hoberdidance") and other details of diction for Edgar's portrayal of Poor Tom, whose psychological tempest reflects the natural madness of the Fool, the actual madness of Lear, and the general madness of the world.

To explore the way Shakespeare amplifies, condenses, or complicates his sources, students may be given portions of both the *Leir* play and the relevant episodes of Sidney's *Arcadia* to consider. It works very well to place Bullough's seventh volume (and other such studies, if the teacher desires) on reserve and then to assign, in sequential order, one segment from *Leir* and one from Sidney to each student; on the first day *King Lear* is considered, the student will read aloud a succinct and specific statement addressing the following questions: (1) What does Shakespeare take unchanged from your segment of *Leir* and the Sidney narrative? (2) What does he add? (3) What does he condense? (4) What else does he do besides add to or subtract from the sources? (5) What artistic or dramatic effects are achieved by what he has done? Before the students submit their written statements, the teacher should have each student read them in sequence, all of the *Leir* material first and then all of the Sidney narrative. Once the reading has taken place, the class will have participated, within the space of about forty minutes, in a group commentary on two of Shakespeare's chief sources for *King Lear*. Furthermore, the teacher now feels confident that anything said in subsequent meetings about sources will not sound remote or intimidating.

The next step is language. To introduce students to the linguistic features of Shakespeare's English, one should make use of the forthright accounts in David Bevington's introduction and glossary in his edition of *The Complete Works*, the first chapter of David Zesmer's *Guide to Shakespeare*, Winifred M. T. Nowottny's "Some Aspects of the Style of *King Lear*," Sheldon P. Zitner's "*King Lear* and Its Language," and David Aers and Gunther Kress's "Language of Social Order: Individual, Society, and Historical Process in *King Lear.*" For most students a sound introduction to Shakespeare's English and its possibilities is available in these works. The students can read and be held responsible for at least the Bevington, Zesmer, or Nowottny discussion. One of these could be incorporated into an examination or quiz question or into an assignment of a paper. The teacher might use all the readings listed as the basis for lecture material and as sources for three or four leading questions to be used in class during a discussion of language.

King Lear features several forms that structure language: blank verse, prose, rhymed verse, and doggerel. Students need to know that these create social and emotional distinctions as well as rhetorical and character contrasts. Even though, as Maurice Charney tells us, "[Shakespeare's] language has the freedom, irregularity, and self-indulgence of spoken English" (*How to Read Shakespeare* 54), it adheres to formal structures of language. The language is stylized, and yet it is extremely flexible. It can be knotty and angular, and it can also be plain.

Such plainness opens and closes *King Lear.* The opening prose exchange between Kent and Gloucester is conversational, even bawdy; Edmund's language here is that of a guarded, concealing formality. Soon all of this gives way to verse and a language of court ceremony and ritual, which in turn generates Goneril's and Regan's deceitful language, Cordelia's disturbing reticence (a "plainness" that Lear links with "pride" [I.i.129]), Kent's energetic bluntness ("To plainness honor's bound," he says [I.i.148]), and Lear's vituperative imprecations. In the subplot too one hears a forthright conversational language as well as relatively formal language, both of which are sometimes used for either deceitful purposes or for blunt communication. This mixture of the colloquial and the formal for deception or bluntness echoes ironically the main plot. Then the Fool enters the play, with his half-cracked language of parody, doggerel, ellipsis, and sardonic wit. He also amplifies the bluntness already associated with Gloucester and Kent in the opening scene. Later the disguised Edgar shows the language to be even more flexible by mimicking various dialects. Finally, out of disguise, Edgar utters the plain but moving lines that close the play.

An assignment for students may involve their finding examples of the various kinds of language discussed above or of still other features. And the teacher may wish to offer some suggestions here, pointing out that the language can be allusive (Aesopian: "thou bor'st thine ass on thy back o'er the dirt" [I.iv.161-62]; Promethean: "O Regan, she hath tied / Sharp-tooth'd unkindness, like a vulture, here" [II.iv.134-35]; Arthurian: "This prophecy Merlin shall make, for I live before his time" [III.ii.95]; biblical: "O dear father, / It is thy business that I go about" [IV.iv.23-24]; Sidneyan: "Have I caught thee?" [V.iii.21]). And it can be paradoxical: "Nothing almost sees miracles / But misery" (II.ii.165–66). The language of rage, anger, coarseness, and madness is at the center of this tragedy, but silences also play a role: "What shall Cordelia speak? Love, and be silent" (I.i.62). After preparing us for the silence, Cordelia utters the word that is at once staggering, sobering, and inciting. Right up to the last moments of the play, Shakespeare stresses the dramatic importance of what is *not* said: Edmund is silent too long about his death orders (Waldo F. McNeir studies this detail usefully in "The Role of Edmund in *King Lear*") and Lear, after howling in response to the Cordelia who now is silent in death (an ironic recapitulation of the opening scene), gazes at her corpse and recalls how "Her voice was ever soft, / Gentle, and low" (V.iii.273–74). By this time it is clear that the silences of *King Lear* are like a vacuum that draws into itself all that is sounded and heard. They are like Edgar's "happy hollow of a tree" (II.iii.2), waiting to be filled with echoes reverberating and amplifying the original sounds.

In addition to the dramatic contrast between silences and sounds is that between two different ways of understanding or using language. In *Shakespearean Meanings* (esp. 237–59 and 276–79), Sigurd Burckhardt develops the complicated but instructive idea that Lear's "wrath and rashness receive the precise definition of a verbal *act*" (241). Lear, that is, desires to eliminate the mediacy of all discourse and hence to "strip off all that stands between him and the truth" (277). He regards Kent as guilty for seeking "To come betwixt our sentence and our power, / Which nor our nature nor our place can bear" (I.i.170–71). Lear willfully seeks immediacy, the direct, confrontational acquisition of truth through language. By contrast, Gloucester understands speech in terms of mediacy or reported indirectness, that is, in terms of mere signs that may or may not point in the right direction; he is easily tricked by means of a forged or "indirect" letter. Lear craves the uncovered, naked truth that is his privilege as one who equates his "sentence" (sovereign speech) and his "power" (the force that creates immediately what speech calls for). He makes the mistake of taking Cordelia at her word. To him the word *Nothing* is understood in its most literal sense: Nothing is nothing is nothing and hence "Nothing will come of nothing." Lear refuses to ponder the word, to go beneath it and mine it for what it may tell him about the woman who uses it. This is too indirect for him, for his very identity as a twin-bodied king made up of a personal self ("our nature") and regal self ("our place") is sustained by his headstrong attitude that speech creates what it states. Assuming, for example, that words of love will immediately or directly create love, he imperiously conducts the foolish contest in the opening scene of the play. But ironically his tragic fall is a direct confrontation with a condition where, says Burckhardt, "all that is sophisticate and indirect, all art and all artful constructs of rational discourse, are stripped away and the bare forked animal alone is left" (278).

More recently, Timothy J. Reiss (applying Michel Foucault's theory of discourse) in *Tragedy and Truth* speaks of *King Lear* as a "clash of different ways of using language, of different discourses, of different ways of conceiving the relation of language to the world, to the speaker and the hearers, to meaning and action" (189). *King Lear* is not only filled with a variety of language, it is also a play about language. The teacher may ask the students to offer details from the play to support this view. If some encouragement is needed to get them started, one may quote the following: "Mean time we shall *express* our darker purpose" (I.i.36); "*Tell* me, my daughters / . . . Which of you shall we *say* doth love us most?" (I.i.48, 51); "*Speak* / . . . Nothing will come of nothing, *speak* again" (I.i.86, 90). These few examples (with italics added) represent only a beginning of a series of references to words, ways of speaking, and other concerns of language found in the play and should stimulate students to come up with several other related passages. Then the teacher may want to point out that, according to Reiss, *King Lear* "shows us people trapped between two different conceptions of what language is and does." Cordelia sees language as referential, intrinsically linking what one says with the world, with meaning; Goneril, Regan, and Edmund use language as an "instrument for the acquisition of power and possessions, for the imposition of the speaker" (189). Lear himself inclines toward Cordelia's conception of language but also wants to practice it in the way that Goneril and Regan do. In seeking to use both, he ends up with neither, and this futile attempt underscores the impact of the play.

The impact of *King Lear* also has been explored over the past forty years through various studies of its figurative and literal imagery. Images abound in *King Lear* and often serve as a chief way of making the play accessible to students. Robert Heilman's *This Great Stage* is the central study of patterned imagery in *King Lear*, and any teacher who deals with the play must know what this critical study has to offer; in addition, one should consult other contributions to the area: Thelma N. Greenfield's "The Clothing Motif in *King Lear*," Wolfgang Clemen's *Development of Shakespeare's Imagery*, and W. R. Keast's strictures regarding Heilman's book in "The 'New Criticism' and *King Lear*."

A certain amount of commentary on networks of images can be done in the classroom, but this should not be overdone. The teacher may specify four or five iterative references each to sight, animals, clothing, and nature. Students might assist in this kind of analysis but should be made aware that the dramatic context of such references must be considered. For example, Lear's "Out of my sight" (I.i.157), addressed angrily to Kent, is linked dramatically to the blindness of the king as it concerns those who love him most. Furthermore, students should realize that images are interrelated: figurative references to sight or sightlessness become associated with the literal image of Gloucester's blinding; and, at the turning point of the play (III.iv.101–09), after many references to clothing in earlier scenes, Lear tears off his own clothing in a gesture that suggests his wish to see clearer the reality of animal nature and its relation to human nature. Students find this use of New Critical analysis appealing, for it gives them the satisfaction of specifying how coherence and unity occur in such a large play as *King Lear*. Also appealing and helpful is the study of the relation between verbal elements in the play and different forms of iconography. Russell A. Fraser's *Shakespeare's Poetics in Relation to* King Lear is extremely useful in preparing a lecture on this matter. Fraser's book may even be placed on reserve should a short paper on iconography in *King Lear* be assigned. The connection between literal or figurative language and pictorial analogues (paintings, engravings, sculptures) for that language, as studied by scholars such as Fraser and Wylie Sypher, never ceases to interest students. Their attention is readily captured by the literal and figurative storm images that become the storm scene on the stage, by clothing references that translate into costumes, and by animal references that support actors' and actresses' portrayal of the bestiality of the evil daughters, as well as the primitiveness of Poor Tom and the dehumanized life of Lear.

When a class has at its disposal the BBC-TV/Time-Life version of *King Lear*, with Michael Hordern as Lear, particular attention can be given to the transfer of word to theatrical production. For example, students can discuss whether the use of Jacobean costumes in the video version is an appropriate approach to the verbal images of clothing found in the play. Another directorial touch is the depiction of Poor Tom. In disguise, Edgar (played by Anton Lesser) wears a crown of thorny nettles and reveals a stigmatalike wound in the palm of one hand. On his other hand is a crawling insect, an object of contemplation during the soliloquy that opens IV.i:

> Yet better thus, and known to be contemn'd,
> Than still contemn'd and flatter'd. To be worst,
> The lowest and most dejected thing of fortune,
> Stands still in esperance, lives not in fear.

This scene is part of a theatrical context that uses animal imagery very well, but we should question the way Poor Tom is made up to suggest Christ or St. Francis. Does this force a Christian reading on the play? Students enjoy exploring this question. At the same time they can explore the iconography of the lower animal world in religious emblems and paintings, which may be the source for how Poor Tom is depicted in the BBC version. The insect-like fiends attacking or hovering over St. Anthony Abbot in various paintings or engravings (Bosch's early painting of the saint in Madrid's Prado or

Schongauer's engraving in New York's Metropolitan Museum, for example) are relevant to this conception of Poor Tom, whose video portrayal serves well as the basis for a short paper on the iconographic tradition and theatrical production. Another short paper might focus attention on the portrayal of the Fool by an older actor (Frank Middlemass) to emphasize the folly of old Lear. The Fool is in whiteface to suggest not only his jester status but also to create a range of suggestions: innocence, illness, death, blankness, and nothing. After the rainstorm the Fool utters his last line ("And I'll go to bed at noon" [III.vi.85]), and the rain has washed the whiteness from his face. A question should be put to the class: Does the washing away of the clownish whiteface represent the cleansing effect of suffering, the wiping away of foolishness, and the acquisition of a new "face" as far as Lear is concerned? With questions like this we move inevitably into a consideration of character.

The characters of *King Lear* represent various levels of society, different ways of using language, and several political and moral attitudes. Furthermore, they are participants in a complex structure of relationships. By using a blackboard diagram the teacher may communicate to students a visual equivalent of Lear's relationships with other characters. Write the characters' names on the board, and then connect Lear's name to each of the others with (1) smooth lines to indicate good relationships (e.g., Lear and the Fool), (2) jagged lines to indicate faulty ones, and (3) a combination of smooth and jagged lines for relationships that either deteriorate (e.g., Lear-Goneril, Lear-Regan) or strengthen (e.g., Lear-Cordelia). Students might participate early in the diagramming until all the characters, except very minor ones, and all major relationships are accounted for. This activity not only introduces students to the characters but also represents, as one student put it, "something to hold on to" when entering the labyrinth of the play. From this point, one may move to a more substantial analysis of individual characters.

Having students deal with characters in terms of basic critical questions is very instructive. What do characters say? How do they say things? What does one character say about another character? How is this said? All four questions are essential and are applicable to the very opening of *King Lear*. Here Kent speaks of the sons-in-law and reveals his uncertainty as to whom the king prefers; Gloucester continues the idea of uncertainty as he too speaks of the sons-in-law. The opening lines provide incomplete exposition through the uncertainty expressed by both Kent and Gloucester, but this also creates important dramatic tension. Kent and Gloucester are in a political position to know whom the king prefers, but neither of them does know. Ironically, Kent does not even know Edmund, never having met him, but will "sue to know [him] better." Kent's line is spoken almost perfunctorily. The intelligent Edmund senses this tone, for his response includes the word *study*, a term that implies calculation, an appropriate frame of mind for the chief Machiavel of the play. We learn, then, a great deal about these characters in a very short space. As the play unfolds, an additional question must be asked: What does each character in the play want? When we begin pondering this question, we are on our way to knowing the characters in *King Lear*.

One feature of the characters we come to know is their associations with certain moral, political, or social principles. Characters themselves become thematic and, as such, help to make *King Lear* a modern parable, something Maynard Mack demonstrates in King Lear *in Our Time*. Although the pre-Shakespearean tradition of the allegorical drama, as Bernard Spivack has shown in *Shakespeare and the Allegory of Evil*, stands behind the dramaturgy of the play and can be seen in the homiletic features of the Fool and the Vicelike wit and shrewdness of Edmund, characters in *King Lear* are not in a strict sense allegorical. And yet we may see Lear as Suffering Humanity, Cordelia as Innocent Victim, Kent as Loyal Service, and Edmund as *Realpolitik*. Shakespeare in *Lear* wants to generalize and to have the play assume a mythic expansiveness. Part of the greatness of *King Lear* is its referential drive, and this drive generates thematic power.

This thematic power resides, certainly, in the play's forceful treatments of human suffering, the bestial within humanity, the primacy of passion, the folly of the world, self-discovery, regeneration, human cruelty toward human beings, the need for ripeness, helplessness, Christian values, pagan values, the perversion of love, the destruction of love, the redemptive power of love, contingency, mortality, gradations of service, errors in judgment and their consequences, the paradoxes of seeing in blindness and reasoning in madness, the Machiavellian version of political reality, division and disorder, the education of the young and the old, the contention between the young and the old, the Apocalypse, the monstrosity of the Freudian id, and nothingness. Obviously, all these themes cannot possibly be dealt with in any given semester that devotes about six meetings to *King Lear*. Whole books have focused attention on important themes in the play—John F. Danby's *Shakespeare's Doctrine of Nature* and William R. Elton's King Lear *and the Gods*, to name just two; therefore, the rubric "be selective" should sound all the more sage and sane.

I usually select one or two themes to emphasize and develop more fully than others in lecture and discussion. One of the most manageable in the classroom is the theme of self-discovery, and I recommend it to teachers of the play. The students respond to its clear development and to its universal and timeless import. Lear has "ever but slenderly known himself" (I.i.293–94), but as Paul Jorgensen informs us in *Lear's Self-Discovery*, his gradual knowledge of self does come; in fact, it follows stages that recall the main topics in treatises of *nosce teipsum* ("know thyself") in the Renaissance:

(1) nature as tutor (Danby's book is important in this regard), (2) the difficulty of acquiring self-knowledge, (3) flattery as a deterrent to self-knowledge, (4) affliction as a stimulus to self-knowledge, and, most important, (5) the study of one's own passions and one's own body as ways to self-knowledge.

Deceived by flattery and taught by nature through affliction, Lear eventually moves, with difficulty, toward subduing passion and quelling his obsessive concern with the physical. Regarding his behavior generally and his treatment of Cordelia specifically, he comes to experience "sovereign shame" (IV.iii.42) and a "burning shame" (IV.iii.46). This realization comes shortly before the climactic recognition scene, in which Lear reveals insight into his own self as well as into the self of Cordelia: "I am a very foolish fond old man, / . . . Pray you now forget, and forgive; I am old and foolish" (IV.vii.59, 84). He answers, at least in part, his own question asked early in the play: "Who is it that can tell me who I am?" (I.iv.230). It is not the complete or the perfect answer; but, by contrast with the blind rashness the old king exhibited in earlier scenes, it is a dignified achievement worthy of a great tragic figure. I find Jorgensen's book most helpful in teaching the play through the theme of self-discovery. The teacher, however, may also want to show students the arguments of some other critics who do not see such optimistic progress in King Lear. For purposes of class discussion or for papers, the teacher may wish to assign students such commentary on King Lear as that in Rolf Soellner's Shakespeare's Patterns of Self-Knowledge and in the essay of Thomas P. Roche, Jr., entitled " 'Nothing Almost Sees Miracles': Tragic Knowledge in King Lear." Lear, according to Roche, has learned nothing: "Not even suffering has taught him anything" (161). Lively discussion and writing result when students take their stands on the matter of self-discovery.

Toward the end of the time spent on King Lear, I find it useful for students to write in class a single sentence stating what they see as the play's most important themes. A model for this brief exercise is as follows:

> King Lear is an apocalyptic play that dramatizes the link between humanity and brute nature and what happens when division in the family, state, cosmos, and individual mind strips humankind of its protective garment, making it intensely vulnerable and subject to the onslaught of the bestial, irrational world and hence forcing certain individuals to discover both a humanity and a self never before experienced.

Not all students will write this kind of statement, but something like this may serve as the teacher's contribution to the exercise after the best student responses have been chosen, reproduced, and distributed. The statements can be evaluated in class as part of the last meeting on *King Lear*. This procedure assists the summing up of the play and leads effectively into the teacher's concluding remarks. It also once again gives the students "something to hold on to" as they anticipate a paper assignment or examination on the play.

This, then, is the *King Lear* of an eclectic approach. I think that the teacher who is disturbed by one critical school's clashing with another does well to reconcile them for purposes of the classroom, to take the best of what each has to offer, and to impart the sum to students.

Teaching a Plural Work Pluralistically

Kenneth S. Rothwell

In teaching a work as plural as *King Lear*, I use a pluralistic approach that considers the play on the printed page as well as on stage and on film.[1] I begin with text and context, as I ask students to identify and define the principal facts, issues, contexts, forces, and dilemmas one needs to know about for intelligent discussion of *King Lear*. To achieve this end, we subject the text to a Cartesian part-whole analysis. Nothing teaches better than the experience of disassembling and reassembling. The French school of criticism and the Yale theorists have opened up enormously sophisticated ways of decentering and deconstructing literary texts. For my own part I have leaned heavily on traditional Aristotelian systems from the *Art of Poetry*. For example, in *A Mirror for Shakespeare*, a study guide written for my students at the University of Vermont, the *King Lear* section, as well as others, is structured around the categories of plot (*mythos*), character (*ethos*), theme (*dianoia*), language (*lexis*), spectacle (*opsis*), music (*melos*). Thus, I establish the "goals" for *King Lear*, as though one could ever resolve them, as follows:

- Plot (*mythos*): To see how Shakespeare has reshaped the legendary tale of a wrathful old king's division of his kingdom among his children (from Geoffrey of Monmouth) into a tragic drama, emblematic of the human condition. To note the labyrinthine echoes and contrasts achieved by redundancy: the same story is told through the experiences of the Lear group (Lear-Goneril-Regan-Cordelia-Kent) in the main plot and through those of the Gloucester family (Gloucester-Edmund-Edgar) in the subplot.
- Character (*ethos*): To observe how the mirror effect created by the twin plots allows manifold opportunities to compare the two fathers (Lear and Gloucester) and the decent with the impudent servant (Kent and Oswald). To notice the way characters may also be said to stand for moral absolutes of good and evil and to examine the functions of clowns and lunatics (the Fool and Mad Tom) as extensions of the personalities of their masters and as agents of paradox.
- Theme (*dianoia*): To explore the multiple ways Shakespeare investigates the mystery of human life in confrontation with wild and inexplicable forces of good and evil. *Lear* is a play about growing old, about suffering, about despair, about alienation, about "the end of the world," and, paradoxically, about the triumph of humanity over all of these horrors.

- Language (*lexis*): To look at the ways Shakespeare succeeds in creating great poetry as well as great drama in the surge and power of words that link the "little world of man" with the ultimate forces of an inscrutable universe.

Having established goals, or priorities, the next step is to compose study questions for guiding the students more or less sequentially through the text. Begun informally as dittoed handouts, my own questions gradually expanded and, after much student criticism, eventually emerged as the *Mirror*, mentioned above. These questions are not designed to circumvent, avoid, bypass, or simplify the text, as is often the case with commercial crib notes, but rather to reawaken interest in it. At their most obvious, even banal, they simply italicize literal meanings ("What is the strange news that Cornwall has heard" [II.i.87]?).[2] Others, though, are expected to stimulate significant thought about the way Shakespeare worked (e.g., "How can Lear's relationship with Goneril and his own daughters be taken as representative of all father-daughter bonds?"). The labor of composing over eight hundred questions for twenty-seven of the plays led to the discovery of what I call the "mirror" principle—or, more accurately, I should say, to "my" discovery of it. Surely the mirror conceit is at least as ancient as the medieval church, where liturgy was thought of as a mirror to life. By the mirror principle, I mean that Shakespeare's plays are viewed as the assembling of a finite set of motifs, situations, and characters into an almost infinite set of mirror relations. The parallel plots in *King Lear* that tell the story twice of faithful and unfaithful children offer a prime example. The technique pervades the canon, however, down to and including even the quips, puns, and equivocations of wordplay. Indeed the mirroring of one situation through the "portraiture" of another (to use Prince Hamlet's word—V.ii.78) creates the illusion of depth and profundity in Shakespeare's work. Audience interaction with text converts that illusion into a reality.

Shakespeare, in other words, not only writes about people and events; even more, he manipulates them to create dramatic effects in the mind of his spectator. Hence it is more intelligent to study his structural tactics than to attempt resolutions of the myriad riddles and crypto-puzzles they spawn. For example, the old (and unanswerable) question of whether *King Lear* is about the triumph of life over death, or of death over life, is less important than the new (and relatively answerable) question of how Shakespeare planted that quandary in the spectator's or reader's mind. Gloucester's "As flies to wanton boys are we to th' gods" (IV.i.36) creates an inverse mirror effect in Edgar's reassuring "The gods are just . . ." (V.iii.171). As in so many of the plays, the contrarieties of *King Lear* have literally been done with mirrors in a kind of Shakespearean magic show.

With some justice, perceptive colleagues will find all this too formalistic in its elevation of dramaturgy over theme. Theme, however, springs from dramaturgy, just as character comes from plot, not the other way around. At the least the approach offers a formula for riveting attention on Shakespeare's text rather than on our own.

Finally, I also felt that in printed form these questions would offer a basis for discussion and for the free exploration in class of matters of greater importance. The questions equip students to be structuralists but do not prevent them from becoming poststructuralists. Here is a sampler from the *Mirror* (283-86), using the third act of *King Lear*:

Act Three

1.   III.i offers another example of a scene that serves narrative more than the dramatic ends as the "Gentleman" describes the mad behavior of the old King (III.i.4 ff.). Kent (now disguised as Caius) hears how Lear strives "in his little world of man" (III.i.10) to "outscorn" the elements. References to a "bear," "lion," and "wolf," also typical of the animal imagery of the play, suggest a world in which men are reduced to beasts (cf. Regan as "serpent-like" [II.iv.161]; both sisters as "tigers" [IV.ii.40]; and Albany's "Humanity must perforce prey on itself, / Like monsters of the deep" [IV.ii.49]). How does this scene also prepare the way for Lear's appearance in III.ii?

2.   In III.ii Lear's cosmic language links the "little world of man" with the storm on the heath. Would there have been sound effects on the Elizabethan stage to supplement this language? What cinematic techniques are used in the Peter Brook film to supplement Shakespeare's words? Compare the Fool's song (III.ii.74) with Feste's in *TN* (V.i.389). The hospitable interior world of *TN* has been replaced by the pitiless exterior world of the "Wind and the rain." What dramatic or thematic significance is implied in the lines by Lear's Fool, "Here's a night pities neither wise men nor fools" (III.ii.12); and Lear's "I am a man / More sinn'd against than sinning" (III.ii.59) and "My wits begin to turn" (III.ii.67)?

3.   The brief III.iii informs us that Gloucester has been mistreated by Cornwall and Regan who have usurped his home. What is the irony in Gloucester's confiding to Edmund that he now leans toward the king?

. . . .

5.   With the entry of Edgar as "mad Tom" (III.iv.39), the style of speech, though in fact obligated to Samuel Harsnett's *A Declaration*

of Egregious Popish Impostures (1603), begins to take on "apocalyptic" features—broken syntax, vivid imagery, discontinuity in thought, allusiveness, hints of imminent disclosure of truth. How does this style fit the major themes of *Lr.*? How does "mad Tom" mirror, or echo, the other Fool in the play both in character and function?

6.   Comment on the meaning of Lear's great line, "unaccommodated man is no more but such a poor, bare, fork'd animal, as thou art" (III.iv.106). Is there any metaphysical significance to the line, "What is the cause of thunder?" (III.iv.155)? In what sense does this line, as Professor Elton argues in King Lear *and the Gods*, reflect the concept of a "vanishing God" (*Deus absconditus*)? In what ways is this similar to *"Terras Astraea reliquit"* in *Tit.* (IV.iii.4)?

. . . .

10.   With the parting words "And I'll go to bed at noon" (III.vi.85), Lear's Fool vanishes never to reappear again. Has his role been usurped by the "counterfeiting" (III.vi.61) poor Tom? Or, was the actor needed to double as Cordelia (cf. V.iii.306)? On what basis does Edgar compare himself with Lear (III.vi.102 ff.) at the close of this scene?

11.   In III.vi, explain the significance of the mock trial. Does it have "metatheatrical" implications? Compare with Falstaff and Hal in *1H4* II.iv.376 ff. Has Lear's language begun to deteriorate? Is it moving toward the "apocalyptic" like Tom's? Can Lear's question, "Is there any cause in nature that make these hard hearts" (III.vi.77), be taken as a vein of skepticism about divine order?

12.   The frightfully cruel scene (III.vii) in which Gloucester is blinded by Cornwall employs "Senecan" elements to make a scathing commentary on the nature of evil in man. Is there any moral justification for the blinding of Gloucester, or is this another example (e.g., the stocking of Kent) of good causes being rewarded by wicked effects? In short, what is the connection between cause and effect? What is the point of having the servant attack Cornwall and then die by Regan's hand? At III.vii.84, does Gloucester resemble Sophocles' Oedipus? In what ways is Gloucester's tragedy a reenactment of Lear's? Comment on Regan's line, ". . . let him smell / His way to Dover" (III.vii.93).

Act Four

1.   In IV.i, how do the references to Gloucester's blindness advance the theme of sight vs. sightlessness (IV.i.19 ff.)? Is Gloucester's despairing (and non-Christian) comment, "As flies to wanton boys are we to th' gods" (IV.i.36), merely a personal expression of his own

fate, or a theme statement for the whole play? For a precisely opposing view, as pointed out by Michael Goldman, compare with Edgar's
"The gods are just" (V.iii.171 ff.). How does Gloucester's experience
in unknowingly having his own son lead him to Dover (IV.i.55)
parallel, or mirror, Lear's relationship with his daughters?

Sets of questions such as these can also be assigned to subgroups in the
class to ensure that the elusive "lively and spontaneous discussion" will
occur at a subsequent class meeting. They are also helpful in assigning
papers built around the mirror principle. Close specifications for papers
forestall plagiarism, a nightmarish problem in Shakespeare studies with its
avalanche of published commentary. Requiring students to pick a key
passage and then show how it mirrors other portions of the text thwarts
derivative work by restricting the assignment to close explication. To that
end, as set forth elsewhere ("Programs"), I have constructed a heuristic
framework of questions to be thought about, though not necessarily
answered seriatim (indeed the latter is to be discouraged). For example, a
student may decide to write about the old king's lamentation over the body
of Cordelia: "Do you see this? Look on her! Look her lips, / Look there,
look there!" (V.iii.311–12). Those lines then should be thought and written
about in the context of one or more of the following questions:

1. What is the simple meaning of the passage (questions of its signif-
    icance can come later on)? That may involve the definition of difficult,
    or archaic, words, for example, *misprision, point device, presently,* or
    vouchsafe.
2. In what context does the passage occur—that is, Who are the charac-
    ters involved? What are they doing? How did they get there? What are
    they wearing? etc.
3. What are Shakespeare's strategies for breathing life into the charac-
    ters? through their own dialogue? opinions of other characters? non-
    verbal gestures?
4. Are there words or phrases that echo, mirror, reflect, or reverberate off
    similar images elsewhere in the same play? At this stage, students are
    entitled to know about Marvin Spevack's one-volume *Harvard Concor-
    dance to Shakespeare,* a treasure trove for image hunters.
5. What major contribution does the passage make to the overall artistic
    design of the play? To look at the matter from another perspective,
    would it make any difference if the passage were deleted by an adven-
    turous stage or screen director?
6. Do any comparisons or contrasts with similar designs, motifs, or scenes
    in this or other plays come to mind?

7. What "personal transaction" can you make with the passage and/or play?

The plural *King Lear* exists, however, not only on the page of the printed book but on stage and screen as well. Outside of major urban areas, few opportunities exist for viewing live Shakespeare performances, hence the need for home-brewed resources. To that end, each Friday a subgroup of my class, aided, cajoled, and coached by a student intern, performs a scene or two, using rudimentary props and costumes—perhaps a blackboard sketch to suggest a castle, or, as in a memorable *Tempest*, a cast outfitted in T-shirts emblazoned with the word "Bermuda." More cautious teachers might consider a variant scheme that I have tried: to videotape a scene or two at the university television station with the help of student volunteers. Much can be learned about filmmaking, and the laundered results can be safely exposed to classroom viewing.

Cinema and television have added yet another powerful weapon to the pedagogical arsenal—Shakespeare on screen. Since 1971, four important films and/or videotapes of *King Lear* have been produced, the first released being the Grigori Kozintsev Russian-language (English subtitles) version, starring Yuri Jarvet in the title role. Shortly thereafter Peter Brook released his movie remake of the 1962 Royal Shakespeare Company production, which, as in the film, starred Paul Scofield (see Hetherington). A decade later, following what seems to be a trend in screen treatments of *King Lear*, two video versions appeared, again almost at the same time. The first was Jonathan Miller's 1982 BBC-TV/Time-Life *King Lear* starring Michael Hordern, one in a series known as The Shakespeare Plays, widely shown in the United States on public television. Hard on its heels in 1983 came the Granada Television *King Lear*, directed by Michael Elliott and starring Laurence Olivier.

If universities had Pentagon-sized budgets and students the stamina, all four versions of *King Lear* could be screened in a ten-hour orgy to reveal the plurality of interpretation that any Shakespeare text invites. Since neither contingency exists, tough choices must be made. Of the two films (not the videotapes by Miller and Elliott), Kozintsev's is the least utilitarian for classroom use. Despite stirring music by Dmitri Shostakovich and translation of Shakespeare's English into Russian by Boris Pasternak, Kozintsev's film proves less appealing to typical undergraduates than does Brook's. By committing an act of double translation—from English into Russian and from drama to movie, Kozintsev sufficiently liberated himself for almost purely cinematic re-creation of *King Lear*. In this respect he produced a masterpiece of filmed Shakespeare comparable to Akira Kurosawa's Japanese-language *Macbeth (Throne of Blood)*. These cinematic virtues notwithstanding, most persons will then turn to the English-language Brook version, for ignorance of Russian can obscure the delights of the Pasternak translation.

Writing of the Kozintsev and Brook films, Jack J. Jorgens in his influential *Shakespeare on Film* points out that the two versions represent "two *King Lears*": Kozintsev's "a story of redemption and social renewal" (237), Brook's "a bleak existential tale of meaningless violence in a cold, empty universe" (236). Brook has filtered *King Lear* through the sensibility of the *auteur* and visualized the verbal in exciting but controversial ways. Godardian devices of cinematic alienation, overtones of Brechtian epic theater, echoes of Artaud's Theatre of Cruelty and Jan Kott's *Shakespeare Our Contemporary* identify the film with the early-seventies Vietnam era. The use of silent film subtitles, rapid acceleration, and lopsided frames (at the end Paul Scofield as King Lear literally falls out of the frame)—all reminiscent of Sergei Eisenstein's *Potemkin*—turn Lear's world into an apocalyptic vision of the postholocaust era. A Mister Kurtz with a white beard, the old king prefigures the Marlon Brando of *Apocalypse Now*. It is a world, as someone once said, that "Shakespeare intrudes on." Students and teacher return to the printed text motivated to analyze the radical ways this imaginative director has transformed words into pictures.

The two recent television productions mentioned above are available on videocassette. As is so often the case, Shakespeare on television may reveal either more or less to the viewer than is possible in the living theater. Reviewing the BBC version, for example, one *King Lear* scholar, Steven Urkowitz, wrote that the actors' "words are unconnected to what we see happening on the screen" ("*King Lear* without Tears" 2). When Michael Hordern as the king tells Cordelia that his "tears do scald like molten lead," his eyes are dry. Ironically, however, Miller, the imaginative director, sought to emphasize actors' faces and words by presenting the production in a "spare, tightly focused fashion" (publicity release, 1982). Settings were designed to be deliberately rudimentary—crumpled black cloths to suggest "the desolation of the heath, " while the Jacobean costumes are almost entirely "in black, grey and white." Miller's choice of costumes is not as anachronistic as one might think; rather, it is an attempt to recapture the ambience of Shakespeare's playhouse where the actors often wore contemporary rather than period dress. In its fidelity to the Peter Alexander text, this *King Lear* runs three hours, which demands a commitment from both students and teachers. In the context of a production actually designed for students rather than for passive viewers, Michael Hordern in the title role displays his usual quietly expert style. Managing exaltation without flamboyance, Hordern achieves a high seriousness appropriate to the occasion. With Hordern is a fine supporting cast that includes veteran

Shakespearean actor Frank Middlemass as the Fool and Penelope Wilton as Regan.

The 1983 Granada Television *King Lear*, directed by Michael Elliott and starring Laurence Olivier, vindicates Peter Ustinov's "wraparound" remarks for the January 1984 premiere on national television that no other production of *King Lear* ever had a better cast.[3] Robert Lindsay's Edmund is a silky villain; David Threlfall's Edgar, passionately sincere; Colin Blakely's Kent, rough-hewn; Leo McKern's Gloucester, an endearing bumbler; John Hurt, a winsome Fool. The three daughters are superb: Diana Rigg, a cruel and sadistic Regan; Dorothy Tutin (curiously reminiscent of Irene Worth in the Brook film), a shrewd and calculating Goneril; and Anna Calder-Marshall, an angelic Cordelia.

At the center, however, is Olivier. Few will miss the self-referentiality that casts the aging monarch of the English-speaking theater in the role of King Lear. In an astonishing display of stamina for a man of his years, aided and abetted apparently by judicious reaction shots when he tired (Perret 1), Olivier employs his uncannily resourceful voice to wring surprising nuances from almost every word he speaks. His "lest it may mar your fortune" to Cordelia does things with *mar* and *fortune* most speakers would never even begin to think of. His nonverbal gestures, like those of the other actors in this production, provide a storehouse for showing how Shakespearean language prompts stage business. After Cordelia's "Nothing, my lord," Olivier's hand cups his ear and moves to his mouth both to reinforce Shakespeare's words and to express feelings that go beyond even Shakespeare's language. In the division-of-the-kingdom scene when Goneril and Regan seek to outdo each other in flattering the old king, Goneril slavishly bows to Lear only to have Regan go her one better by both bowing and kissing the king's hand.

These ocular virtues are partially undercut, however, by the deletions needed to compress the action into two hours and thirty minutes. A speech sliced in half may result in somebody's favorite line vanishing, such as Albany's "Humanity must perforce prey on itself, / Like monsters of the deep" (IV.ii.49). In other instances whole scenes (e.g., IV.iii and IV.iv) disappear. There are also inexplicable alterations, which seem to be rooted neither in the notorious discrepancies between quarto and First Folio texts nor in any obvious anxiety to modernize the language. One sometimes suspects lapses by the actors—for example, *think* for *look* at I.iv.71; *forgot* for *mistook* at II.iv.11; and *remission* for *remotion* at II.iv.114.

In color, the Granada version turns a studio set into a fairly convincing landscape for the scenes of the old king wandering the moors, where at one point he decks himself in flowers and sacrificially consumes the entrails of a quivering rabbit raw. The fertility of that landscape, which contrasts with the sterility of the Brook and Miller envisionments, endows the text with a redemptive sense. Olivier, looking cherubic after being shorn of his white beard, as though he had come full circle from old age to infancy, joins Cordelia for a final scene evocative of a pagan sacrifice. With both father and daughter enrobed in pure white, the ritualized pattern of their deaths suggests the propitiation of dark gods. That motif is further underscored by the Stonehenge-like settings framing the production, which, though shot entirely in a studio, also manages to provide a plausibly fertile green world when the old king must deck himself with flowers. Even so, the gap between the sham of the studio and the authenticity of Shakespeare's language is never quite bridged. Whatever its drawbacks, however, simply having the record of Laurence Olivier in performance gives the production an enduring value.

The plurality of *King Lear*, then, as it appears on the page, on the stage, and on the screen, emerges in multiple ways to provide a never-ending series of challenges and opportunities for teachers and students alike.

NOTES

[1]Portions of this article have been adapted from previous work I have published in *Teaching Notes* and the *Leaflet* (see Works Cited).

[2]All citations of Shakespeare's works are from the Evans edition.

[3]The Olivier *King Lear* received its American premiere at the New York City Museum of Broadcasting in spring 1983, as a part of the Britain Salutes New York Festival.

SPECIFIC APPROACHES

An Approach through Theme: Marriage and the Family

Lynda E. Boose

No play of Shakespeare's—and perhaps no work in literature—is as painfully difficult to teach as is *King Lear*. None prompts as much agony—personal, metaphysical, and pedagogical—as does the play that John Keats defined as "the fierce dispute / Betwixt damnation and impassioned clay" (lines 5-6 of "On Sitting down to read *King Lear* Once Again"). While everything about Hamlet's situation makes him a figure with whom students can readily identify, almost nothing in the experience of *Lear's* tragic hero invites such parallels. In preparing to teach the play, one cannot avoid being conscious of the unbridgeable gap between our students' experience of life and the enormous age and pain of the irascible old king who is himself responsible for most of the suffering and for whom there is no time left in which to make amends, begin again, or redeem the past—no opportunity, in other words, to do any of those things that our students' youth, their middle-class affluence, and the optimistic premises of their American culture assume to be inalienable rights. Even deciding to teach this awesome play is painful, for it compels the instructor to send students on a journey that will be filled with repeated loss, disappointment, and seemingly limitless suffering. Lear's challenge to the storm—"Pour on, I will endure"—all too accurately defines the response the play demands of its readers. Yet through the old king's paradigm of pain and endurance, the readers, the actors, and the characters they play ultimately do come

59

together in a synonymity of experience—one defined by the tough heroism explicit in Lear's eulogy: "the wonder is he [and we] have endured so long" (V.iii.315; this and subsequent quotations of *Lear* are from Muir's Arden edition).

Approaching *King Lear* from the perspective of marriage and the family has the particular advantage of providing students with a familiar reference point. But, furthermore, such an approach actually roots the play in the center of its tragic maelstrom. For in *Lear*, family issues are less a reflection of those in the political world than they are the genesis of them. The spotlight *King Lear* places on the family should be evident from the way conversations about the kingdom are repeatedly interrupted and displaced by those that thrust family rivalry—specifically, sibling competition for the father's love—to the center of the stage. In the opening scene, first the presence of Edmund and the subject of his bastardy versus Edgar's legitimacy usurp Gloucester's and Kent's anxieties about the forthcoming division; next, the competition among the king's three daughters again usurps the political issue and reduces the kingdom to merely a prize within the family game of "who loves the parent most"—a game with which anyone who grew up with siblings may be all too familiar.

Approaching the text through a focus on family issues enables a teacher to use any of several critical methodologies: archetypal, psychoanalytical, ritual, feminist, historical, structural, or a combination of several of these. Since the family is an institution with a definable structure of rules, it seems appropriate to study its significance in *Lear* by analyzing how the play's characters and narrative design dramatize the inherent codes of family—the rituals, taboos, distributions, and hierarchies that themselves depend on age, positional relationship, and gender.

The organization of the Elizabethan family and the society it mirrored was, like our own, patriarchal and patrilineal, transmitting authority and kinship through only the father. Unlike the contemporary family, however, it also transferred inheritance through primogeniture, a design that allowed the family to retain material power intact by passing it exclusively through the first male child. Social historian Lawrence Stone has defined the aristocratic sixteenth-century family as governed by a paternal authoritarianism through which the "husband and father lorded it over his wife and children with the quasi-absolute authority of a despot" (*Crisis* 591). Families in *Lear* fit Stone's definition. In terms of the play's reiterated principles of judicial distribution and division, the world of *King Lear* is a world of patriarchy, asymmetrical distribution, and polarization that divides like-gendered siblings, wife and husband, and fathers from children of either sex. And the text structurally accentuates the negative effects of the authoritarian patriarchy by its elimination of mothers and its refraction of the patriarchal image into a double-plot symmetry that places two such families, one consisting of father and daughters and the other of father and sons, into mirror relation.

In each of the two plots, the children are divided into the starkly archetypal categories of good and bad. Though in both plots the fathers initially love their good child best, they disastrously reverse their judgment, disinherit and cast out the good child, and in anger endow the bad ones. Also in both, however, even supplanting the favored child and getting all the father owns leaves the unfavored ones unsatisfied. For after they have acquired all, the evil children turn from the rationally explicable goal of self-acquisition to an irrational lust to deprive that is enacted in forms of gratuitous violence against the father, against the sibling who has already been dispossessed, and, in the Lear plot, even against one another. Lear's "pelican daughters" and Gloucester's bastard son have an insatiable greed for power, inheritance, and titular rule that masks, by implication, a set of more primal, inarticulate needs lurking potently beneath the text of this play like its "monsters from the deep." Ultimately, the needs of the unloved and the illegitimate express themselves in inverted forms of desire aimed symbolically against genital acts of fathering: thrusting the father and the child he favored out of the house and locking its gates, draining him of all he possesses and preventing him from begetting the fortune of the rival sibling, and violently castrating his authority by cutting off his "knightly train" (Willbern 245), clawing out his eyes, and emasculating his psychic image of virility. Eventually, Edmund even seeks to kill Lear, and Regan seeks to maim Gloucester as the insatiable rage of the neglected child overwhelms the play and vents itself indiscriminately against the world of the fathers.

In its exploration of the good-and-bad-child motif, *King Lear* goes far beyond the archetypal sibling dichotomy of the fairy tale, for it inscribes the image of filial monstrosity inside the context of an inverted quest for love. The quest is horrifically savage, yet it nonetheless rings with a pathos we cannot miss in the dying Edmund's wish to construe the evil sisters' murderous lust for him as an affirmation that "Yet Edmund was belov'd" (V.iii.238). It is not only the apportioning of justice and material goods that *Lear*'s world of patriarchal rule has "ta'en too little care of" nor only those commodities that cry out for a "distribution to undo excess." The play's repeated quantifications of "more" and "less," "all" and "nothing," accumulation and dispossession, continually rephrase the point that the power to bestow or abate, enlarge or scant, whether measured by the size of a kingdom or the number of knights, represents, on its most important level, the power to confer or withhold love.

While not only Lear and Gloucester but most of Shakespeare's fathers clearly fit Lawrence Stone's authoritarian model, family relations in the plays do not match Stone's related thesis that the Elizabethan family virtually lacked emotional bonds. And while Stone's contention that second and third sons were of negligible value seems accurately reflected in the Gloucester family, his assertion that daughters "were often unwanted and might be regarded as no more than a tiresome drain on the economic resources" (*Family* 121) is clearly inadequate to describe the father-daughter relationship either in this play or in the twenty-one others of Shakespeare where it occurs. Perhaps historians have been overhasty to infer that, since the daughter was the least economically useful member of a patrilineal and primogenitural institution, she was also the least desired. Instead of measuring what the daughter does not materially contribute to the family, we might consider just what she threatens to subtract from it. For if she is classified as the family's most expendable member, it may be because she is actually its least retainable. To an institution that fears loss, the daughter's presence by definition constitutes a threat to its maintenance of closed boundaries. She is always the transitory member of the group and is thus analogous to what social anthropologist Victor Turner defines as a "liminal" or threshold person within cultural space (94–130), whose very presence asserts a breach in the genealogical fence of family enclosure. In multiple ways, she signifies all that the father desires and simultaneously cannot have. She exists only to be lost—or, as Polonius recognizes about Ophelia, "I have a daughter—have while she is mine" (*Hamlet* II.ii.106).

If we consider what myths or rituals define Western culture's authorization of a son's or a daughter's independence, we will discover a telling difference. The son's struggle for individuation is legitimized within mythologized stories that at once reassuringly narrate the prodigal son's inevitable return and simultaneously threaten the father with usurpation. The biblical tales of the prodigal son and of King Herod, the Cronos-Zeus and the Oedipus myths, Freud's theory of the primal horde, and Shakespeare's *Henry IV* dramas describe the son's circular pattern and its accompanying threat—a pattern that is implicit anyway in a patrilineal system of family or a religious structure in which the Son is simultaneously the Father. Gloucester's immediate willingness to believe that his firstborn and favored son Edgar secretly contemplates patricide is understandable when placed in context of the father-son myths that prophesy it. Nor does the prophecy go unfulfilled in *King Lear*. For within the structure of the play, the agent of old Gloucester's death is indeed the guiltless Edgar: appropriately enough, the father's heart, caught between the extremes of joy and grief, "bursts smilingly" at the instant he learns that the armed man kneeling for blessing who has guided his enfeebled steps is no other than the son who will replace him.

One of the challenges in teaching Shakespeare is to get students to go beyond making black-white moral distinctions and discover the less obvious similarities that can be obscured by apparent difference. Since students invariably, if unconsciously, draw on their own experience of family when analyzing the filial patterns in a text, they may gain greater insight into conflicts in their own families by realizing the extent to which a character's needs and ends are predetermined by factors like gender and positional order. Once readers realize that the apparent difference separating legitimate and firstborn Edgar from illegitimate Edmund is a distinction that is nearly erased by Shakespeare's choice of character names so similar as to invite transposition, they may be able to see the structural parallels that bring these two characters together and imply a common humanity. The two sons follow one pattern, perhaps best defined as the pattern of the son. Having been cast out by the father and displaced by the rival brother, each struggles violently to get back into the family enclosure and inherit the privileges of the father—the father's name, titles, and designation as his replacement—the very privileges that, by the law of primogeniture, structurally preclude the possibility of brotherly love and set up the competitive, ultimately fratricidal rivalry that this drama plays out.

Whereas both the favored and the unfavored son ultimately pursue the same goal of appropriating the paternal holdings, the three daughters have names and patterns that more strongly distinguish them according to the loved-unloved dichotomy. The two wicked daughters are bound together by their names as well as their needs, for "Regan" is no more than an abbreviated anagram for her older sister, "Goneril," while "Cordelia" stands alone and carries a name that allusively suggests the heart. As distinct from the favored son, what the daughter who has been loved tangibly needs from the paternal storehouse is actually best expressed by Cordelia's "nothing." What she needs is not appropriation of the father's name and titles along with a bequest that will fix her within his house as heir to his identity but, in fact, a release from the father's structure and permission to pass out of it.

Should students search for myths that authorize a daughter's departure from the father's house or foretell her displacement of his authority, they will be hard pressed to find any. The daughter figures prominently in folktales, but traditionally she must wait within the father's castle to be liberated by a prince who wrests her from her implied captivity. Invariably, the daughter's independence is preceded by triangulation that places her between the father and the rescuing lover. Because her departure is a separation and a genuine passage outward, it is not contained within the circle of return and thus requires a more potent form of authorization than does the son's. Instead of merely being narrated, it is enacted with a form defined by Arnold van Gennep as a "rite of passage," a specific category of ritual that contains three sequentially fixed phases classified as separation, transition, and reincorporation.

The church marriage service—which has changed negligibly since Shakespeare's time and is as familiar to us as it was to him—constitutes the separation phase, which severs the daughter from the retentive father and authorizes her transition into a new identity as wife. Viewed from the perspective of its ritual implications, the separation of daughter from father is, in fact, what the marriage service is about. It contains the paradigm of all the conflicts that define the father-daughter bond and reassert their power precisely at the moment of ritual resolution.

A detailed analysis of the symbolic implications of the marriage rite and their relevance to *King Lear* is available elsewhere in my work. By focusing on the structure of this familiar ritual, however, students may themselves be able to see why, throughout his career, Shakespeare used it as the key dramaturgical subtext of his father-daughter relations. They may also see why, as a consequence of the truth of symbolic logic, ritual custom dictates that the one who bears the *cost* of a wedding is, by definition, the father of the bride. What the ceremony authorizes is not, as it might seem, the transfer of a passive female object from one male to another. The ritual is a communal coercion of the father that forces him to deliver to God's agent a daughter whom he has not touched and whom, at the altar, he must transfer as a gift to the rival male who stands at her other side. Once he has done so, the ritual script forces him to acknowledge that his role in both the ceremony and his daughter's life is ended: he must retire from the stage and, sitting mutely in the audience, watch her forsake his name and the family he governs as she transfers her commitment to "obey, serve, love, honor, and keep" (Booty's edition of the 1559 *Book of Common Prayer* 292) to his replacement, the male whom the service privileges as the violator of sexual taboos the father has been forced to observe. And lest the importance of these ritual father-daughter dynamics be regarded as merely a historical anachronism, it helps students to recognize that, even in our own time, when women hardly feel they need their fathers' permission to marry, daughters still choose to reenact the same ritual, virtually unchanged. The psychological significance of a daughter's departure from her patrilineal house still dominates the way we feel about—and therefore enact—a ceremony that ostensibly seems designed only to unite the bride and groom.

A major problem students often have with *King Lear* is understanding Cordelia's stance in the opening scene, the event that sets the tragedy in motion. To them, it frequently seems that, regardless of Goneril's and Regan's obvious flattery, Cordelia's determination to yield "nothing" to a father who only wants reassurance of her love is indicative of a coldly uncompromising nature. What Lear is really attempting to do (and why his request is not as harmless as it seems) should be clear once the wed-unwed distinctions among the sisters and the significance of Cordelia's pending marriage are taken into account. In this crucial scene, the issue of dividing the kingdom is repeatedly conflated with that of marriage, which divides daughters from their paternal family. In fact, Lear has called his court together for the announced intent of performing two seemingly unrelated divestitures: to allocate his kingdom as his "daughters' several dowers" (I.i.43) and at last to give Cordelia in marriage to one of her two princely suitors who "Long in our court have made their amorous sojourn, / And here are to be answer'd"(46–47). When it is understood that the dowry— the material sign of a daughter's separateness from her family—functioned historically as a virtual prerequisite for her marriage, the contradiction inherent in Lear's demands should be evident. The pledges demanded by the father as a dowry condition would psychologically invalidate the vows to be "plighted" the husband, thus nullifying the daughter's separation and reconstructing it into a return to the father. When Cordelia defines the contradiction in her wily father's seemingly harmless request for love, she illustrates it in her sisters' statements and then links the "plight" of the unwed daughter—who owes obedience to the father—to the "plight of troth" (or pledge of truth) designed to resolve it in the wedding:

> Why have my sisters husbands, if they say
> They love you all? Happily, when I shall wed,
> That lord whose hand must take my plight shall carry
> Half my love with him, half my care and duty:
> Sure I shall never marry like my sisters,
> To love my father all.   (I.i.98–103)

What Cordelia's pending marriage has forced Lear to face and what the aged, apparently widowed king is trying to forestall is the very human fear of crawling toward death alone, unloved, and without family. It is the desire to prevent this threat that motivates him to call together his whole family and attempt to bind to him not only the loved child who is about to depart but even the two unloved ones who have separated from him and owe primary loyalties to husbands and homes of their own. Since the territory he parcels out has clearly already been preallocated, his gambit of awarding the "largest bounty" to the rhetorician who wins his land-for-love game is false bait. It does, however, reflect his desire to reinclose all three daughters within the psychic territory of paternal rule by setting them into competition for the privileged position of loving him most. His kingdom is the bait. When Goneril's and Regan's greed to acquire material signs of the father's love prompts them to pledge themselves "in all-but-incestuous terms" (Barber 197), they do what Cordelia is determined not to do. They acquire a "dowry" that, by uniting them with their father, severs them from

their husbands and results in the psychic annulment that the play drama-
tizes in both sisters' marriages.

Instead of relinquishing his daughters, Lear has attempted a substitution
of paternal divestitures. To the two married sisters he has offered a dowry
that unmarries them; to Cordelia's dowry he has attached terms designed
either way to prevent her from marrying. For Cordelia to accept his dowry
would negate her marriage; to refuse it leaves her dowerless and hence un-
able to wed. Thus when Lear disinherits her, he casts her away not to let
her go but to prevent her from going. Likewise, his bequest of state is not
the transfer of rule it purports to be, for the self-deposed king clearly in-
tends to retain monarchical power and "manage those authorities / That he
hath given away" (I.iii.18-19). And in this deliberate inversion of divesting
and dividing his public paternity in order to retain his private one intact,
Lear violates both spheres of patriarchal authority. From this scene on, inverted images of Lear's paternal relation to his daughters and his kingdom
pervade the drama through the king's ceremonial invocations of sterility
against the daughters he has generated and the land he has ruled.

Once cued to notice the structural principles of inversion and circularity
that are set out in this first crucial scene, students can often trace the way
most of the important issues in the play recapitulate these designs. The
other defining design of the play is its ritual subtext; as students alert to this
point may themselves notice, the dialogue among Lear, Cordelia, and her
two suitors resonates with phrases and actions traditionally associated with
marriage. This subtext shapes our expectations of what *should* be happening and allows us to recognize the parodic nature of what is in fact transpir-
ing. While Cordelia and France appropriately echo the sacred language,
the father of the bride repeatedly violates it in his attempt to thwart the
linear movement of the daughter's ritual passage and convert its forward
progression into a circular return back to him. Beneath Lear's image of
fatherhood as the "barbarous Scythian, / Or he that makes his generation
messes / To gorge his appetite" (115-17), lurks the monstrous appetite of
the father who devours the flesh he begets and thus converts even the act
of fathering into an expenditure that returns to feed him. The father's unnatural appetite is implicit in the regression motive Lear reveals in his plan
to set his rest on Cordelia's "kind nursery" (123), an image in which the
father has imaginatively returned to infancy and pictures himself nursing
from his own daughter—a sublimation that absorbs the guilty father's
desires into the infant's unconsciously oedipal ones and thus reestablishes
the father's incestuous proximity to his daughter. The monstrous cycles of
appetite are the extension of the circular terms of Lear's dowry proposal.
And yet—in a paradox quintessentially Shakespearean—this monstrosity,
too, is born out of the retentive impulses of love.

Cordelia's departure with France seems to break the pattern of circularity that holds the daughter in family bondage. But when we consider that Cordelia returns at the end of the play and describes her life with France as one of "mourning and importun'd tears" (IV.iv.26) for the father to whom she is still psychologically bound, it becomes tragically apparent that Lear's refusal to obey the ritual and give up his daughter has effectively negated the daughter's natural pattern and enclosed the family within the sterile cipher of "Nothing." Choosing father over husband, Cordelia returns to ask him to "look upon me, Sir, / And hold your hand in benediction o'er me" (IV.vii.57–58)—a plea that summarizes the inchoate cries for love that emanate from every child and every parent in this play. Through the dramatized inversion of ritual patterns, the play's tragic circles find their counterpart in the psychological needs that create them, and the final scene stages the most sterile of family images: a dead father with his three dead daughters, the wheel having come full circle back to echo the opening scene.

The internecine violence released within the patriarchal world of *King Lear* leads the institution of family to "within a foot / Of th' extreme verge" (IV.vi.25–26); the only two who survive to emphasize its sterility are Albany, a widower, and Edgar, an unmarried son. Sisters have killed sisters, brothers, brothers; fathers have decreed the death of sons, sons of fathers; daughters have maimed fathers, fathers cursed daughters into sterility; wives have plotted to murder husbands. Even in acts of love, such as Cordelia's self-sacrifice and the poignant beauty of her reunion with Lear, what is repeatedly scripted within the text is the compulsive self-annihilation of the patriarchal family—an annihilation generated, paradoxically, by the family's possessive attempts to preserve itself intact.

Conspicuously absent from this play—as students will undoubtedly note—has been the mediating presence of the mother. If readers search her out, they will find that beneath the patriarchal text, she does exist within an allusive "maternal sub-text" (Kahn) of images that associate the maternal with ideas like "pity," "feeling sorrow," "conception," and "kind nursery"—ideas that repeatedly connect her absence to a value structure that is likewise missing from the brutal savagery of the *King Lear* universe. She emerges overtly in Lear's attempt to prevent tears at Regan's humiliation of him, an attempt that images the expression of sorrow as a metaphoric pregnancy beginning to swell to the heart and show, despite his efforts at suppression:

> O! how this mother swells up toward my heart;
> *Hysterica passio!* down, thou climbing sorrow!
> Thy element's below. (II.iv.54–56)

Especially given the emphasis this drama places on the necessity to *feel*, the absence of the maternal within Lear's patriarchal kingdom becomes a powerful metaphor for a fertility that must be conceived by the heart, an image signifying all that, like the mother, is missing in the cruelly retributive world of the play. The toughness of this drama takes its readers, as it took Edgar, beyond the limits of imagined endurance; much as we would like it to, it will not give us, even at its conclusion, any comforting models of social or familial rebirth that we can pass out to our students as palliatives for the experience of having suffered through it. Yet while a play may be *about* its characters, it is *for* its audience/readers. And it is to the relationship between the audience or reader who is located outside the text and the values that are absent from it that I turn at the conclusion of this painful play. For, by leaving us with the latent image of pregnancy, the image of "conceiving" announced in the play's first pun (I.i.11), the play implicitly poses a new and potentially generative circle. All that is metaphorically subsumed by the maternal is absent from the text because it has been located in the reader: our capacity to feel has been defined as the womb where new conception must occur. And if the students we teach have opened themselves to this powerful play's seemingly implacable determination to violate them and bring them to "feel what wretches feel," the play has implanted in them a particular ripeness, a conception that is best modeled within the drama by Edgar's willingness to define himself as

> A most poor man, made tame to Fortune's blows;
> Who, by the art of known and feeling sorrows,
> Am pregnant to good pity.   (IV.vi.218–20)

An Archetypal Approach

Ann E. Imbrie

The value of the archetypal approach to *King Lear* rests in its ability to adapt to the demands of the individual teacher or course as well as to the needs of a variety of students. For the teacher who favors discussion as the primary classroom technique, this approach has the advantage of encouraging participation among students of varying intellectual abilities and degrees of literary sophistication. The archetypes themselves—many evoking memories of familial relationship—engage the personal experience of even the most unsophisticated students; the ways in which Shakespeare combines and subverts these archetypal patterns will suggest the play's complexity to those students who bring greater literary expertise to their study. The teacher who feels more comfortable with a lecture format will find a wealth of material about which to generalize, both in the play itself and in the major documents of archetypal theory from Carl Jung to Northrop Frye. In addition, because archetypal criticism tends generally toward comparative analysis, the approach suits in-class oral reports and outside reading assignments, as well as paper topics that ask the students to reach beyond the play to the patterns it shares with other literary works. For the same reason, the identification of archetypal patterns provides access to the play's difficulties when it is taught in introductory courses and literary surveys or in genre courses (e.g., drama or tragedy). Furthermore, because the archetypes can be contained and recognized in the play itself, without necessary reference to other works of literature, this method aids the teacher of *King Lear* in an undergraduate Shakespeare course as well.

Before outlining some practical suggestions for using this approach in the classroom, especially in directed discussion and in oral reports, I should establish some definitions. I distinguish two distinct but related kinds of archetypes present in the play. The first we may call the literary or artificial archetype, defined by Northrop Frye as "a typical or recurring image . . . which connects one poem with another and thereby helps to unify and integrate our literary experience" (99). Such archetypes are conventions that literature both creates and transmits. Examples of literary archetypes in *King Lear* include the blind seer, the proud king's abasement (Hornstein), the suffering servant, the wise fool, the demon-god or *dioboia* (Bodkin 326; see also Frye 147–49), the descent to the underworld, the demon-woman, the wheel (Wheelwright, *Metaphor* 125–27), the sacrificial victim (*pharmakos*), the tyrant-father, and many others. Unless one is teaching *King Lear* in a larger literary context—say in a course in tragedy or myth— the identification of such archetypes may fall to the teacher alone; because recognition of these conventions requires knowledge external to the play itself, they may prove less successful subjects for discussion and discovery by the students.

A second kind of archetype, however, which we may call the natural or psychological archetype, is available to most students regardless of their prior literary experience. These archetypes exist in our hearts, like something we long for or have long forgotten, and, at least for practical purposes in the classroom, establish connections not between one literary work and another but between the readers' personal experience and their experience of a particular text. These archetypes tend to be located less in particular images or symbols than in patterns of experience that the play reproduces. In *King Lear*, I would distinguish three basic archetypes of central importance that help define the relationships among the characters and reveal the play's structure: the parent-child relationship (the oedipal father, the usurped parent, the rejected child), romantic love, and sibling rivalry. For introducing and defining these psychological archetypes, I have found it most useful to refer the students to highly conventionalized popular literature, especially the fok and fairy tales, which, in Northrop Frye's terms, provide "an unobstructed view of archetypes" (116).

The English fairy tale "Caporushes" (Steel 280–89) offers the closest analogue I know to the main plot of *King Lear*. It is probably best to assign the short tale as outside reading or to ask a student to report on it, comparing the folktale with the play as a means of beginning discussion. "Caporushes" presents a streamlined version of *Lear's* opening scene, reducing both its cast of characters and its psychological complexity to the essentials: an aged father with three daughters, a love test, the rejection of the youngest and most favored child because her expression of love seems insufficient ("I love you as fresh meat loves salt," she says). The tale, then, follows the fortunes of the rejected daughter, who must prove herself in the world by overcoming a series of obstacles before she wins the love of a prince and is reunited with her father to live happily ever after. The aged king himself suffers blindness before he learns the error of his ways and recognizes the value of his rejected child, at which time his sight is magically restored to him. The simplicity of the fairy tale directs the students' attention to the archetypal characterization in Shakespeare's play. Lear's irrational response, pinpointed carefully through the function of Kent, is a familiar fairy-tale type, motivated by psychological impulses deeper and more mysterious than those reason can explain. Similarly, Goneril and Regan are not individuated any more than the wicked stepsisters are in "Cinderella," of which "Caporushes" is a less familiar version. An insistence on psychological realism, which many students expect from having studied modern novels, can be an interpretive trap for students approaching *King Lear* for the first time; seeing the play as a fairy tale, at least initially, can divert their expectations appropriately. Comparison between *King Lear* and "Caporushes," then, can preserve the fairy-tale simplicity of Shakespeare's play (and make the primitive setting and the feudal social structure more immediate) while suggesting ways in which the dramatist complicates the archetypal matrix he uses. Shakespeare complicates the type of the wicked sisters by giving Goneril and Regan both some good lines and some good insights. He also lifts out the sexual issues barely implicit in the fairy-tale love test by shading Goneril's and Regan's responses to their father's demands with romantic colors as well as by offering the marriage auction for Cordelia's hand as an immediate parallel to the love test. In addition, he extends and deepens Lear's character by developing his "economic" definition of love (suggested in the fairy tale), which continues throughout the play to provide a moral analogue to the fairy-tale father's physical blindness. Comparison with "Caporushes" will also raise questions about the structure of Shakespeare's play, particularly about the relation between its two plots. The heroine of "Caporushes," for example, combines in herself both Cordelia and Edgar (she disguises herself in "natural" weeds and accepts the abasement of poverty), just as the physical blindness of the father figure in the fairy tale suggests both Lear and Gloucester.

A less limiting way of introducing both the idea of the archetype and the particular archetypes that underpin *King Lear* is to encourage the students to produce their own fairy tale. Before they have even read the play, I begin a discussion by starting the story off: "Once upon a time there was a great king who had three daughters, the youngest of whom he loved best. One day he decided to find out if they loved him in return, so he asked the eldest, 'How much do you love me?'" I then ask each student in turn to contribute a detail to the story until we come to the "happily ever after" ending; students who are already familiar with the play are asked to observe but not participate. Students must monitor one another by rejecting and refashioning any detail that does not fit the fairy-tale pattern. Although this exercise in the "collective unconscious" has its dangers (one never knows what the students will say), it has the advantage of illustrating concretely what an archetype is. Because students call forth the story as if from memory, the teacher need not attempt abstract definitions of the concepts. I have found surprising and fruitful conformity among the responses to this exercise. Without fail, the most loved child is rejected; the ensuing story traces her course toward recognition by the rejecting parent; through the intervention of some magical force, the rejected child marries a handsome prince and is reunited with her father; and all live happily ever after. When, in a moment of self-conscious perversity, one student announced the untimely death of the heroine, he was booed—affectionately, of course—by his classmates. Once the pattern of the fairy tale has been established, the students should then read the play. Through this process, they will see immediately Shakespeare's departures from the model and can suggest sophisticated reasons for them.

Unlike the usual fairy tale, for example, *King Lear* focuses on the fate of the rejecting parent rather than on that of the child, a departure from the form that seems fully appropriate to the intended (adult) audience of the play. As an "adult fairy tale," *King Lear* locates the psychological and sexual interest in the parent who must endure hardship in order to resolve internal conflicts. Students are often surprised to learn that many psychoanalysts (e.g., Bettelheim) see the fairy tales as nonthreatening ways in which the child can work out oedipal conflict, resulting in a purgation of "dangerous" feelings not unlike catharsis. Students enjoy discovering an adult analogue in *King Lear*, in which the father entertains incestuous longings for his daughter; hence, the violence of his initial rejection of her (according to "Caporushes," because "he always loved her best"), his sexual revulsion in IV.vi, and Cordelia's insistence throughout the play on maintaining the appropriate relationship between father and daughter ("I love your Majesty / According to my bond, no more, no less"; "Why have my sisters husbands if they say / They love you all?"). That Cordelia marries France at the beginning of the play—rather than at the end after having endured hardships as the heroine of a fairy tale would—suggests as well that the oedipal conflict is located in the father. The daughter is already prepared for a romantic attachment to a man of her own generation. The familiar patterns of the fairy tale, then, can suggest in the structure of *King Lear* a play of one set of archetypes (the unconditional familial bond, the child's resistance to the parent, the parent's fear of usurpation by the child) against another (appropriate romantic love). This same conflict of archetypes can help define the two sisters' relationship with their father, on the one hand, and with their husbands on the other, as well as the adulterous triangle of Edmund-Goneril-Regan. Lear's "Come, let's away to prison" is the "happily ever after" ending he envisions for himself and his daughter-wife, a sentimental ending this adult fairy tale cannot allow (Mack 113–14). It remains for the final scene with its pietá of the grieving father (an emblem if not exactly an archetype), to resolve this archetypal conflict between generations on which the play is structured.

Using the typical fairy-tale structure as a way of approaching the complexities of *King Lear* can also raise significant thematic issues. In the usual fairy tale, the world seems stacked against the good child, and the story requires the intervention of some magical force to tip the balance in the child's favor. To the young audience of the fairy tale, this motif builds confidence in the workings of the world, and the magic is finally not unreasonable because it is psychologically necessary. The absence of the gods in *King Lear* (for "gods" read "fairy godmother" or some magical force) again locates the play firmly in a more realistic adult world. The gods may not kill us for their sport, but neither do they protect us—a recognition that forces on adults a sense of responsibility for their own choices, a central theme in the play. Similarly, the poetic justice of the "happily ever after" ending of fairy tales, in which the good are rewarded and the wicked punished, appeals to the child's innocent respect for justice. G. K. Chesterton's remark that children love justice because they have not lived long enough to desire mercy provides an appropriate explanation for the inversion in *King Lear* of a just order. The child's sense of justice flavors Lear's naive certainty that he is "a man more sinned against than sinning"—"So what?" we adults ask, somewhat cynically. Similarly, the grace of Cordelia's "No cause, no cause" suggests the adult's will to mercy. If there is fairy-tale magic or justice in the play, it lies not in the organization of society at large or in the ways of the world but in the care we take of one another. The enormity of our pain at the end of the play may tell us that even as adults we still long for the poetic justice of the fairy-tale world, simply because it is easier than accepting the demands of personal relationship. Apparently, Nahum Tate could not relinquish that longing, and neither could generations of playgoers. Students find it interesting that Tate's *King Lear*, with its romance plotting and happy ending, held the stage for over 150 years of the play's history. Compared to Shakespeare's, Tate's version of the story is a child's play, a literary fairy tale that reduces the play's power by explicating or removing the disturbing archetypes, making the story neat, reasonable, and overly particularized. Tate's redaction can be used successfully (again, through oral reports or outside reading assignments) to convince students of the appropriate tragic realism of the original and to ensure the tragic response the play demands.

The archetypal patterns of familial relationship will also illuminate the versions of sibling rivalry in *King Lear*. In this archetype, as it is represented in the fairy tales, siblings rival one another for the affection of the parent, with the weak, despised, stupid, silent, or rejected (and usually the youngest) child finally winning that recognition by defeating the other siblings. This pattern defines the relationship among the three sisters in the main plot; in addition, Goneril and Regan are clear rivals, first struggling not so much to win the father's affection as to usurp his place and then trying to win Edmund's love. Similarly, Edmund's usurpation of his brother's birthright and his father's status, familiar as an archetype through the Jacob and Esau story, structures the familial relationship in the secondary plot. Edgar, the despised child, wins out through patience and acceptance of his lowly status, even as Cordelia takes her rightful place in her father's heart by refusing to usurp his place as her sisters do. Thus, the sibling-rivalry archetypes highlight the relationship between the two plots. Although the questions of primogeniture and legitimacy may seem distant issues to many students, Edmund's villainy and his pride in his own bastardy can be viewed with more understanding—and some sympathy—through reference to the archetypal fear of adoption, a memory most students have and a fear many children overcome, as Edmund does, through an assertion of pride in their extrafamilial status. A complicated pattern of sympathy and judgment of the two brothers in the subplot reflects Shakespeare's mixture of sibling-rivalry archetypes, his setting up of certain responses only to undermine them.

While the archetypal approach cannot confront equally well all the issues in the play (e.g., the political and social satire), it seems to me especially appropriate to the study of this particular play, surely the most elemental and as such the greatest if not the best of Shakespeare's tragedies. As Philip Wheelwright suggests, "Certain particulars have more of an archetypal content than others: that is to say, they are 'Eminent Instances' . . . stirring in the soul something at once familiar and strange" (*Burning* 89). *King Lear* is one such "eminent instance," both familiar and strange to students asked to tackle it. The archetypal approach provides experiential contact for the students with characters and situations otherwise removed from their own—the primitive setting, a perverse and magnificent king "four score years and upward," a daughter too good to be true, and sisters too wicked to believe—and can thus help them overcome the distance between themselves and *Lear* by encouraging them to see a familiar universality in the play's arrangement of strange particulars. It allows for close scrutiny of the text as well as for speculative and personal discussion. But while this approach gives the students access to the play, in no way does it diminish its mystery; in fact, because the "universal idea cannot be divorced from the given context, cannot be logically explicated, without distorting it" (Wheelwright, *Burning* 88), the archetypal approach collapses under our experience of the play itself, freeing, without sufficiently explaining, our responses of awe and compassion and grief.

King Lear in a Literature Survey Course

Ann Paton

In a literature survey course with many nonmajors, connecting students with the work is an ever-present challenge. One useful approach to teaching *King Lear* in such a course is to build on students' experience as well as on works previously studied, both ancient (the Bible, classical tragedy) and modern (mystery plays, *Everyman, Dr. Faustus*), discussing archetypes as well as theatrical, religious, and cultural traditions.

Students readily sense the "once upon a time" atmosphere of the play's first scene: once upon a time there was a king who had three daughters; the youngest was the fairest of them all, and her two sisters hated her. Three is the pervasive archetypal number: here are three daughters and a kingdom divided into three parts. Among those present are the familiar suitors for the hand of the youngest princess; as usual, the worthy suitor wins her hand, though in this case France need not slay a dragon—he merely has to defy one: Lear. What modern students glibly identify in both plots as sibling rivalry is an ancient phenomenon. Of course, one recalls Cain and Abel. Sibling rivalry, then, is traced as far back as Eden, and it recurs in countless tales, legends, and television shows.

One also may focus on the recurring theme of paternal rejection. Lear pronounces curses on Cordelia and later (I.iv) on Goneril. In a patriarchal society, to be disowned by one's father is a terrible thing. Noah's curse on Ham (Gen. 9) is an early example, as is Abraham's casting out of Ishmael (Gen. 21). Today, if the child of a strict Muslim or Orthodox Jewish family departs from the faith, the family may act as if that child no longer exists. Lear's actions, however, are not religious but manipulative, perhaps analogous to a modern parent's threat to cut a child out of a will.

Opposite to paternal rejection is the paternal blessing. Near the end of the play both Cordelia and Edgar ask their fathers' blessings (IV.vii.58 and V.iii.194, respectively). This motif is, again, ancient and patriarchal (e.g., Jacob blessing his sons in Gen. 49 and the parable of the prodigal son in Luke 15). One may ask students whether there is any modern equivalent to this blessing. A variation of the patriarchal theme occurs in the many tales where the father figure is the king (as Lear is both), and the plot involves exile or return. In each case the archetypal pattern is alienation from, or restoration to, the community, be it family or kingdom, that provides the individual's identity and sense of belonging.

An archetypal figure is the blind soothsayer, who, according to tradition, can "see." Probably the most familiar example is the soothsayer in *Oedipus*; in that play, Oedipus, when he "sees" the truth about himself, punishes himself by putting out his own eyes. The same interplay of mental and physical vision occurs in *King Lear*. The theme of sight and blindness—introduced in I.i.52 with Goneril's vow that she loves Lear "dearer than eyesight" and then strongly pursued in I.i.155 with Lear's "Out of my sight!" and Kent's "See better, Lear"—is continued throughout the play, as Gloucester's physical blindness constitutes a counterpoint to Lear's mental blindness. At the beginning, Gloucester, like Lear, has no consciousness of wrongdoing; he is, in fact, rather proud of having a bastard son. Furthermore, like Lear, he is deceived about his children. Only after he is brutally blinded does Gloucester perceive the truth, both about himself and his sons and about the universe, where people are not as flies to wanton boys, to be killed by the gods for their sport, but are responsible beings, whose wrongdoings bring their own retribution. Through suffering and through the "psychotherapy" of his attempted suicide he learns patience, is reconciled to Edgar, and finally can die "smilingly."

Though never physically blinded, Lear undergoes a similar process. At the beginning of the play he is "in the dark" about his own proud nature, the characters of his daughters, and the suffering of the "poor, naked wretches" in his kingdom. Like Gloucester, he must be plunged into utter darkness, the mental darkness of lunacy, before he can emerge into the light of understanding. A Lear who can suggest to Cordelia that they go to prison as two birds to a cage may seem not to understand the reality of evil, but in fact he has lived through and passed beyond that reality to one more transcendent. From his darkness he has gained insight into himself as fallible man and negligent king and into the evil of Goneril and Regan. But he has also come to see the value of love and grace (embodied in Cordelia) and of life lived not in pomp but in simplicity. Thus, in both main plot and subplot Shakespeare has made powerful use of the archetypal figure of the blind soothsayer.

Discussion of these universal, archetypal, mythic elements is productive because it stimulates students to think and to relate the play to their own lives, experiences, and studies. They may participate in discussions relating *King Lear* to what they know of sociology, psychology, anthropology, children's stories, television programs, films, family life, work experiences, and everyday social situations. They then perceive that the archetypal elements occur in *King Lear* and recur in much of literature simply because they recur in human experience, whatever the century or culture.

The emphasis on universals shows that Shakespeare's genius transcends the boundaries of time and place. In addition, more scholarly comparisons of *King Lear* with some works read earlier in the survey course demonstrate how that genius was nourished by theatrical, religious, and cultural traditions.

Mystery plays, for instance, were still being performed when Shakespeare was young, and students may better understand *King Lear*, including its artistic form, purposes, and themes, with some knowledge of Shakespeare's heritage from the Middle Ages. I find, too, that such comparisons help students see the value of a chronological survey of literature, for through such a comparative survey they perceive that the tendency of Renaissance drama toward inclusiveness (multiple settings, long time spans, and characters from all social strata) was inherited from medieval rather than classical drama and that medieval plays had accustomed English audiences to drama in verse. Most important, students need to know how medieval religious drama provided thematic materials that Shakespeare transmuted into secular Renaissance terms.

The medieval mystery cycle was designed to display the entire history of humankind, from the Creation to the Last Judgment. The central event was the birth of Christ, come to reconcile fallen humanity to its Creator. Thus, *The Second Shepherds' Play* celebrates the entrance of redeeming grace into a fallen world. The world into which Christ is born is a place where the poor are oppressed by the rich, exploited by their employers, nagged by their spouses, and chilled by the weather. The good, simple shepherds are deceived by the rascally Mak and also by a false lamb/baby before they find the true baby/Lamb. At the end of the play their circumstances have not changed. They are still oppressed, exploited, and cold, but because God has sent his Son to provide grace to redeem humankind, they are singing. This plot line, which moves from suffering to a joyous conclusion, anticipates the movement of Shakespeare's major comedies, but it appears in *King Lear* as well. The fallen nature of humanity, rudimentary to medieval Christian belief, is fully displayed in *King Lear*, and Lear goes through the pattern of sin and suffering, the principal subject of the mystery cycles. Some would also say that he proceeds to the redemption that completes the pattern.

But what of even larger grace? A teacher (and students) may cite France's generosity of spirit; the loyalty of Kent, the Fool, and Edgar; the slaying of Cornwall by a servant who can no longer stand aside as a spectator of evil; and Edmund's strange, inexplicable final gesture when he tries to save Cordelia and Lear. These are signs of grace, but Cordelia is the chief agent of it. In this secular drama she represents the divine grace of the mystery play: redemptive, self-sacrificing love that can restore human dignity and assure suffering humanity that ultimately the destructive powers of evil cannot prevail. True, she dies, but the grace she embodies is that unconquerable power which restores Lear's soul. Of course, the debate about the presence and nature of redemption in this play is still endless. Some see a lack of universal and divine grace yet allow that a grace is offered by Cordelia and accepted by Lear on a human, worldly level. At any rate, without Cordelia's luminous presence, the world of *King Lear* would be hopeless indeed, just as the shepherds' world would be without

Christ. Thus *King Lear*, in a secular mode, sets forth the themes of sin, suffering, and redeeming grace that were central to medieval Christianity and were the subject of *The Second Shepherds' Play.*

Everyman also provides a striking comparison with *King Lear.* Both are concerned with the values one should live by, the constant theme of the medieval morality plays. Everyman, like Lear, has been self-serving and unconcerned about his fellow human beings (as attested by the feeble condition of Good Works at the beginning of the play). Edmund Creeth in *Mankynde in Shakespeare* shows how Lear's disenchantment with Goneril and Regan parallels Everyman's abandonment by Fellowship, Kindred, and Goods. Even as Everyman is eventually deserted by the externals to which he has devoted his life, so Lear is stripped of all the externals that have defined his role and perverted his system of values. Instead of adhering to "goods," both Everyman and Lear must gain humility. The loss of these externals is so traumatic that Lear goes mad, but in his poverty and madness he is finally willing and eager to grapple with the vital questions: what is humankind, and how should a human being live?

Willard Farnham in *The Medieval Heritage of Elizabethan Tragedy* gives an enlightening treatment of the development of the morality play and its contribution to later drama (e.g., a search for the meaning of suffering, the conflict of vice and virtue, and freedom of choice as a shaper of character). By Shakespeare's time the protagonist was not an abstraction but an erring human being. The Shakespearean tragic hero is, through his choices, the shaper of his own destiny, and what is important is what happens to the inner man. To Everyman, grace comes through confession and contrition, mediated through ecclesiastical channels. Lear's spiritual pilgrimage follows similar steps but is expressed in terms of this world. As noted earlier, Lear through anguish attains new insight. He loses his world, but he gains his soul through confession and penitence. He comes to a full realization of Cordelia's love, and in the end it is her forgiveness that frees him from the "wheel of fire." The setting of *King Lear* in pre-Christian Britain does not invalidate this point. After all, Cordelia echoes Christ's words in IV.iv.23–24, "O dear father, / It is thy business that I go about," and Lear is told by a gentleman, "Thou hast one daughter, / Who redeems nature from the general curse / Which twain have brought her to" (IV.vi.200–02).

Marlowe's *Dr. Faustus* also provides interesting parallels. The central issue, moral choice between good and evil and that choice as determinant of the soul's destiny, is clearly the *Everyman* issue, and *Dr. Faustus* treats the same choice in more obviously Christian terms than *King Lear* uses. Faustus knows very well the dangers of pride (I.iii.70–72), but he aspires to reach beyond the proper bounds of humanity; he thus makes his particular choices, for which he finally assumes full responsibility. When he signs the covenant with Satan, he uses Christ's own words, so his sin is deliberate, an intellectual, volitional evil, quite different from Everyman's unthinking hedonism or Lear's irrational passion.

The influence of the medieval morality plays on *Dr. Faustus* may be seen in the presence of the Seven Deadly Sins and in Faustus's glimpses of right even after he has chosen wrong. Still more obvious are the allegorical Good and Bad Angels speaking to the soul of Faustus (humanity). In *King Lear* Shakespeare has created a more subtle version of the same with Lear (humanity) between Cordelia (Good Angel) and Goneril and Regan (Bad Angels). Finally, the sense of apocalypse that pervades *King Lear* is in *Dr. Faustus* concentrated in the awful reality of a soul's being carried off to Hell, for Faustus, unlike Everyman and Lear, has chosen to reject grace.

These suggestions of universals and comparisons are by no means exhaustive and are meant to be stimulating, not reductive. Teachers have their own styles, and every class is different; but if, as teachers of literature, we truly believe that great literature speaks to human beings in every age, the ideas expressed here may at least help students begin to hear the glorious voice of *King Lear*.

Sight and Perception in *King Lear:*
An Approach through Imagery and Theme

Frances Teague

When I teach *Lear,* I spend time talking to students about particular images in an act; then we follow an image pattern through the play, deriving from this analysis a better understanding of the play's major themes. Such an approach helps students grasp the meaning of the term *image,* shows them how imagery functions, and compels them to pay close attention to the text. This focus is essential because all too often students find themselves overwhelmed by the play: there is too much in it for them to comprehend. The brighter students recognize the profundity of Lear's tragedy, but when they try to discuss their insights in class, they inevitably digress. One student may begin by raising the issue of parent-child relationships. Before the class can fully explore that issue, another student has asked if all the gods in the play are malevolent, a third wants to know why Lear sees more clearly in madness, and one of the slower students asks for help in figuring out how to tell Edmund apart from Edgar. By turning the class into image hunters, I give them a focus for their discussion. Of course, one must caution students against hunting imagery to the exclusion of any other critical approach. An instructor has to take responsibility for integrating the students' findings with a coherent reading of *Lear.*

To study the imagery, I divide the class into five groups and ask each to be responsible for a particular act; I reserve the first scene of the play for myself and assign it to no one. Each group has two tasks: first, to study the assigned act and cull from it all images and references concerned with sight; second, to answer in class any questions other students may have about the act. While I use sight imagery in my teaching and discuss only that pattern in this essay, the play is rich in other patterns that students may explore. Different catalogs might be made of patterns of animal, religious, age, clothing, sterility, madness, or nature imagery. (The end of this essay includes a short list of critical works that can guide teachers to a fuller treatment of these other patterns.)

Often students assume they know what an image is or else feel embarrassed about asking for a definition of the term. So, a week or so before we begin the play, I ask them what the word *image* means. Generally the class tells me that an image is a picture in words or that images are all metaphors. Because critics use a broader definition, I ask the class to compare what some handbooks of critical terms say. For example, in *The Study of Literature,* Sylvan Barnet, Morton Berman, and William Burto write:

A few decades ago it was commonly held that images evoked pictures . . . and it was sometimes held that images were not literal but were produced by figurative language . . . , but today it is agreed that images involve any sensations (including those of heat and pressure as well as those of eye, ear, etc.) and that the literal sensory objects in the work are images.   (307)

C. Hugh Holman's *Handbook to Literature* has a similar definition of image: "a literal and concrete representation of a sensory experience or of an object that can be known by one or more of the senses" (263). A definition that proves popular with students is the one given by poet and critic John Frederick Nims in his textbook *Western Wind*: an image is "a piece of news from the world outside or from our own bodies which is brought into the light of consciousness by one of the senses" (3). When students tell me they like Nims's definition best, I point out that he is using imagery in it and that their preference shows the power of imagery.

On the first day of our study of *Lear*, I take the class through I.i, carefully explaining the events and the implications of each event. We concentrate particularly on lines that refer to sight. The first of these is Goneril's vow that she loves her father "dearer than eyesight" (Evans ed. I.i.56). Later, when Cordelia refuses to quantify her love, Lear warns her to "avoid my sight!" (124). His rejection leads to his exchange with Kent:

> LEAR.   Out of my sight!
> KENT.   See better, Lear, and let me still remain
>   The true blank of thine eye.   (157–59)

When France asks what Cordelia has done, she defends herself, saying she lacks "A still-soliciting eye" (231), and as she goes with France, she tells her sisters, "The jewels of our father, with wash'd eyes / Cordelia leaves you" (268–69).

Some of these images fit the definitions of the term that students usually give, although "Out of my sight" and "avoid my sight" are marginally metaphoric. Yet as a group the images extend beyond metaphor or word picture, drawing on the power of irony and establishing a major theme in Shakespeare's play. The metaphor in Kent's lines, for example, is compound. Lear has compared his angry decision to a "bow [that] is bent and drawn"; when Kent asks Lear to "let me still remain / The true blank of thine eye," he refers to the center of an archery target as well as to the center of the king's vision—that is, Kent's role as true and loyal subject. Further, he urges Lear to "See better," in order to understand more fully what Cordelia's answer means. But Lear's understanding is faulty; he is spiritually blind to Cordelia's merit and chooses not to see. Thus he commands both Cordelia and Kent to avoid his sight. Lear's refusal to listen to Kent's defense is made particularly ironic when the king calls on Apollo, the god of light and justice. Although he swears by Apollo, he remains unenlightened about the merits of his child or his servant and so behaves unjustly. Kent's rejoinder that Lear "swear'st thy gods in vain" will reverberate throughout the play, as Lear realizes his own injustice and experiences injustice from his other daughters with no assistance from his gods.

Cordelia's lines in the scene are also metaphoric and ironic. She says that her sight is both deprived and enriched because she lacks "A still-soliciting eye, and such a tongue," both of which her sisters have. In equating speech and sight, she echoes what Goneril has said earlier: "Sir, I love you more than [words] can wield the matter / Dearer than eyesight. . . . " Goneril offers insincerely to exchange her most valuable senses, her speech and sight, for Lear's love. Cordelia says she lacks such speech and sight, but by saying so she proves that she can see her sisters more clearly than her father does and speak the truth more fully than her sisters do. Her claim of inadequacy establishes her superiority. Further irony lies in Cordelia's reference to her sisters as "the jewels of [her] father" whom she leaves "with wash'd eyes." Her eyes are washed with tears of sincerity; because her vision is cleansed, she sees her sisters' hypocrisy. When Cordelia calls her sisters Lear's jewels, she alludes to Cornelia, mother of the Gracchi, who gave up wealth and power for her children whom she called her jewels. Unlike Cornelia, Lear surrenders his kingdom to his children only to find that his sacrifice brings him disaster.

In that first class, I emphasize the play's irony, both verbal (as the characters say one thing but mean another) and dramatic (as the characters' speeches hint at what is to come), and I make it clear that Shakespeare has a larger purpose than simply retelling an old story. Lear is spiritually blind, and his lack of vision leads him into chaos and suffering. His gods do not grant him clear vision, and Goneril and Regan deceive him, yet the king himself chooses his blindness. He limits his own vision when he orders Cordelia and Kent into exile, out of his sight. The consequence of his action furnishes matter for the rest of the play; the question of who bears responsibility for his injustice remains unanswered.

The students who have cataloged the references to vision and perception in the rest of act I present their findings on the second day. They point out, among other things, Gloucester's gullibility in believing Edmund's false letter (I.ii), Lear's failure to recognize Kent (I.iv), and the king's comments on sight and perception as he complains of Goneril's unkindness (I.iv.71, 227, and 296–308). My central point about act I is that characters fail to recognize one another both physically and morally. Gloucester and Lear fail to see their children as evil (or virtuous), just as Lear fails to penetrate Kent's disguise. Last of all I discuss Lear's speech to Goneril:

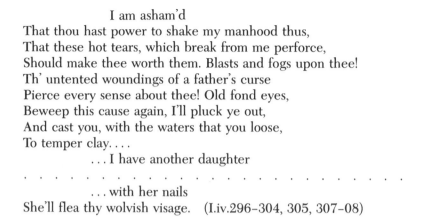

> I am asham'd
> That thou hast power to shake my manhood thus,
> That these hot tears, which break from me perforce,
> Should make thee worth them. Blasts and fogs upon thee!
> Th' untented woundings of a father's curse
> Pierce every sense about thee! Old fond eyes,
> Beweep this cause again, I'll pluck ye out,
> And cast you, with the waters that you loose,
> To temper clay....
>   ... I have another daughter
>
> ·
>   ... with her nails
> She'll flea thy wolvish visage.   (I.iv.296–304, 305, 307–08)

This speech contains so many sight images that reverberate throughout the play that one probably cannot discuss it exhaustively. Although Lear is beginning to see more clearly, he still errs in his valuation of Regan. This speech lets the audience hear him come near the truth, although he makes mistakes. Tears will recur, for example, in II.iv, when Lear refuses to weep and allow his daughters' cruelty to touch him. Yet Cordelia's tears in act IV both indicate her valuation of her father and help heal the king by closing "the eye of anguish." The "Blasts and fogs" fall on Lear in the heath scene, not on his daughters. Lear does not blind himself, nor does Regan flay Goneril's face, but Regan does help Cornwall pluck out Gloucester's eyes. This speech, in short, foreshadows later action and provides a good transition to the next day's work on act II.

Discussion of the second act proceeds directly from that of act I. In the first act characters failed to recognize one another, and in II.i–iii, characters repeatedly mistake another's identity or fail to see through a disguise. In II.iv, the Fool's song suggests that both Goneril and Regan are blind to Lear's needs. Lear describes and curses Goneril in terms of her vision, while he appeals to the kindness he thinks he can see in Regan's eyes. But the Fool's vision is clearer than Lear's: Lear has no power over his daughters, an impotence that is made plain when he unsuccessfully orders Oswald, "Out . . . from my sight!" Unlike Cordelia or Kent, Oswald will not go, and the act ends with Lear's refusing to weep as the storm begins.

Act III presents the most devastating scenes in the play: the storm scenes and the blinding of Gloucester. If students are focusing on the imagery of sight, they will naturally concentrate on the latter scene, particularly since the mad babble in the storm episodes confuses them. Thus students often do a fine job explicating III.vii but fail to present the rest of the act effectively. The instructor then has the reponsibility of showing the class that Gloucester's blindness parallels Lear's madness, that both characters turn away from the external world to find a clearer moral vision within themselves. Although sight imagery is explicit in III.vii, it can also be found implicitly in the storm scenes, especially in references to the dark night and the rain. Nature seems to weep for Lear as he rejects tears and enters the darkness of insanity. The king tells Kent he hardly notices the storm because "this tempest in my mind / Doth from my senses take all feeling else . . . " (III.iv.12–13), a sentiment that Edgar echoes when he first sees his blind father in IV.i. An overwhelming evil drives smaller problems from men's minds.

In the fourth act, both Lear and Gloucester move through infirmity to a spiritual reawakening. Furthermore, in this act sight imagery suggests the possibility of happiness and justice. Students will not realize this possibility on their own; the instructor must point out the awful irony of the fourth act when it is considered with act V. Gloucester's blindness leads to his reunion with Edgar and allows Edgar to trick his father at Dover into a belief in "the clearest gods." Though Edgar's action saves his father from despair, the old man dies in act V; the gods will not save him. News of Gloucester's blinding clears Albany's vision. Seeing the evil of his wife and the forces allied with her, he vows to revenge Gloucester. Yet in act V, he recants and fights with his wife against Cordelia's army. Cordelia's tears and care restore Lear to sanity in act IV, but in the end both Lear and she are captured, and Lear reverts to madness. Act IV suggests the possibility of hope, but that hope is denied in act V. Given the play's ending, Lear seems to be right when he tells Gloucester, "What, art mad? A man may see how this world goes with no eyes" (IV.vi.150–51). He insists that there is no justice in the universe. He himself is mad as he asks Gloucester, "What, art mad?": the greatest irony of all is that a madman can see what will happen more clearly than the other characters or even the audience. In his fit, he brags that when he comes upon his daughters and sons-in-law, "Then kill, kill, kill, kill, kill" (IV.vi.187); the terrible truth is that the good as well as the evil will be killed.

By act V, students may well feel exhaustion. Because the last session devoted to this demanding play can be flat and tired, the instructor has to follow the catalogers' presentation energetically. The teacher should point out that, by the play's end, moral and physical disguises are abandoned and that all the characters now see more clearly. I also go back to I.i to show the class how the meaning of those opening images has been changed and enriched by the rest of the play. At V.iii.258, Lear equates speech and sight as Goneril did in I.i. But she did so insincerely; he does so to mourn Cordelia's death. Neither Goneril nor Lear can respond adequately: she is too false, and he too grieved. His sight plays tricks on him as he calls for a mirror, thinks he sees a feather stir, and tells Kent his sight is poor. The other characters watch Lear and comment on his plight, but Lear is intent on watching Cordelia. As he dies, whether he thinks she is alive or not, his last words urge the others to look at her. Though he is physically and mentally broken at the end, his spiritual vision is clear: the real tragedy is not his anguish, but the death of Cordelia and her virtue. When Edgar ends the play with the words, "we that are young / Shall never see so much nor live so long," he is right. No one else can attain the clarity of vision that Lear reaches through his suffering.

By tracing the imagery of sight, students learn several important lessons. First, they discover what an image is and how Shakespeare uses imagery to unify his play and to imbue it with symbolic meaning. Second, by concentrating on one of the play's strands, they limit their critical focus without reducing the play. *Lear* can overwhelm students unless they have something to help them organize their ideas and to keep them from digressing; tracing imagery offers a coherent approach.

Several tools will help an instructor who wants to use this approach. Anyone who wants a class to trace an image pattern should introduce students to a good concordance and teach them how to use it. A teacher will find interesting discussions of imagery in G. Wilson Knight's *Wheel of Fire* and Caroline Spurgeon's *Shakespeare's Imagery and What It Tells Us*; Spurgeon's belief, however, that the imagery offers biographical insights into Shakespeare's life is not generally accepted. Robert Heilman's *This Great Stage* remains the standard work on imagery in *Lear*; an answer to it may found in W. R. Keast's "Imagery and Meaning in the Interpretation of *King Lear*." Kenneth Muir's article "Shakespeare's Imagery—Then and Now" provides a good survey of works on the subject, while volumes 13 and 33 of *Shakespeare Survey* both concentrate on *Lear*.

An Approach through Dramatic Structure

James E. Hirsh

One feature of my approach to teaching *King Lear* is to discuss with students the paradoxical structure of the play. In a highly systematic way, *King Lear* threatens our sense of order, system, and structure by repeatedly forcing us radically to restructure our responses as the play progresses. I begin my unit on the structure of the play by demonstrating what an incompetent piece of work it is, at least when measured against the traditional and presumably commonsensical conceptions of dramatic structure with which most students are familiar. *King Lear* violates the unities of action, time, and place: its episodic double plot covers a considerable time period and abruptly shifts locale. "The number of essential characters is so large, their actions and movements are so complicated, and events towards the close crowd on one another so thickly, that the reader's attention, rapidly transferred from one centre of interest to another, is overstrained" (Bradley 206). If one is not confused by something in *King Lear*, one has simply not been paying attention. This apparently loosely organized play, furthermore, does not exhibit the structure conventionally attributed to a tragedy. As discussed below, the play has a confusing exposition, a falling action when it should have a rising action, a misleading climax, a rising action when it should have a falling action, and seems headed for a tragicomic resolution rather than a tragic catastrophe.

I believe it is a mistake either to apologize for these supposed shortcomings or to pretend the play fits the conventions. Instead, students and I work through *Lear* together to determine what Shakespeare may have been after, to determine why such a supposedly great playwright may have intentionally made all these seeming blunders. To this end, we try to reconstruct the experience that the play seems designed to evoke in an audience. What does an audience make of what happens on stage as it happens? What kind of structure does a playgoer provisionally give to the dramatic events, and how does this provisional structure change as the play proceeds? Only a selection of moments from the play can be examined in detail in class, and only a smaller selection can be briefly mentioned here by way of illustration.

As we closely examine the opening scene, we keep in mind the conventional notion of exposition. As soon as possible and as smoothly as possible, a playwright is supposed to give us our bearings, to let us know who's who and what's what and especially whom to root for and whom against. Shakespeare does so with seemingly conventional economy at the very beginning of *King Lear*. As one of the entering characters introduces his two companions to one another, Shakespeare simultaneously introduces the audience to all three, but mainly to the talkative character who makes the introductions. He is a crude and insensitive old man who embarrasses his illegitimate son before a third person by making coarse allusions to sexual intercourse with the young man's mother ("there was good sport at his making"). We sympathize with this unfortunate young man, who is admirably forbearing under the circumstances, and hope that the old man will eventually get his comeuppance. Later in the same scene we are introduced to another old man who is even more disagreeable—foolish, choleric, cruel, and tyrannical—and who treats a child even more insensitively. All this would be conventionally successful exposition, except that the victimized young man turns out to be a cold-blooded villain and the insensitive old men later become pitiable victims. If Shakespeare intended to let us know whom to root for as soon as possible, he has clearly bungled the job. If he wanted to demonstrate the fallibility of human perceptions and judgments, however, he might have decided to do so not merely by dramatizing Gloucester's and Lear's misjudgments of other characters but also by dramatizing our similar fallibility. Instead of giving us our bearings, the opening scene deprives us of our bearings, our ordinary perspective, and our confidence in our assumptions, and the rest of the play systematically subverts our attempts to recover them.

As we work through the play in class, we come across other examples of Shakespeare's incompetence. In addition to bungling the exposition, he mishandles what seems to be a major turning point in the action. After overhearing a "plot of death" against Lear, Gloucester hurriedly sends him to Dover to "Both welcome and protection" (in scene 13 [III.vi]). This moment is crucial in several respects. Until now the main crime against Lear has been the two sisters' humiliation of him—their insidious attacks on his perquisites and his dignity. They do close the doors of Gloucester's castle on him, but only after Lear himself has chosen to go out into the storm. Now, however, we learn of a murder plot against Lear, and at the same moment, we also witness Lear's rescue from this plot. This moment is almost equally important as a turning point because Lear is now headed somewhere. Since the first storm scene, he has been wandering about directionless or has been shuffled about with at most a very immediate and temporary goal: shelter from the storm. Not only is Lear now headed somewhere, he is finally headed in the right direction: toward his one loving daughter. After Lear's humiliation and after the anguish of the storm scenes, his fortunes have clearly hit bottom and are now on the way up, due to Gloucester's lucky eavesdropping and timely intervention. The worst is over. The sympathetic characters are beginning to work together and have frustrated the latest plot devised by the evil characters. The subplot will presumably follow the same pattern. Gloucester will escape Edmund's treachery, as Lear has escaped the "plot of death."

And then in the next scene Gloucester's eyes are put out. We assumed we had reached the turning point of the play only to be shocked by a new calamity. Like Edgar at the beginning of scene 15 (IV.i), we had assumed the worst was over. Again, in order to give us an experience that reflects, however dimly, that of a character onstage, Shakespeare has made the low point of his subplot more shocking than the low point of his main plot.

But by the time Edgar encounters his blinded father, Shakespeare has managed, however incompetently, to bring both his plots past their respective turning points in what promises to be a tragicomedy. The overall tragicomic structure becomes more and more apparent as the play progresses. After his initial cruelty toward his one loving child, Lear met with similar cruelty himself. His intense sufferings drive him to the point of madness and would seem to expiate his crimes. Because of his madness, his sufferings continue even after his initial arrival among Cordelia's friendly forces. But his adversities seem to effect a kind of moral redemption; indeed, his suffering is intensified and prolonged by his sense of guilt. By the time Lear is restored to and comforted by the loving child he had mistreated, we feel the rightness of this upward movement toward a tragicomic conclusion. Gloucester undergoes a similar process. Although an audience's initial identification of the turning point was premature because the subplot had not reached bottom, the general upward direction of the action (despite complications) after Gloucester's blinding—coupled with our sympathy for Lear and Gloucester, who surely have suffered enough for whatever crimes they may have committed—encourages us to hope and even to expect that this upward movement will continue. Thus the play encourages us to expect a tragicomic dénouement in which, perhaps after some temporary setbacks and further last-minute complications, the good characters finally triumph over the evil characters. And, indeed, Lear eventually recovers enough to join Cordelia at the head of an army.

But Shakespeare botches the ending. Of all the incompetent features of *King Lear*, the final scene is the most incompetent. Cordelia's death is the result more of Albany's forgetfulness than of any error committed by her or even Lear. It is not the inexorable working out of tragic fate. As Bradley complained, the catastrophe "does not seem at all inevitable. . . . In fact it seems expressly designed to fall suddenly like a bolt from a sky cleared by the vanished storm" (204). The final scene is so incompetent that no less a critic than Samuel Johnson found it unbearable and preferred the revision by Nahum Tate. As the work of a genuinely competent playwright, Tate's happy ending satisfies the tragicomic expectations set up by the earlier part of Shakespeare's play, and Tate's version held the stage well into the nineteenth century.

My students and I examine the final scene as closely as we examined the first. One effect of this scene is to reproduce even more forcefully an effect produced earlier. The audience experiences, even before Edgar does, the horror of the realization that "the worst is not / So long as we can say 'This is the worst'" (scene 15 [IV.i]). But in the very act of assenting to Edgar's assertion, we denied it by assuming that, by that time, we *had* seen the worst—namely, the blinding of Gloucester—but the shocking entry of Lear with the lifeless Cordelia in his arms is even worse. We are forced to experience something worse than the worst—again.

Although *Lear* does not have a conventional dramatic structure, our classroom discussions are intended eventually to show that it does have an artistically purposeful structure, or rather an antistructure that depends in part on the audience's familiarity with conventional dramatic structure. The play is also bound together by a multiplicity of intricately superimposed structures, from verbal echoes and patterns of imagery to the famous parallels between the main plot and the subplot. No one becomes aware of all these patterns, but every playgoer notices some, and I discuss with a class as many as possible. Furthermore, every scene in the play has its own demonstrable internal structure, sometimes simple and clear, sometimes complex and deceptive. The patterns within scenes and the juxtapositions and patterns among these units—each separated from the next by a distinct break in the dramatic continuity: a cleared stage—are major elements in the play's overall structure.

One of the most interesting patterns in the play involves a series of five scenes, all with the same simple format. In each, two characters enter simultaneously after a cleared stage, engage in a single continuous dialogue, and then leave simultaneously. (No other Shakespearean play has more than three such scenes.) These five scenes are arranged in a clearly symmetrical pattern. Goneril and Oswald are the participants in scene 3 (I.iii), Regan and Oswald in scene 19 (IV.v)—the first and the last of these "duets" each involves one of the two major female villains in the play and the same servant. The middle duet of the five (12 [III.v]) is an encounter between Cornwall and Edmund, the two major male villains in the play. In contrast, the intervening scenes of this type (8 [III.i] and 17 [IV.iii]) both depict conversations between Kent and the Gentleman, two unselfish characters who attempt to aid Lear. This pattern is reinforced and given greater significance by many details. For example, in the first scene Goneril gives Oswald the first overt commands in the two villainous sisters' campaign to humiliate Lear, whereas the last of the five portrays the first overt expression of one sister's antagonism for the other.

Many individual scenes reflect the paradoxical structure of the play as a whole. After the confused exposition and abrupt transitions of the opening scene, the second scene has a nicely symmetrical structure, with five clearly defined segments (a structure that resembles the large-scale pattern of duets). The opening, middle, and final segments are soliloquies by

Edmund, and each of the other two depicts an encounter between Edmund and one of his dupes, first Gloucester and then Edgar. But what this orderly scene of exposition exposes is our own earlier misjudgment of Edmund.

Not only are some individual events in this play painful and frightening to contemplate, but so are some of the patterns formed by those events. Parallels between the opening and closing scenes, for example, seem as cruel and gratuitous as the death of Cordelia itself. The unstable division of the kingdom in the opening scene is paralleled by Albany's attempt to divide the kingdom at the end, but this time no one even accepts rule. In the opening scene Kent is banished by Lear on the threat of death; in the final scene Kent imagines he is called by Lear on a journey toward Lear, toward death. Lear banishes Cordelia in intense and unassuageable rage in the opening scene and suffers intense and unassuageable grief at his separation from her in the final scene. Cordelia's self-injunction to "be silent" in the opening scene is paralleled by her silence at the end of the play. She says "Nothing" when Lear asks her to speak in scene 1 and says nothing when asked to speak up by Lear at the end ("What is't thou sayst? Her voice was ever soft"). Lear's pathetic fantasy about life with Cordelia after his retirement ("I lov'd her most, and thought to set my rest / On her kind nursery") is paralleled both by his pathetic fantasy of life in prison with Cordelia near the beginning of the final scene and, near the end, by his sporadically recurring fantasy that she is still alive. This structure of parallels intensifies the painfulness of the play.

By means of orderly patterns that in their very multiplicity make the play more confused, more disorderly, *King Lear* disrupts our sense not only of orderliness but even of the value of orderliness. One goal of my classroom approach is to forestall my and my students' impulse to derive from the play what it seems magnificently structured to deny: a comforting sense of order.

A few of the issues raised here I explore at greater length in *The Structure of Shakespearean Scenes*. Three of the four works that have most influenced my approach to teaching the structure of *Lear* are "The Ending of *King Lear*" by Nicholas Brooke, "Some Dramatic Techniques in *King Lear*" by William H. Matchett, and King Lear, Macbeth, *Indefinition, and Tragedy* by Stephen Booth. The fourth work is *Shakespearean Tragedy*, which is still valuable after eighty years partly because Bradley described, often with great particularity and eloquence, those features of *King Lear* that violate Bradley's own criteria for dramatic structure, features that make *King Lear* a disturbing masterpiece rather than a comfortingly competent play.

"Mapping" *King Lear* in a Drama Survey Course: A Guide in an Antiformalist Terrain

Maurice Hunt

When taught as part of a survey of English drama to 1642, *King Lear* allows an instructor not only to demonstrate the evolution of Renaissance dramatic tragedy but also to acquaint students with a revolutionary function of art. Most undergraduates assume that lasting drama, especially Shakespearean plays, are organically unified works of art designed to teach memorable lessons. They often believe that art is ordered while life is chaotic and that a harmonious arrangement of experience constitutes the distinctive value of art. As a rule, they expect that the teacher of Sackville and Norton's *Gorboduc*, Marlowe's *Tamburlaine*, and Jonson's *Sejanus* will once again explain how aesthetic parts "fit together" to create a "perfect" whole. By assigning Aristotle's *Poetics* early in the survey, I help students explore the critical basis for their usually unexamined assumptions. Once they have fully grasped the concept of dramatic formalism, students generally are more appreciative of the traditional idea that *King Lear*, in so many ways, violates.

In the light of this pedagogical goal, Aristotle's ideas of dramatic wholeness and magnitude receive emphasis during class discussion of the *Poetics*. The doctrine of magnitude, in Aristotle's opinion, depends upon artistic proportion or order: "Again, a beautiful object, whether it be a picture of a living organism or any whole composed of parts, must not only have an orderly arrangement of parts, but must also be of a certain magnitude; for beauty depends on magnitude and order" (203; 7.4). By asserting that a "whole" dramatic tragedy has a beginning, a middle, and an end, Aristotle implies that

> the plot, being an imitation of an action, must imitate one action and that a whole, the structural union of the parts being such that, if any one of them is displaced or removed, the whole will be disjointed and disturbed. For a thing whose presence or absence makes no visible difference, is not an organic part of the whole.   (204; 8.4)

The strict concatenation of fatal events in Sophocles's *Oedipus Rex* illustrates for students Aristotle's principle of organic wholeness as well as his idea of a model complex tragedy. When taught in conjunction with the *Poetics*, *Oedipus Rex* reveals how a reversal of the situation (*peripeteia*), coinciding with a recognition (*anagnorisis*), concludes the complication of the play and initiates the swift unraveling (dénouement).

Because of its formalist qualities, *Gorboduc* suitably begins that phase of the drama survey course leading to *King Lear*. With its compact and streamlined single action, its set declamations representing opposed viewpoints, its *nuntius* bearing heavy news, its curse on the house of Brut, its imitation of the classical chorus, and its ritualistic tone, *Gorboduc* of all English drama perhaps most closely resembles those classical plays from which Aristotle induced his critical maxims. The formal speeches of King Gorboduc and Arostos and of Philander and Eubulus, respectively for and against the transfer of royal rule from father to sons, are mirrored in act II in the conflicting advice of Hermon and Dordan and of Tyndar and Philander to Ferrex and Porrex respectively. Gorboduc's *peripeteia*, his learning of Ferrex's conspiracy against the younger brother, predictably occurs (by the iron law of tragic rise and fall) in the middle of the play and coincides with his Solonic *anagnorisis*—"O no man happy till his end be seen" (III.i.1–28). Tragic wholeness also characterizes *Tamburlaine I and II*, though less rigorously so. The Scythian shepherd methodically rises and falls on fortune's wheel, his proud ascendancy occurring precisely at the midpoint of Marlowe's expansive ten-act structure—the conclusion of part 1. These and other plays, such as *Hamlet*, thus can give students a fairly detailed understanding of how sixteenth-century English playwrights practiced formalist techniques of drama.

Immediately prior to teaching *King Lear*, the instructor might assign *Hamlet*. Few critics have improved on A. C. Bradley's description of the five-part structure of *Hamlet*, whose midpoint *peripeteia* (the killing of Polonius) quickly produces *anagnorisis* (Hamlet's idea that he is a doomed scourge operating in a divine plan). These events punctuate sets of stratagems and counterstratagems that occupy much of acts II and IV respectively. Hamlet's successful trapping of Claudius with *The Murder of Gonzago* ends the first set, Claudius's lethal commanding of Hamlet to England begins the second, and the reversal of the situation and the recognition stand between these two rhythms, which are framed in turn by a first-act exposition and a fifth-act catastrophe (40–78).

Turning to *King Lear* after a formalist study of *Hamlet*, students are curious about the nature and extent of the protagonist's tragic education. A reading of *Hamlet* usually confirms students' non-Aristotelian assumption that the hero of tragedy, dramatic or otherwise, achieves philosophical knowledge at the price of (often on the condition of) death. The basis for their post-Romantic assumption is explained by Thomas P. Roche, Jr., in "'Nothing Almost Sees Miracles': Tragic Knowledge in *King Lear*." Hamlet's late understanding of a divinity that shapes our ends, of the providential fall of a sparrow, and especially of the importance of readiness for life and death appear to offset, even to redeem, some of the tragic pain that makes it possible. During my classes devoted to *Lear*, students understand that Lear also undergoes an instructive experience, even though Shakespeare's antiformalist method, raising expectations of order in the tragedy only to undermine or deny them, makes Lear's learning less than a clearly defined education.

The key issue in opening the play to undergraduates involves Lear's game of giving away his kingdom. My point of departure is Lear's belief that love is a measurable, exhaustible quantity, which merits a quantitative reward. A certain size of love, judged by the magnitude of affirming speech, gains a proportional amount of land. These ideas, as well as those in the remainder of this paragraph, are suggested by Robert B. Heilman in chapter 7 of *This Great Stage: Image and Structure in* King Lear. I point out that Cordelia apparently shares Lear's quantitative view of love. Not only does she say, "my love's / More ponderous than my tongue" (Evans ed. I.i.77–78), but she also loves Lear according to a bond in which he enjoys only one-half of her affection. At this point, I read the speech in which Juliet protests that her love for Romeo is as deep as the sea—that the more she gives to him, the more she has, "for both are infinite" (II.ii.133–35). In other words, I remind students that love can be a boundless quality. A reading of sonnet 116 can also convey this concept. Students thus can understand that Lear's, and possibly Cordelia's, tragic error could be an imperfect idea of love.

Next, I observe how, in later scenes of act I, Lear's daughters cruelly attack his requirement of a hundred knights, reducing it to fifty, twenty-five, ten, five, and finally zero. Considered from one viewpoint, Lear experiences the repercussions of his quantitative idea of love. Goneril and Regan restrict Lear's substance even as he imposed limits on his love for his daughters. Having reached Lear's "O, reason not the need" speech, I ask students to consider Lear's experience as educational—both for him and for us. I then introduce the idea of charting Lear's moments of insight, explaining how students might create "maps" of them.

By "mapping" the play, students can initially focus their assumptions about aesthetic order and tragic learning. Student maps are simply charts of speeches in which Lear appears to express tragic knowledge. At an appropriate moment during the second class period devoted to *King Lear*, I ask students to record act, scene, and inclusive line numbers of passages that reflect Lear's insights into himself or his world. I also encourage undergraduates to write a one-sentence paraphrase below the record of each passage. Each record and paraphrase forms a unit; linked together by straight lines, the units form a map—a chart of Lear's educational pilgrimage.

Some students record ten or twelve different speeches in which Lear voices tragic insights; others may note only three or four. Most students usually record Lear's intuition of true need ("O, reason not the need") and his prayer on the heath (III.iv.28–36). Other speeches that often appear in student maps involve Lear's vision of "unaccommodated man" (III.iv.101–09); his understanding of the relation between authority and power, his "seeing feelingly" (IV.vi.150–59); his realization that the human condition requires patience (IV.vi.176–83); and his final dark questioning of the meaning of Cordelia's life. Also frequently noted are his early insights into his foolishness in divesting himself of his kingdom and in banishing Cordelia. Surprisingly, many students overlook single lines in the play: "I did her wrong" (I.v.24) and "I am a very foolish fond old man" (IV.vii.59). Often undergraduates record Lear's terrible view of divine justice (III.ii. 49–60) and his arraignment of Goneril and Regan (III.vi.20–56), uncertain whether these speeches reflect understanding or ignorant rage. Throughout the process of recording passages, I assure students that a definitive map does not exist. What is important is the realization that Lear has meaningful insights, that some insights are more important than others, and that the insights can be plotted in relation to one another.

Several studies can help the teacher identify dramatic passages containing Lear's insights. In "Lear's Schoolmasters," Manfred Weidhorn provides an overview of the king's progress in learning by describing five stages in Lear's education. Chapter 8 of Heilman's book and Paul Jorgensen's *Lear's Self-Discovery* also include discussions of Lear's chief acts of knowing. After students have realized that Lear's learning can be plotted, and after they have mapped it throughout the play, I note that Edgar arranges a learning experience for Gloucester. Edgar wishes to cure the blinded Gloucester of despair, convincing him through a staged "miracle"—the trick at Dover Cliff—that life is precious and that the gods intervene to preserve it. Understanding that he has been "the superfluous and lust-dieted man" who "slaves" the laws of heaven, Gloucester clearly has the capacity for self-knowledge. He responds to Edgar's instruction, promising to "bear / Affliction till it do cry out itself / 'Enough, enough,' and die" (IV.vi.75–77). Nevertheless, I observe that the stiff Gloucester proves to be a forgetful pupil. On the occasion of Cordelia's and Lear's quick defeat, Gloucester, for example, lapses, content to "rot" where he sits.

I emphasize that Edgar himself does not feel successful in achieving his educational aim with regard to his father. In summing up his pilgrimage, Edgar states that his delayed revelation of his identity, necessary for his "teaching," should be regarded as a fault. He realizes that his untimely disclosure of his identity contributed to Gloucester's premature death (V.iii. 195–200). Having stressed this fact, I then turn to those earlier speeches of Edgar's in which he desires to use tragic experience for his own comfort. Edgar believes that viewing Lear's tragedy can make his pain "light" and "portable," simply because that which makes him "bend makes the King bow" (III.vi.109). He assumes that the play's chaotic events have places within an order, that of the wheel of fortune. It is worth observing that this expectation of order causes Edgar occasionally to appear unempathetic; the fortune's-wheel view of tragedy requires a dispassionate consideration of a king's fall. Consequently the tragic lesson is an intellectual one. Anticipating an order in events, Edgar objectively states that "[t]he lamentable change is from the best, / The worst returns to laughter" (IV.i.5–6), only to encounter his ravaged father and be forced to deny his "wisdom." Chastened, he admits that humankind cannot imagine the worst to which it may sink. Painfully, Edgar must endure hearing Gloucester ironically paraphrase his naive idea of tragic order: "That I am wretched /Makes thee the happier" (IV.i.65–66).

During my presentation of Edgar's attitudes, I suggest that reading or viewing *King Lear* within Edgar's orderly frame of reference is easy—almost instinctual in fact. But I emphasize that Shakespeare, through Edgar's and Gloucester's roles, appears interested in encouraging certain expectations of order and learning that are subsequently never fulfilled. At this point, I introduce students to the antiformalist perspective (avoiding, however, the use of this phrase). I explain that we often project forms onto experience, whether actual or artistic, in order to make it reflect our preconceived notions of coherence. I then indicate that art, clearly perceived, sometimes challenges and shatters our artificial ordering of the world, disorienting us before leading us to more truthful visions. Morse Peckham's *Man's Rage for Chaos: Biology, Behavior, and the Arts* constitutes an introduction to antiformalism; this study can supply concrete examples of the phenomenon for the teacher. Finally, I ask students whether they, like Edgar, have imposed a distorting order on Lear's tragic insights.

My intention is to prepare students for the dramatic regressions that follow Lear's moments of insight. Lear's education cannot be portrayed as an unbroken curve upward, though many students plot such a map. Lear's knowledge of true need and patience is overwhelmed by rage and destructive urges (II.iv.272–86) and by a pride that leads to madness (III.ii.1–24). In III.iv, his great prayer dissolves in the mad idea that Tom O'Bedlam's daughters have reduced Tom to nothing. Imagining the wretch to be as foolish as himself, Lear no longer feels pure empathy. In general, I highlight the "madness-in-reason" quality of several of Lear's insights. His intuition of the relation between authority and power degenerates, for example, into the nihilistic claim that "none does offend" (IV.vi.168). E. A. J. Honigmann, in *Shakespeare: Seven Tragedies*, defines Lear's "blurred vision" and describes his mind as an inner landscape that is difficult to assess because the king often avoids knowing and being known.

Students thus can realize that Lear's progress in knowledge is a broken course, marked by many lapses. At this juncture, they may further refine their maps. Teachers may wish to reassure them that dramatic qualifications of Lear's insights do not negate those insights or make them invalid. In fact, they might explain that student maps represent guides in an antiformalist terrain. My next-to-last segment concerned with *Lear* consists of a detailed survey of this terrain. Teachers can gain an understanding of the antiformalist features of *Lear* from the following studies: John Holloway, *The Story of the Night*; Nicholas Brooke, "The Ending of *King Lear*"; Michael Goldman, *Shakespeare and the Energies of Drama*; Richard Fly, *Shakespeare's Mediated World*; Edward Pechter, "On the Blinding of Gloucester," and James Black, "*King Lear*: Art Upside-Down." Fly shows how scene, language, and character in *King Lear* decompose or deteriorate: how Edgar's view from Dover Cliff collapses before nothingness; how Lear's character fragments into the "shadows" of fool and madman; and how the ritual speech of the opening scene declines to howls, curses, and the numbing repetition of the single word *never*. Holloway observes that the play could end with act IV and explains that in the fifth act Shakespeare keeps raising formal expectations that the tragedy will end, only to shock onlookers with renewed savagery. Edmund, Edgar, and Albany in turn try to provide ending speeches for a tragedy, only to fail as disaster continues, seemingly with a life of its own. Brooke identifies at least six false endings to the play. Even Bradley, dependent on Aristotelian aesthetics, admits that *King Lear*, marked by an unparalleled first-act crisis and reversal of the situation, a demise of the protagonist dangerously stretched over four acts, and a curious fourth-act rising action, does not illustrate a neat five-phase development. In order to make the play fit into his formalist scheme, he is forced into naming Goneril, Regan, and Edmund de facto protagonists.

With the exception of Bradley, all the above-named critics discuss episodes or speeches in *King Lear* in which Shakespeare leads us to anticipate order or success only to thwart it. For example, readers expect Cornwall's intervening servant to preserve Gloucester from total blindness, but they see Cornwall finish his gruesome task because the servant has reminded him that Gloucester has one eye left by which he can see justice done. They expect Tom O'Bedlam's moralizing about the sin of adultery to be directed to the lustful Gloucester, but they hear it applied instead to Lear. They expect Cordelia and Lear to be on the "right" side, but they see them invade Britain under the flag of the traditional enemy, France. They expect Edgar's promises to bring Gloucester comfort, but they see Edgar reenter immediately with the news that Lear and Cordelia have lost the battle. They expect Albany's prayer—"The gods defend her!"—to prevent the strangling of Cordelia, but, horrified, they see Lear enter straightaway with his dead daughter in his arms. They expect that

Kent will be recognized and rewarded for his faithful service, but they hear Lear's vague dismissal of the man instead. They expect to hear a strong speech of continuity at the end of the play, like that delivered by Fortinbras, but they listen instead to Edgar's disturbing suggestion that the younger generation can only sustain the mutilated state before suffering an early death. Obviously, reversals of expectation abound. Taken as a whole, such reversals convince students that Shakespeare was intent on dramatizing events and attitudes that repeatedly block attempts to find either a just or pleasing order in the play.

Nevertheless, *King Lear*, in the last analysis, is not a nihilistic play. A teacher can conclude by observing that undergraduates have recorded genuine insights into the superfluousness of social class and rich garments, into the need for patience and absolute charity, and into the arbitrariness of earthly justice. *King Lear* is not a nihilistic play, because father and daughter achieve a mutual understanding of the quality (as opposed to the quantity) of love. This quality can be heard in those tender words of Cordelia spoken to her awakened father. It can also be heard in Lear's prayer and in his response to "unaccommodated man" in act III. Finally, it can best be appreciated in the reconciled king's wish to withdraw to prison, away from the world of his victorious enemies, with only his beloved Cordelia as his resource. This sensitive speech, in which Lear desires to sing joyfully, lovingly, like a bird in a cage, expresses his new qualitative knowledge of love. This knowledge makes possible Lear's final insight, in which he sees (or thinks that he sees) Cordelia's soul escaping at her lips. Such speeches will always provide an effective conclusion to a discussion of *King Lear*. They are also especially meaningful outer limits for student maps of a rugged and surprising tragic world—a world that seems even more unconventional when students immediately turn to a play like *Sejanus*, predictably crafted according to neoclassical method.

Shakespearean Tragedy in a Renaissance Context: *King Lear* and Hooker's *Of the Laws of Ecclesiastical Polity*

Bruce W. Young

When I was asked to teach a section of Harvard's introductory survey, I found that all sections of the course were to use the same syllabus and anthology. Fortunately, the anthology I was to use, *The Norton Anthology of English Literature*, is well suited to the approach I take. It includes *King Lear*—in fact, it is the only anthology used widely in historical surveys to do so—but it also includes a wealth of material by lesser writers of the same period, much of which can be used in connection with Shakespeare. Teaching *King Lear* as part of a British literature survey has its disadvantages, most prominently the absence of the context that a dozen or so other Shakespearean plays would provide. But it offers one advantage in return: the presence of other works from the Renaissance that provide another kind of context. The most important of these works for the approach I take is Richard Hooker's *Of the Laws of Ecclesiastical Polity*. I have found other writers useful as well, but a look at Hooker will be sufficient to illustrate my approach. In essence, I set passages from Renaissance writers—in this case Hooker—alongside passages from *Lear*, with the aim of helping students to become aware of ideas, attitudes, and thematic patterns that the works have in common. At the same time, I point to differences in the treatment the writers give to similar themes. This approach derives from my conviction that by setting *King Lear* in its Renaissance context, teachers may help students to a richer and more informed understanding of the play.

The *Norton Anthology* has labeled one of its selections from Hooker "The Law of Nature." *Nature*, as many have noted, is also one of *Lear*'s most important words. But when we think of *nature* in *Lear*, we must remove the overlay of ideas that have become attached to the word in the three and a half centuries separating us from Shakespeare. For the Renaissance, *nature* meant primarily the created universe, usually viewed in one of three ways: as a structure of laws, as the material substance governed by these laws, or as the active power giving the universe its life and motion. The passages from Hooker in the *Norton Anthology* allude to all three. Hooker conceives of nature as a great, harmonious structure, normally productive and life-giving, with "celestial spheres" following their "wonted motions," "the times and seasons" pursuing an orderly course, and the winds, clouds, and plant life of "this lower world" all carrying out their usual functions (1037). This harmony, according to Hooker, extends, or ought to extend, to human life as well as to the other elements of the world. Just as other creatures

have prescribed natures, so humankind has what Hooker calls "the law of [its] nature." Human beings are made aware of this law by their "natural discourse," or reason, through which they hear the "voice" of Nature, teaching "laws and statutes to live by." As with other creatures, if human beings obey the "law of [their] nature," good follows; if they disobey it, the result is misery and confusion (1038–40).

Nature appears in many guises in *King Lear*, but among them are those stressed by Hooker: nature as an ordered structure and as a life-giving force. Most of the characters see themselves as part of an interconnected structure governed by divine power (see, for example, Lear's reference to "the orbs / From whom we do exist and cease to be" [I.i.107–10]). Moreover, they attribute the powers of life to nature: Lear speaks of "Nature's molds," which contain the "germens," or seeds, of life (III.ii.8–9), and refers to nature's normal "purpose" of making the womb "fruitful" (I.iv.254–56).

Like Hooker, the characters in *King Lear* assume that nature, besides ordering the world in general, also prescribes right behavior for human beings. Hospitality, gratitude to benefactors, loyalty and kindness between parents and children—all these are felt to be "natural." Lear speaks of the "offices," or duties, "of nature" and associates them with the "bond of childhood, / Effects of courtesy," and "dues of gratitude" (II.iv.172–73). Gloucester (though mistakenly) calls Edmund a "Loyal and natural boy" (II.i.85) and expects the "sparks of nature" to kindle filial piety in him (III.vii.89). On the other hand, disloyalty to king and father is called "unnatural" (III.iii.1).

The events of the play show, of course, that nature can be anything but harmonious and life-giving. But even the disharmony and death in *Lear* are viewed by most of its characters as departures from nature's established norm. When Lear curses Goneril, for instance, he asks nature to "suspend" its normal "purpose" and either make his daughter sterile or else give her a "disnatured" child (I.iv.254–62). Here again, Hooker can be helpful in making explicit the assumptions at work in the play, for despite his emphasis on nature's harmony, he recognizes that in the world of actual experience nature may be a scene of chaos and destruction. Lear's invocation of the destructive powers of nature—"Blow, winds, and crack your cheeks! rage! blow! / . . . And thou, all-shaking thunder, / Smite flat the thick rotundity o' the world!" (III.ii.1, 6–7)—is paralleled by Hooker's vision of chaos. Hooker imagines a world of confusion and sterility in which the "frame" of heaven "loosen[s] and dissolve[s] itself," the "celestial spheres . . . forget their wonted motions," the seasons blend in a "disordered and confused mixture," and the earth, "defeated of heavenly influence," ceases to bear fruit—all the presumed result of nature's failure, "though it were but for a while," to observe "her own laws" (1037). The world, as Hooker conceives it, is "so compacted that as long as each thing performeth only that work which is natural unto it, it thereby preserveth both other things and also itself"; yet it is the very intricacy and connectedness of the natural order that make ruin the inevitable consequence if "any principal thing . . . but once cease or fail, or swerve" (1039).

Such chaos is not, for Hooker, the normal or usual order of things. Yet the imperfection he sees in nature—especially in human nature—means that some degree of disharmony is to be expected. "Swervings"—that is, departures from law—are, he says, "now and then incident into the course of Nature," because the "matter whereof natural things consist" is corrupt and imperfect, so that it sometimes proves "uncapable" of perfect harmony (1038). Human nature, too, is corrupt: "deformities" and "festered sores" mark our moral natures, and "the natural understanding" of whole nations has been "darkened" (1042). At times, Hooker presents this view with a bluntness that almost anticipates Hobbes, asserting, for instance, that "the will of man" must be presumed generally "to be inwardly obstinate, rebellious, and averse from all obedience unto the sacred laws of his nature" and that man must be held "in regard of his depraved mind little better than a wild beast" (1040). This last phrase recalls the profusion of animal imagery in *Lear*—the frequent comparison of human beings to dogs, wolves, tigers, serpents, boars, and so on—used, as in Hooker, to suggest human corruption.

But the resemblance between *Lear* and Hooker on this matter extends beyond imagery. Lear's indictment of humanity and the social order in III.vi and IV.vi, though presented as the ravings of a madman, has its roots in the concept of human depravity. Besides being prone to evil, human nature is also weak, subject to sickness (II.iv.99–106; IV.vi.103–04: " I am not ague-proof") and to the decline that comes with age (II.iv.139–41). Human beings are exposed to the evils of others and to the fury of the elements (III.i.1–15; III.iv.29–33): we are told, during one of the scenes on the heath, that "The tyranny of the open night's too rough / For nature to endure" (III.iv.2–3).

Edmund is the play's prime example of the corruption of nature and the misuse of its powers. Nature, for Edmund, is the opposite of law. He invokes Nature as his goddess because he has acquired from her (he claims) "more composition and fierce quality," more of the energies of life, than conventional procreation could give "a whole tribe" of legitimate offspring (I.ii.1–15). He later uses the word *nature* to describe his individual characteristics, specifically his tendency toward ruthless self-promotion: he will do one last good deed "Despite of [his] own nature" (V.iii.243).

Obviously, Hooker does not share Edmund's view. Yet, like Edmund, Hooker sometimes uses the word *nature* to mean "individual endowment," including the sort of energy and strength Edmund possesses. In a passage that could apply to Edmund, Hooker asks, "For hath not Nature furnished man with wit and valor, as it were with armor . . . ?" Where Hooker differs from Edmund is in warning that this natural endowment may be used "as well unto extreme evil as good" and in asserting that to use it for evil is contrary to natural law (1041–42). For Edmund, disloyalty and self-seeking are "natural"; nature includes the wildest of energies and is unbound by law. But for Hooker, this view of nature is one-sided: Edmund and the "nature" he invokes would be examples of "nature depraved" (1040).

For both Hooker and Shakespeare, chaos and destruction enter into the world of nature through the violation of natural law. When human beings transgress the "law of [their] nature," Hooker writes, "tribulation and anguish" follow (1039). The laws Hooker is thinking of include the very ones broken in *Lear*: the laws of loyalty, kindness, and filial piety. *King Lear* is largely, in fact, a play about the violation of the natural order and the consequences of such violation. The consequences turn out to be just those Hooker describes: "strife, contention, and violence," and finally misery and ruin (1041). Or as Gloucester puts it: ". . . in cities, mutinies; in countries, discord; in palaces, treason. . . . Machinations, hollowness, treachery, and all ruinous disorders . . . " (I.ii.97–103). The major violators of natural law eventually incur retribution: Goneril, Regan, and Cornwall fall prey to the destructive forces they have unleashed, and for Edmund, too, the "wheel" finally comes "full circle" (V.iii.173).

But Shakespeare complicates this pattern of cause and effect by making the misery several characters experience exceed anything they can possibly have deserved. The very structure of the play rests on the assumption that the characters' actions have consequences: Gloucester's adultery produces a bastard who seeks his death (see V.iii.169–72); Cordelia's words (or lack of them) wrench Lear's "frame of nature / From the fixed place," turning the natural love of a father to hate (I.iv.245–49); Lear's foolishness and pride set off the chain of events leading to his misery and madness. Yet no interpretation of Lear, Gloucester, or Cordelia can reasonably make their faults commensurate with what they suffer. Much of the play's power, in fact, derives from this apparent contradiction between justice and the operation of natural law.

While it would be a mistake to try to explain away this tension, I am convinced that, even in this case, seeing the play in its Renaissance context adds to rather than detracts from its power. Here again, passages from Hooker help us understand *Lear*, for Hooker recognizes the tension between nature and justice and even makes that tension part of a coherent view of the world. Besides the general principle of natural law, Hooker notes three subordinate principles that influence nature's operation, making it something rather more complicated than a simple instrument of "poetic justice" in which individuals' earthly happiness and suffering are measured strictly according to their good and evil deeds. The first of these principles is that the effects of an evil deed are not limited to the doer. If any "principal" element of the natural order "fails" or "swerves," Hooker writes, the "sequel thereof" will be "ruin both to itself and whatsoever dependeth upon it" (1039). The world is so interconnected, in other words, that the effects of one person's deeds may help or harm many others.

The second principle is that we may be carried into evil by circumstances or by the acts of others "against our wills, or constrainedly." "In such cases," Hooker says, " . . . the evil which is done moveth compassion; men are pitied for it, as being rather miserable in such respect than culpable" (1039–40). Hooker's words are echoed by Lear's claim that he is "More sinned against than sinning" (III.ii.57–58) and by the whole series of horrors perpetrated by the play's characters against one another.

The third principle affecting nature is its corrupt and imperfect state, a state whose cause is to be found in humanity and in its original violation of divine law. Nature's corruption, says Hooker, is a consequence of "divine malediction, laid for the sin of man upon those creatures which God had made for the use of man" (1038). Human sin has this effect because of the place humanity holds in an intricately interconnected universe. According to Hooker, "man . . . [is] a very world in himself" (1039)—a microcosm, in other words, so connected with the cosmos that his violation of law produces chaos in the world as a whole. Here a teacher comparing Hooker and *Lear* may wish to introduce supplementary material to show that Hooker's concept was standard in the Renaissance. Theodore Spencer, for instance, in his summary of the Renaissance view, exactly repeats Hooker's idea: "when Adam fell, Nature fell too" (25). Further substantiation is offered by John F. Danby and Geoffrey Bush: both writers discuss the Renaissance view of nature as an ideal, but also as a fallen reality.

For Hooker, the world's fallen condition helps explain its seeming injustices. The mere fact of living in a fallen world means that one is exposed to violence and misery not of one's own making. And this fallen condition cannot, according to Hooker, be expected to yield itself fully to human attempts to improve it. Though human laws and governments may curtail some of the evils of nature's fall, they will never do so perfectly:

> . . . the stains and blemishes found in our state, . . . springing from the root of human frailty and corruption, not only are, but have always been more or less—yea, and for anything we know to the contrary will be till the world's end—complained of. . . .   (1036)

Again, Hooker was not alone in this opinion. The common view, according to Theodore Spencer, was that both nature and human nature are "incurably corrupted" (26). Indeed, it was felt that nature would decline, rather than improve, until the end of the world, when, after cataclysmic destruction, all things would be "made new" (see Shakespeare's sonnet 55; also Spencer; Danby; and Bush).

In *King Lear* Shakespeare joins Hooker, and Renaissance thinkers generally, in assuming that nature has undergone a fall and that nature's fallen condition derives from humanity. Nature, says a "gentleman" in *Lear*, is under a "general curse" brought about by human wrongdoing (IV.vi.201). As in Hooker, a human being is a microcosm—the "little world of man" (III.i.10)—whose condition affects and is affected by the larger cosmos. The chaos we see in individuals, including "The tempest in [Lear's] mind" (III.iv.13), is paralleled by chaos in society and in the cosmos. Furthermore, the play (like the *Laws*) asserts that nature is in decline. By the end of the play, wasted by age and by what he has suffered, Lear is called by Gloucester a "ruined piece of nature." As Gloucester goes on to point out, Lear's condition reflects that of the world as a whole, for, like Lear, so shall "This great world / . . . wear out to nought" (IV.vi.133–34). This story of human weakness and decline takes place in a world that is itself in decline, so much so that Kent and Edgar, viewing the final events of the play, wonder if they are witnessing "the promised end"—the end of the world—or only an "image of that horror" (V.iii.262–63). Thus, even in a play unquestionably pagan in setting, Shakespeare draws freely on the Christian idea of the Apocalypse, the era of tribulation and judgment that will accompany the end of this fallen world.

In most important respects, then, Shakespeare's picture of the world is similar to Hooker's, and both use the word *nature* in closely parallel ways: *nature* may refer to the ideal structure of the world, the laws that should govern human behavior, the energies that normally sustain the life and motion of the world (but that may be turned to violence), the unique endowment of individuals, and the fallen and corrupt condition in which both individuals and the world as a whole participate.

The parallels between *Of the Laws of Ecclesiastical Polity* and *King Lear* thus include shared assumptions about the nature of reality. By "parallels" I do not, of course, mean exact repetitions. But even where differences are concerned, the two works make an especially illuminating pair. Hooker presents the orthodox view in eloquent but straightforward prose. Shakespeare, through a much different literary medium, both expresses and challenges important aspects of the orthodox view. The ideas in *King Lear* are less consistent and harmonious than those articulated by Hooker—

partly because *Lear* attempts to reproduce some of the richness and contradiction of reality, partly because a playwright understandably takes
greater interest in setting ideas in conflict than in organizing them into a
consistent system. But, despite these differences, the ideas in the two
works are much the same and present a view of the world and human life
that Shakespeare and Hooker shared with most of their contemporaries.

Teaching with a Proper Text

Michael Warren

Enter Cordelia, Doctor, and others. (Q1)
*Enter with Drum and Colours, Cordelia, Gentlemen,
and Souldiours.* (F1)
Enter, with Drum and Colors, CORDELIA, [DOCTOR], *and*
SOLDIERS. (Evans, *Riverside Shakespeare* IV.iv)

Special problems attend the determination of a text for teaching *King Lear*; similar problems may yet attend the teaching of other Shakespeare plays, although the issues for those plays may not be so critical. Simply stated, recent research has called into question the authority and validity of *all* available modern editions of the play, and therefore of the criticism based upon them. It proposes instead two versions of *King Lear*, each susceptible of distinctive interpretation.

I

There are three early publications of *King Lear*: a first quarto (Q1) published in 1608; a second quarto (Q2) published in 1619, but with a title page that is falsely dated 1608; and the printing of the play in the First Folio (F1) in 1623. Q1 and Q2 are relatively similar. Q2 is generally regarded as a reprint of a copy of Q1 with some alterations in spelling, punctuation, and lineation but few authoritative alterations in substantives (words as units of meaning, by contrast to accidentals, which include spelling, punctuation, etc.); consequently, it is of little concern here. The variations between Q1 and F1, however, are great and very important. Q1 contains a scene, sequences, speeches, and lines that F1 does not; F1 contains sequences, speeches, and lines that Q1 does not. Speech assignments, stage directions, and individual words vary extensively from text to text. Q1 contains approximately 300 lines that are not in F1, and F1 contains approximately 100 lines that are not in Q1 (F1 is about 3,300 lines long). The traditional and conventional view of these two texts of *Lear*, expressed in the textual notes of almost all standard editions of the play, is that each is an imperfect recension of the original play that Shakespeare wrote; that that original play contained all the Q-only material and F-only material; and that all variants between the two texts are the result of corruption in one or the other. Editors have generally attempted within this hypothesis to identify the distinctive qualities of these two texts, to explain their features, and in the light of the explanation to eliminate the identified corruption and to restore thereby, however approximately, the original form and details of Shakespeare's play. Various explanations have been advanced for the apparently imperfect state of Q1; some relation to foul papers (Shakespeare's "original draft") has customarily been proposed, but actors' memorial contamination has also been detected in it. F1 has usually been regarded as less corrupt than Q1; scholars have traditionally proposed its origin in a copy of either Q1 or Q2 that had been modified by comparison with a theatrical promptbook. Consequently F1 has been considered the more authoritative text—that which approximates more nearly the supposed authorial original—and it is F1 that has been used as the copy-text for most editions. However, since Theobald's edition of 1733 all edited publications of the play have conflated the two texts, printing "all that Shakespeare wrote." Where substantive variants have occurred, editors have proceeded eclectically, choosing on the basis of hypotheses of origins and transmission "the better reading" from either text. Thus a modern edited text of *King Lear*, such a text as most Shakespeareans have habitually read, studied, taught, acted, or directed, is a play that did not exist in print until 117 years after the death of its author. (G. Blakemore Evans provides an excellent statement of the standard editorial process in relation to *King Lear* in "The Editing of a Shakespearean Play," a section of his highly recommended introductory essay "Shakespeare's Text" in *The Riverside Shakespeare*.)

Recent research has challenged the authority of this construct as representing "Shakespeare's *King Lear*." A number of scholars have attacked the hypothesis that Q1 and F1 are variously corrupt recensions of a single original and have proposed instead that the two versions are separate and distinct works on the subject of *King Lear*: see Michael J. Warren, "Quarto and Folio *King Lear* and the Interpretation of Albany and Edgar"; Gary Taylor, "The War in *King Lear*"; Steven Urkowitz, *Shakespeare's Revision of* King Lear; P. W. K. Stone, *The Textual History of* King Lear; Peter W. M. Blayney, *The Texts of* King Lear *and Their Origins* (Vol. 1: *Nicholas Okes and the First Quarto*); and the essays in Gary Taylor and Michael Warren, eds., *The Division of the Kingdoms: Shakespeare's Two Versions of* King Lear. In looking beyond the isolated variant to patterns of variation, and considering particularly their implications for characterization, interpretation, staging, and performance, these scholars have proposed that the two texts are sufficiently different to be regarded as separate entities and, therefore, should not now be conflated, since they were not together in the first place. In this view there is not a single play but an earlier version, represented by Q1, and a later version, represented by F1; moreover, with the "ideal" text discredited, neither early printed text appears corrupt to the degree that has usually been assumed, although each has its idiosyncrasies and problems. In fact, it has now been proposed that Q1 derives directly from foul papers, while F1, although still thought to be printed from some combination of materials relating to Q1, Q2, and a promptbook, is discerned as revealing the intervention of Shakespeare's revising hand (Stone and Blayney do not subscribe to the identification of Shakespeare as the reviser).

The implications of this new hypothesis are clear: for 250 years Shakespeare's *King Lear* plays have been obscured by a construct of mistaken scholarship; the standard editions are invalid and misleading; we now need to think of two versions of *King Lear*; and we lack editions of those two versions. Two early attempts at parallel-texts reprints of Q1 and F1 exist, edited by Alvey Augustus Adee and Wilhelm Viëtor, but they are rare, and not wholly reliable. However, we do have access to good photographic reproductions in book form of both Q1 and F1. W. W. Greg reproduces the Gorhambury copy in *King Lear 1608 (Pied Bull Quarto)*, now out of print; Michael J. B. Allen and Kenneth Muir reproduce the Huntington Library copy in *Shakespeare Plays in Quarto*. The Folio text is reproduced in *The Norton Facsimile: The First Folio of Shakespeare*, ed. Charlton Hinman. Both of the sources still in print are, unfortunately, quite costly, although they should be present in the libraries of most universities and colleges. No separate editions of Q1 and F1 have yet been prepared, and so the teacher of *King Lear* must resort to special approaches.

II

Teaching *King Lear* to advanced undergraduate students and graduate students involves a problem of access to materials. Such students must clearly be taught in a way that keeps the textual issue foremost: they need to be introduced to the problems of establishing texts, to confront two versions, and to study two plays. They will need to study the earliest printed originals, presumably with the commentary that a conventional edition with text, apparatus, and textual and critical introduction and commentary provides (in this respect the Muir edition is the most useful, although the collation is selective). Advanced students, then, will consult the library's photographic reprints regularly; in this connection *King Lear* is a particularly valuable subject for study in graduate courses, since it introduces the student to bibliographical matters that raise questions in critical, editorial, and educational theory. However, both advanced students and their teachers may also take advantage of the method that I propose for use with classes of less specialized students.

King Lear is widely taught in courses where the students are far more diverse and where the object is not to train students in the study of literature but to introduce them to a major work of European literature; such courses customarily use one of the many editions of the play currently available, or a complete edition of Shakespeare's works, or else *The Norton Anthology of English Literature*. To such a heterogeneous and presumably less sophisticated group the debate concerning the text may, perhaps, not be relevant, although it can prove fascinating to them and should certainly be mentioned. However, the question of teaching with a proper text does present itself, for no one will teach error willingly. In this case, then, two questions arise. First, which version shall one strive to teach, Q or F? Second, how shall one approximate the chosen version in any degree?

The version to be taught is a matter of individual choice: current scholarship confirms the statement on the Q1 title page that Q1 represents the form of the play that was initially acted, and research also suggests that F1 is the form of the play acted after it had been revised by Shakespeare in the years 1609–10. Each may contain some transmissional corruption—Q1 has some notably confused passages, and F1, while superficially freer from error, may contain misprints and other nonauthorial interventions, since error is common in printed plays of the period. However, a choice has to be made if only one *King Lear* is to be taught. My own inclination is to teach F1, primarily because I hypothesize that in its revised state it is close to Shakespeare's final desires, but also, secondarily, because the teaching text is relatively easily prepared. Such labor of preparation is exacting, but also exhilarating and instructive.

When F1 provides the copy-text for an edition—and both editions based on Q1 (ed. M. R. Ridley and Jay L. Halio) are out of print—the text produced consists of F1 material into which passages not present in F1 have been introduced. At certain points also the editor will have preferred individual Q1 readings where the two texts vary, judging that the earlier text preserves the earlier form of which F1 contains a corruption. The editor may also have introduced some emendations in problematic passages and will have adjusted the stage directions to conform to his or her view of the action. The speech prefixes will have been regularized, the spelling and punctuation modernized. Most editions include not only a note on the text but also a selective list of variants indicating which material derives from Q1 only or where Q1 readings have been preferred to those of F1, although only in the Muir edition does this notation of variants appear on the same page as the text; whatever the location of this notation, however, its presence makes the task of adaptation easier. Moreover, some editions (notably those edited by Evans, Harbage, and Bevington) place the Q1-only material in brackets, in the way that most editions tend to bracket editorial additions to stage directions. Indeed, the Evans edition marks selected problematic readings by brackets also. By using the apparatus provided and by constantly checking one's work against *The Norton Facsimile* of F1, one can eradicate from a conventional edition of *King Lear* the Q1 elements that complicate and distort the F1 version. Students, then, may still work from a modernized edition that provides notes and other aids to interpretation.

If this procedure is followed, certain features of the conventional text will be conspicuously absent. For instance, III.i will be much shortened, and it will be especially clarified by the removal from Kent's long speech of lines 30–42, "But true it is. . . . This office to you" (I cite the numbering in Evans). The mock trial will be eliminated from III.vi (lines 17–56), as well as Kent's and Edgar's last speeches (lines 97–101, 102–15). The conversation of the servants after the blinding of Gloucester will be cut (III.vii.99–107). The confrontation of Albany and Goneril in IV.ii will appear in abbreviated form (lines 31–50, 53–59, 62–69 being omitted); the whole of IV.iii will be deleted; and the last act will undergo (among many important small modifications) an alteration of Edmund's role during the Herald's activities and the omission of Edgar's report of his meeting with Kent over the body of Gloucester (V.iii.205–22); the attribution of the last speech to Edgar will no longer be a matter for debate.

This list is just a selection of major changes; numerous smaller changes will also be necessary, although in a few cases the teacher may wish to consult the discussions of alternative readings in the critical literature concerning the play, especially *Shakespeare's* King Lear: *A Critical Edition*, ed. George Ian Duthie; the Cambridge *King Lear*, ed. George Ian Duthie and John Dover Wilson; the Arden *King Lear*, ed. Kenneth Muir; and the works of recent scholarship cited earlier in this essay (Taylor and Warren's *Division of the Kingdoms* contains an index of passages discussed and a similar index to all the other recent works except Blayney's, which contains its own index). The teacher should remember, however, that any discussion of variants will be influenced by the general textual hypothesis that informs a work.

The resulting edition no doubt will be less than perfectly satisfactory for teaching. To dictate a whole series of modifications to a textbook, or to place a master copy for consultation in advance at a specified location, is not a desirable activity prior to teaching a play to a general audience of students, but it is necessary (at least temporarily), and it allows one to teach with a confidence of integrity in the endeavor. Several forthcoming publications will help considerably. *The Complete Oxford Shakespeare*, projected for publication in 1986 in separate modernized- and old-spelling formats, will contain two *King Lear* plays. Subsequently, the Oxford English Texts edition, with full critical and textual apparatus, will also follow the hypothesis that there are two versions. Volume 2 of Peter W. M. Blayney's *The Texts of* King Lear *and Their Origins* will contain an edited text of Q1. I myself hope to produce a new parallel-texts presentation of Q1 and F1.

New editions will be produced, and old editions—presumably including *The Norton Anthology of English Literature*—will need to be revised. Soon teachers will be able to choose to teach either the earlier or the later *King Lear* to general students, and advanced students and scholars will benefit from the amplitude of commentary that these editions will provide upon their problematic originals, Q1 and F1.

A Theatrical Approach:
King Lear as Performance and Experience

J. L. Styan

I shall not use space to argue further the virtues of teaching a play by performance methods or to discuss the many ways of doing so: many have attested to the vivid immediacy with which a text can be brought to life when students act out a few lines, even at first reading and even with books in hand. Students who have no training as actors will usually surprise themselves when they lend their bodies and voices to a scene to demonstrate how a point in a play is to be seen and heard and communicated. Instructors can facilitate this process by not casting the parts themselves but dividing the class into small working groups, each of which discusses, casts, and rehearses a brief scene out of class. Presenting such makeshift performance at the next meeting of the class, if necessary with two or more teams in competition, invariably stimulates pertinent discussion. Getting the text off the page is the kindest thing a teacher can do to a play, and I would argue that no playwright profits more from this approach than Shakespeare, and no play is more rich in scenes and incidents that illustrate his range of skills than *King Lear*. Of all plays, this one offers so much to talk about, but I would never think of teaching it at any level (freshman to doctoral) without the use of performance.

A theatrical approach can draw attention to two qualities in this play. First, it permits the instructor to refute point by point the hallowed argument that *Lear* is "too huge for the stage" (Bradley 200) or, more specifically, that "the plays of Shakespeare are less calculated for performance on a stage, than those of almost any other dramatist whatever" (Lamb 28). In practice, one is astonished at the degree of particularity with which Shakespeare has imagined each scene in performance and proposed the "controls" that can ensure a maximum response. In scenes of more naturalistic behavior, like that of Cordelia's waking the king from his madness, the playwright supplies, moment by moment, a guide to the detailed gestures and movements that will make the scene work: at such times, *Lear* becomes a play of minutiae, of pins and buttons and feathers, despite its grand scale. At another extreme, specifically ritualistic scenes that make full use of the Globe platform—as when the king divides his kingdom, or strips off his royal garments to look like a Bedlam beggar, or enters with his dead daughter in his arms—are exactly visualized, so that the implicit directions in the text invite both demonstration and discussion of the scenes' intentions. I like to think that Shakespeare was himself responsible even for the precise insertions in the Folio of those cues for offstage effects, *"Storm still"* (meaning "more storm"), each like a voice from God.

A second justification for a performance approach in class has to do, perhaps surprisingly, with the carefully calculated shape of the whole play. We can assess this shape as we progress from disliking Lear to sympathizing with him and as we trace his passage on the "wheel of fire" from the tyranny and discord of the early court scenes to the madness and chaos on the heath and then to the humility and harmony of the prison. By making sure that the segments chosen to study and perform trace the orchestration of changes through the whole play, the instructor can successfully convey the relentless advance of the action through its pattern of moods and tones, working simultaneously on narrative, moral, psychological, and musical or poetic levels. The simplest way for the class to enjoy a direct experience of the tragedy while keeping the total picture in view is to work on a sequence of scenes showing strongly contrasting views of the king: first as tyrant on his throne; then as abused father, in a scene with either Goneril or Regan; then as insane but demonstrating his new-found "reason in madness"; and finally as tragic victim. When time was short, I have managed this kind of sampling by placing four Lears in the four corners of the room to read four contrasting speeches, which at least suggest how the poetry changes as the play develops.

Even a plan that samples the major dramatic shifts of feeling and response will not embrace all of the special features of this play. Time is well spent on the study of such elements as its physical horror (the blinding of Gloucester and the connection with Elizabethan bearbaiting), the uses of the popular ingredient of disguise (the extraordinary sequence of roles required of Edgar, with the reason for each), and the black-comic or grotesque thread that runs through the play (best exemplified, perhaps, by the scene of Gloucester's attempted suicide from Dover Cliff, although the Fool's commentary as his master's alter ego or Edgar's frantic performance as Poor Tom, the sane man's idea of the madman, would also serve).

If *King Lear* is not too huge for the stage, it may be so for the curriculum. However, it is comforting to report that none of the play's individual scenes is too huge for the classroom, where the usual institutional bareness and total lack of theatrical features may even enhance its simple and powerful poetry and drama. The following is a condensed list of the scenes or segments I have used for class performance at one time or another. The asterisks mark those scenes that I have found most effective with beginning students.

Muir edition reference	*Subject*	*Performance points*
A. I.i.1–23	Introducing Edmund	stage space, character
B. I.i.34–93	°Dividing the kingdom	ritual stage, contrast of character

Muir edition reference	Subject	Performance points
C. I.i.283–308	The sisters plot against the king	use of prose vs. verse
D. I.ii.1–46	Edmund and the letter	address to audience
E. I.iv.45–100	Oswald insults the king	use of entrances, movement, group responses
F. I.iv.197–239	°Goneril confronts the king	stage space, contrast of voices
G. II.iv.1–27	Kent in the stocks	use of prose vs. verse
H. II.iv.184–288	Goneril joins Regan	visual and vocal devices, Lear's progress to madness
I. III.ii.1–36	King and Fool in the storm	use of poetry, mime
J. III.iv.1–36	°Lear before the hovel	use of platform, address to audience
K. III.iv.37–112	The king meets the beggar	use of platform, symbolic action
L. III.vi.1–88	The mad trial	ironic comedy
M. III.vii.1–93	Blinding Gloucester	ritual use of the stage
N. IV.vi.1–74	°On Dover Cliff	comic use of the stage
O. IV.vi.80–189	Blind man meets madman	character contrast
P. IV.vii.17–84	°Waking Lear	movement, space, gesture
Q. V.iii.1–40	The king and Cordelia in prison	contrast in groups, voices
R. V.iii.221–57	Death of the sisters	sequence of entrances
S. V.iii.257–326	Death of Lear	pace, tone, character

From this list of scenes I have selected a few points of performance that have afforded unexpected insights into the meaning of the action when students, usually working in competing groups, have tried out different ways of playing them. All quotations are from Muir's edition of the play.

A. *Introducing Edmund.* This important incident, coming immediately before the opening court scene, is often overlooked. Yet it not only announces the scene to come but prepares the audience to look with keener eyes to the parent/child relationships about to be portrayed. To make the point, one should first have the three men, Gloucester, Kent, and Edmund, enter as a group, so that the father talks about his bastard son in the son's presence:

KENT.   Is not this your son, my Lord?

GLOUCESTER.   His breeding, Sir, hath been at my charge: I have so
often blush'd to acknowledge him, that now I am braz'd to't.

KENT.   I cannot conceive you.

GLOUCESTER.   Sir, this young fellow's mother could. . . .

The class will judge that there is far more force and meaning if Edmund
makes a separate entrance and stands apart while he sees the older men
talking about him and laughing. When his father calls him over to meet
Kent, everyone will hear an innuendo in Edmund's voice:

GLOUCESTER.   . . . Do you know this noble gentleman, Edmund?

EDMUND.   No, my Lord.

GLOUCESTER.   My Lord of Kent: remember him hereafter as my hon-
orable friend.

EDMUND.   My services to your Lordship.

B. *Dividing the kingdom.* Several issues here. The image of Lear will be
determined from the start by the way he enters, sits on a throne, and gives
his orders. The text ambiguously invites both senility and vigorous old age;
it is best to try the spectrum of possibilities (in Peter Brook's production,
Paul Scofield as Lear failed to enter on cue or from the expected direction
but pushed through the assembled courtiers from one side, powerfully conveying his individuality). The teacher may try different places and sizes for
the map: on a table, on the wall, on the floor.

The major contrasts in Goneril and Regan and their opening speeches
will be effectively supported if the sisters are placed opposite one another
and visibly respond to one another's lines, so that we watch their reactions
as well as Lear's. An icy smile from Regan on her line "Only she comes too
short" should cap this silent exchange between the sisters.

To arrange Cordelia outside the symmetrical frame of the court not only
allows her to speak her asides directly to the audience but also makes her
known well in advance of her answer to the king. "What shall Cordelia
speak? Love, and be silent" also prepares us a little for the shock to come
and makes Lear's expectant "Now, our joy . . . " doubly tense with its irony.
Irony and tension will be redoubled if the king descends from his throne to
say his lines to Cordelia, or invites her to sit beside him, or even on his
knee. After the ritualistic address to Goneril and Regan, Lear's change in
style and tone to one suggesting a more intimate relationship with the
audience and affection for his youngest daughter (preparatory to the colloquial style of their exchange of "Nothing"s) can be intensely moving. A
game with their repeated "Nothing"—divided by pauses, spoken in a
variety of tones and inflections, marked first by Lear's amusement, then by

his anger—provides a true lesson in Shakespeare's stagecraft. It can also, of course, introduce a pertinent discussion on the idea of "my bond."

F. *Goneril confronts the king.* This segment may seem unwarranted, but Granville-Barker's preface suggested its virtues years ago, and I have found it useful for illustrating the range of Shakespeare's verse in the play: Goneril's smooth, paragraphic lines, Lear's broken iambics, the Fool's little jingles and his prose. More than this, the playwright is here showing his control of the space on an open stage and the uses to which it can be put. Goneril enters, but that she does not speak for twelve lines should alert us to a special effect intended. She probably stands glowering in silence at her point of entrance, while Lear and the audience try to interpret her thoughts. The Fool meanwhile comments on them *both*, perhaps passing between them: most texts include the stage direction *"To Goneril"* before his "Yes, forsooth, I will hold my tongue; so your face bids me, though you say nothing," but this direction is Pope's and is not in quarto or First Folio; it certainly inhibits the Fool's freedom of movement (which matches his freedom of speech: "That's a sheal'd peascod," "So out went the candle," and "Whoop, Jug! I love thee" are little springboards for his rapid changes of posture and direction). And one small point: Lear's five-syllable line, "Are you our daughter?" should be spoken with the weight of five feet, after which his mind shows its first signs of breaking.

H. *Goneril joins Regan.* It is worth drawing attention to the sequence of Lear's almost subliminal questions about Kent in the stocks as they increase in significance for him:

> Who put my man i' th' stocks?
> Who stock'd my servant?
> How came my man i' th' stocks?
> You! did you?

They provide some steps for the actor on his path to madness, as well as marking, by a kind of counterpoint, the development of the king's response to Shakespeare's calculated sequence of highly offensive signals in the action: Goneril's tucket, the entrance of Oswald, Regan's showing the letter from Goneril, the entrance of Goneril herself, the greeting she receives from Regan (Lear: "O Regan! will you take her by the hand?"), and finally Cornwall's cold admission, "I set him there, Sir."

Shakespeare's habit of providing a sequence of steps for his actors by which the progress of the scene may be measured also emerges later in the same scene. The repetition of "Return to her?," "Return with her!," "Return with her!" invites more than discussion of the structure of a major speech; it also touches his new status as a father without a family and a king without a kingdom. Another sequence of steps follows in the wrangling over the number of his knights: "I and my hundred knights," "what! fifty followers / Is it not well?," "I entreat you / To bring but five-and-twenty," "What need you five-and-twenty, ten, or five . . . ?," "What need one?" Soon after this, the Folio gives first notice of the weather: *"Storm and Tempest."*

J. *Lear before the hovel.* To play out this extraordinary scene may be sufficient commentary in itself. It makes evident use of the actors' moving on the empty stage, first to sustain the image of the storm, then to order Lear's movements to a downstage position, presumably in the center of the Globe theater, before the onset of madness:

> Thou 'ldst shun a bear;
> But if thy flight lay toward the roaring sea,
> Thou 'ldst meet the bear i' th' mouth.

Lear's prayer to "poor naked wretches" prepares the audience for the imminent appearance of Edgar as Poor Tom (described in detail long before in II.iii), and this shocking entrance, preceded as it is by the running and shouting of the Fool, is itself ironic as an enactment of madness when Edgar enters running and shouting with false exaggeration. When Lear tears off his robes ("Off, off, you lendings!"), the two threads of the play, Lear's and Gloucester's, begin to intertwine in one astonishing image of "unaccommodated man," and the change is reinforced by the king's rejection of his former, "sophisticated" companions for the company of Poor Tom: "First let me talk with this philosopher."

M. *Blinding Gloucester.* One or two points may be missed because of this scene's sensationalism. The action seems to begin at breakneck speed, and as the scheme to punish Gloucester is prepared, one should not overlook that his son Edmund is party to it, remaining on stage in frightening silence: nodding? smiling? Then one must not forget that he departs with Goneril, under the eyes of her jealous rival Regan—leaving her in a particularly nasty frame of mind before the torturing starts.

The text provides exact details on how Gloucester is to be blinded, and it is important that the victim be tied to a chair if the visual analogy with bearbaiting is to be supplied. The repetition of the line "Wherefore to Dover?" can even be made to sound like the yapping of dogs. Finally, one must not stop short of the blind man's exit. The Folio's *"Exit one with Gloucester"* can be variously interpreted as pushing, pulling, or kicking him, but that he should crawl on all fours like an animal is clearly indicated by Regan: "Go thrust him out at gates, and let him smell / His way to Dover."

N. *On Dover Cliff.* Point by point, this scene offers a series of prime topics for class discussion, particularly on the relation between the fates of Lear in his insanity and of Gloucester in his impulse to suicide. The presence of the comic in the play also emerges unavoidably here. First, was there, or was there not, a "cliff" on the platform of the Globe? If there was none, what kind and degree of laughter is implied by the action, and with what effect on our perception of suicide? Again, only performance can identify the kind of comedy expected by the opening lines of the scene:

> GLOUCESTER.   When shall I come to th' top of that same hill?
> EDGAR.   You do climb up it now; look how we labour.
> GLOUCESTER.   Methinks the ground is even.
> EDGAR.   Horrible steep.

Only performance can bring out the force of "you are now within a foot /Of th' extreme verge" (here the lineation in the Folio should be checked for its "white spaces"—the arrangement of lines for its suggestion of pause or business by the first actors).

There are many questions. What is the reason for Edgar's asides? What will the actor do on the injunction "Go thou further off"? At the moment of his prayer, how much will an audience empathize with Gloucester? And will any laughter cease? On the quarto direction *"He falls,"* what response would the actor aim for? Put a teasing question: what would the consequence be if Gloucester had entered with a walking stick and had thrown it over the "cliff" before he jumped? Edgar must leap to stop it clattering to the floor of the stage. And finally, is Edgar's statement that "Thy life's a miracle" true or false? I believe that the answer will turn on the degree of comedy admitted in performance.

P. *Waking Lear.* I have used this simple and moving scene divorced from the play in a number of drama classes, because it illustrates so well Shakespeare's control of the stage and the audience. We should note especially how he first changes all the external signals, those of costume ("We put fresh garments on him," i.e., the last of Lear's three changes), music ("Louder the music there!"—and it is proper to ask what kind of music will best contrast with the sounds of the storm), lighting (Lear asks, "Fair daylight?," after the long night of the heath scenes), and vocal style (Lear's pyrotechnic prose has become simple, smooth, sometimes monosyllabic verse).

It is good to discuss why the King must enter "in a chair" (the focus is to be on the act of waking, and the question everyone must ask is what the new king will be like) and where on the platform it should be placed (the intimacy of the relationship between father and daughter suggests that it must be downstage close to the audience). Where should Kent and the Doctor stand in relation to Lear in his chair? (I believe the ritual element in the scene demands that father and daughter be isolated.) The text is excellent for the way it prompts a delicate physical contact between Lear and Cordelia, traced through "this kiss," "these white flakes," "Was this a face . . . ?," "This thin helm," to the point where he touches her cheek on "Be your tears wet?" Cordelia will find that she must kneel in order to caress and cradle Lear's head, and trial and error will test the intended pattern of gestures that bring the two of them centerstage, kneeling to each other symbolically. It is an easy error to interpret Cordelia's "No, Sir, you must not kneel" as a direction for him to return to his chair; he is kneeling at this point, of course, and must remain so, as the source play, *The True Chronicle History of King Leir*, confirms.

S. *Death of Lear.* One final comment on "Howl, howl, howl!" These are Lear's half-animal noises, to be made and heard as noises, not his order to the court to join in his lament. The three words are most effective when they are divided by the king's movements—the first heard offstage by the courtiers as they run in all directions and freezing them to the spot; the second given upon Lear's entrance upstage *"with Cordelia in his arms,"* so that the crowd falls back; the third spoken to the audience after the king comes down to us as if to offer us the sacrifice of his daughter. As in the first court scene, all three daughters are again on stage, and again Cordelia is distinguished from the other two—only now all three are dead. And Lear himself seems to return to an earlier state of confusion in the face of the unpredictable and inexplicable processes of life.

A Theatrical Approach: Readers' Theater

John B. Harcourt

The focus of my Introduction to Shakespeare course is a four-week "readers' theater" unit on one of the major tragedies; every fourth semester, we come to *King Lear*. This unit begins around the midpoint of the course, after we have considered in some detail and more traditionally three or four plays written earlier in Shakespeare's career. If *Lear* is in the offing, these early plays are likely to feature ominous fathers or father-surrogates: *Titus Andronicus, A Midsummer Night's Dream, Romeo and Juliet, The Merchant of Venice.* The students thus begin the unit knowing something about Shakespeare and his times, the Shakespearean theater, the shape of the Shakespearean play, the resources of language that it employs, and the tensions within the family and the community upon which it so frequently centers.

Why approach *King Lear* as readers' theater in an introductory Shakespeare course designed to give undergraduates from many different majors an overview of Shakespeare's dramatic production? Perhaps that last phrase points to the answer: my emphasis, especially in this unit, is on Shakespeare as actor-director-scriptwriter-shareholder in the leading theatrical company of his time. As far as we can discover, he had little interest in securing readers for his plays. It is something of a shock to students that he did not rush to sign a contract with a publisher as soon as he had completed a script, that he apparently had little or nothing to do with the publication of the sixteen plays that appeared in quarto editions during his lifetime, that even in these cases the texts supplied to the printer were most often the "foul papers" rather than the official promptbooks, and that neither the playwright nor members of his company bothered to proofread the pages as they came off the press. A parallel can be drawn with the present-day writer of television or movie scripts, most of which will never appear in book form. Throughout the course, therefore, I emphasize Shakespeare the playhouse professional, writing on demand for the immensely successful commercial venture in which he was a partner. Such demythologizing, while obviously far from the complete story, is a salutary corrective to the impressions of the Bard too often derived from high-school English classes. Coincidentally, deemphasizing the printed page corresponds quite realistically to the situation of the students, the vast majority of whom will never pick up an edition of Shakespeare after their formal education is completed but many of whom may, if we do our work well, occasionally watch Shakespeare on television or take in a performance or two at a summer festival. I have shaped my course in the hope that what we do together in the classroom will motivate those postgraduation experiences of living Shakespearean theater and make them more meaningful than they might otherwise be.

Shakespeare, then, must be approached on his own terms—in terms of the patterned experiences that emerge as actors say and do things in that ritualized event we call theater. Clearly, limitations of time and resources preclude our mounting a full performance even of part of a Shakespearean play. But a practical solution is to employ readers' theater—a highly stylized presentation before an audience by a group of readers who use books or scripts and who do not act in any theatrical sense, although they may turn or move about and even occasionally use a prop or two, or a hint of costuming such as a crown. The device of having separate readers divide the lines of a single character so as to present different aspects of that character can be an important part of a readers' theater presentation. One reader, for example, speaks lines from I.i, I.ii, II.i, and III.iii that establish Edmund's deferential-hypocritical relationship with his father (and also with Edgar in I.ii and with Cornwall in III.v). A second reader with quite different vocal tonalities highlights Edmund the Machiavel, while a third shows him as lover, cynically weighing the merits of the two women who are pursuing him. A fourth reader focuses on the new emotions Edmund experiences in V.iii ("Some good I mean to do / Despite of mine own nature"). In another presentation, the readers may detach lines from their specific dramatic contexts and arrange them in a sequence that points up a pattern of repeated images, themes, or key words. The word *nothing* occurs more than two dozen times in the play; reading these lines seriatim forces the audience to consider the function of this leitmotif in the play's larger structure. Or a group may choose lines that refer to clothing—the actual putting on or taking off of garments or the metaphors implied in words like *invest, divest, dismantle.* Discussion can then relate the clothing images to the overarching theme of appearance versus reality. However the readings are organized, the crucial fact is that we move from scanning with the eyes only, in the privacy of dormitory or library, to an aural and oral experience—readers and audience together encountering Shakespeare *as sound.* Such readers' theater presentations can fit into any syllabus; they can be given anywhere an audience gathers around a group of players.

To begin the unit, I designate four students, usually but not always drama majors, to function as group leaders for the readers' theater project. The class is then divided into four sections of six to eight members each, selected alphabetically, without regard to gender or academic background. To avoid excessive overlapping in the performances, I give each group a specific aspect of the play to consider. For example, a group may be assigned a set of closely related characters to work with or may address a specific pattern of images. To prepare their presentations, the groups meet separately wherever they are able to find space on a crowded campus.

At the first group meeting, the leader announces which feature of the play that group is to focus on and assigns to each member three or four readings from an extensive bibliography that I have provided (the list contains book-length studies of *Lear* as well as articles immediately relevant to that group's primary concern). We use the Muir Arden edition (from which I quote) because its introduction, notes, and apparatus are especially well adapted to our study of the play. For about two weeks, the groups pursue their topics through reports on the assigned readings and discussion of each member's findings.

Then each group prepares its script, almost always a montage of episodes or passages from throughout the play. Group members subject the script to intense scrutiny to determine the precise sense of every word and phrase, the correct pronunciation of unfamiliar words and names (it takes some effort to make the point that *Gloucester* rhymes with *roster*). In addition to the notes in the Arden *Lear*, basic references such as the Furness New Variorum edition, Kittredge's extended notes in *Sixteen Plays of Shakespeare*, the Duthie-Wilson Cambridge Shakespeare *Lear*, Schmidt's *Shakespeare-Lexicon*, Partridge's *Shakespeare's Bawdy*, and, of course, the *Oxford English Dictionary* are consulted.

In rehearsals, special attention is given to students with no prior dramatic experience. I require that every member of the group have ample speaking lines and that the drama majors function more as coaches than as stars. Happily, the very artificiality of readers' theater permits the lines of a given character to be distributed among several readers, irrespective of gender.

Performances—some highly formal, some far less so—take place wherever each group sees fit: in the classroom, the chapel, the recreation rooms, the lobbies. Performance time is strictly limited to twenty minutes. For the rest of the period, the members of the audience engage in dialogue with the members of the cast, who remain onstage. Discussions are lively, and, at the end, I attempt a brief summation and establish a link with the next presentation, reserving the detailed critique of the performance for a meeting with the group itself. Within a week, group members individually submit reports that list their research and detail their specific contributions to the group's activities. In the space provided for suggestions, most students state that the readers' theater project was for them the high point of the course—for many, the first time that Shakespeare had ever come alive. Alumni, returning sometimes after many years, continue in that belief.

Topics for the unit vary from year to year. In Year A, the focus may be on character. One group may address itself to Lear's relationships with his daughters; another, to Gloucester's problems in discriminating between his sons; a third, to the affinities between Cordelia, the Fool, and Mad Tom; a fourth, to the carefully demarcated stages in the development of Lear's madness.

In Year B, our interest may be directed to the basic patterns of imagery in the play, again with a fourfold division: images of sight and blindness; those that relate human behavior to that of birds and animals; the powerful images of sexuality and sex nausea; and images of mutilation and torture. Isolating these images from their contexts of plot and character and presenting them linked in an unbroken sequence wonderfully clarifies their function in the symphonic structure of the play as poem.

In Year C, I may make Shakespeare's dramaturgy our primary concern. One obvious focus is the interrelation between the main plot and the subplot: a rapid oscillation between bits of Lear scenes and parallel bits of Gloucester scenes can make essential dramatic points more effectively than extended commentary can. Another dramaturgical device, which a second group can investigate, is the repeated use of trial or near-trial scenes: Lear's trial of his daughters in I.i; Cornwall's stocking of Kent in II.ii; Lear's bitter comments on justice in III.ii and IV.vi; the mock trial in III.vi; the interrogation and torture of Gloucester; the trial by combat in V.iii. An area for a third group to examine is Shakespeare's use of a framing device in the construction of *King Lear*. Through identical blocking, the readers can make their audience experience visually as well as aurally the two striking scenes so widely separated in actual playhouse performances—a kingly father with three living daughters grouped about him in I.i and then the same father, surrounded by his three dead daughters, in V.iii.

A fourth group may be asked to concentrate on one of Shakespeare's most successful (and most frequently utilized) stage effects—the visual overlapping of successive scenes. Again and again, he arranges for the new character or characters to be seen proceeding from the rear entrances down the deep Globe stage, while, up front, the scene the audience has been attending to draws to its conclusion, so that a simultaneous awareness of something ending and something beginning is achieved. This kind of dramatic counterpointing is easy to realize in readers' theater by the simple expedient of having the new characters stand or turn to face the audience while the others are still reading their lines. As we listen to Goneril and Regan hatching their plot against their father at the end of I.i, we already see Edmund, letter in hand, with "Thou, Nature, art my goddess" about to form on his lips and defiance already registering in his expression. The fused images establish the spiritual kinship between Lear's older daughters and Gloucester's younger son. Likewise, at the ending of I.ii, Edmund departs with the observation "All with me's meet that I can fashion fit," precisely as our attention turns to Goneril and her Machiavellian instructions that Oswald "breed occasions" by coming "slack of former services." And at the conclusion of III.iv, Edgar's "I smell the blood of a British man," with its echoes of the fairy-tale ogre, is heard just as one of the play's actual monsters, Cornwall, looms into view for his "I will have my revenge ere I depart his house." Examples of this technique may easily be multiplied, and the ensuing impression of continuous and indeed overlapping dramatic episodes corrects the students' habit of thinking of the play as atomized into discrete scenes and acts.

The vast literature on *King Lear* can be organized by critical schools, and, in a Year D, these discordant and sometimes mutually exclusive interpretations can be parceled out to the readers' theater groups. A first section, directing its attention to the New Critical *Lear*-as-dramatic-poem perspective, will probably organize its script around the image clusters, with Robert B. Heilman's *This Great Stage: Image and Structure in* King Lear as its principal reference. Another group, exploring Freudian insights, will turn to Norman N. Holland's *Psychoanalysis and Shakespeare* and M. D. Faber's *Design Within: Psychoanalytic Approaches to Shakespeare* and will emphasize the episodes suggesting oedipal hostility between Gloucester and his sons and a powerful incest motif in Lear's relationship to Cordelia. A third set of readers may combine existential criticism, such as Jan Kott's *Shakespeare Our Contemporary* or Thomas McFarland's *Tragic Meanings in Shakespeare,* with the Christian-versus-pagan controversy, as developed in Roy W. Battenhouse's *Shakespearean Tragedy: Its Art and Its Christian Premises* and William Elton's King Lear *and the Gods* respectively. Readers' theater treatments of this issue may concentrate on the episode beginning *"Re-enter* LEAR, *with* CORDELIA *dead in his arms,"* with successive readings that draw on Marvin Rosenberg's summary of the range of interpretation in *The Masks of* King Lear. A final section, tackling the feminist readings of *Lear,* may respond to Linda Bamber's insight that Lear "projects onto women what he refuses to acknowledge in himself" (14) or Marilyn French's contention, in *Shakespeare's Division of Experience,* that Shakespeare's understanding of character was polarized according to gender.

Critical approaches are not exhausted, of course, by the four just mentioned. A group once demonstrated the value of source criticism by juxtaposing scenes from the old *Leir* play with corresponding segments of the text as we know it: Shakespeare's transformation of the carefully plotted and skillfully motivated opening of the earlier play into the mysterious and unpredictable I.i of his own work became clear and opened immediately into the question of why the playwright had so studiously avoided using the materials that lay ready to his hand. Textual criticism presents formidable obstacles in an undergraduate course, but, next time around, I am planning to use the readers' theater format to test Steven Urkowitz's challenging thesis, as expounded in his *Shakespeare's Revision of* King Lear, that Shakespeare wrote, at different times, two quite different *Lears*. Presenting in performance first the quarto and then the Folio version of selected scenes may indicate to what extent the two seventeenth-century texts represent stages in the dramatist's conception of his play that cannot really be coalesced into the "composite" text we all know.

Thus, each semester we experience once again the paradox that, while on one level we cannot adequately say a Shakespearean line without understanding its meaning, it is equally true that reading it aloud may reveal that meaning—and, of course, what we hear and see *is* ultimately the meaning. Ideally, therefore, I should like to end the *Lear* unit with a videotape of the entire play, presented without a single word of comment from anyone. Those of us who presume to teach Shakespeare need to remind ourselves as well as our students that, if at last we do not find the meaning in the words and actions of the play, we shall not find it anywhere. A readers' theater approach can move us a long way towards that awareness.

An Approach through Visual Stimuli and Student Writing

Jean Klene, CSC

Charles Lamb once commented that acting the title role of *King Lear* is "impossible" (37). It sometimes seems equally impossible to teach the play. I and countless others attempt to do so, however, and I shall share some of my methods in this paper. I teach *Lear* in a one-semester survey course that includes representative Shakespearean comedies, histories, and tragedies in their chronological order, and I use slides in order to create interest, stimulate ideas, and provoke questions about the play. Students then use the ideas and questions (examples of which are given later in this essay) in an exercise we call an "investigation." The investigation requires that the students reread the play and, while doing so, write (1) the question they are investigating, (2) quotations from each act that answer the question (or help shape our ideas about a topic or theme), and (3) a summary of what they have discovered. Finally, they seem to enjoy sharing the results of these quests during class periods.

Students must read the play in its entirety before the first class devoted to it. To stimulate discussion I show two different kinds of slides: scenes from productions by the Royal Shakespeare Company (*Shakespeare: New Productions*)—mainly because they are available, not because they are ideal—and famous paintings borrowed from the art department. These slides help students focus their attention on scenes providing historical and theatrical enrichment, even though the RSC photographer did not always choose the scenes we might consider crucial. Viewing several productions of *King Lear*, however, does give some sense of theater and theater history, a sense most students do not have when they begin a course on Shakespeare's plays.

First, we look at slides from the 1968 and 1976 productions directed by Trevor Nunn, and discuss how the visual images enhance understanding of the play. For example, in the opening court scene of the 1968 production, the symmetrical placement of characters suggests perfect order in the court: Lear sits in the middle under a golden canopy draped to the floor, behind his daughters; Regan and Goneril sit in front of him on either side with their respective husbands standing behind them; and Cordelia sits directly in front of her father—clearly, his "joy." Yet even this arbitrary order seems destroyed when we finally discern the Fool's pixielike head peering out from between the skirts of Cordelia and Regan. The pageantry of this first scene prompts us to discuss the way the sumptuous clothing suggests the rich quality of courtly life. "Robes and furred gowns" do seem to "hide all." When I ask about the costume changes to come, students

125

mention Lear's disheveled dress on the heath, and someone inevitably will remember lines like "Come, unbutton here" or "Off, off, you lendings," especially when I ask about the relation between clothing and the question of kingship. After discussing the significance of clothing in the play, the students realize that the subject will make a fruitful topic for further study.

The last slide of the 1976 production, in which a tattered Lear kneels, holding the dead Cordelia in his arms, illuminates the contrast between the first and the last scenes of the play; indeed, I flip back to the first slide in order to underline the contrast of not only clothing but also posture, atmosphere, and attitudes.

I also use slides of works by Renaissance artists such as Pieter Brueghel (c. 1525–59). These paintings raise some of the same questions that Shakespeare's plays do. Brueghel's *Blind Leading the Blind*, for example, illustrates the well-known biblical warning and helps students visualize Gloucester's plight; at the same time, it underscores chief themes of the play: sight or perception and the vulnerability of "poor unaccommodated man" under flawed political leadership. The same painter's *Justicia* raises problems about the methods of interpreting and administering justice, for though the lady Justicia is blindfolded for impartiality, she ignores totally the abuse of human beings suffering from the execution of the law. Art historians—like Shakespeareans—disagree about particular points of interpretation but generally agree that Brueghel asks hard questions about justice.

By the time we have looked at a number of slides and talked about various issues, students have an idea of what questions they can use on rereading *King Lear*; and they proceed to write their investigations, due at the beginning of the third class. They know that the work requires three elements: a question, quotations with occasional critical comments, and a conclusion. They ask questions like the following: How does Shakespeare integrate sight and blindness with major themes? How does he characterize Cordelia (or someone else)? How does he raise questions about human nature? about evil? about attitudes toward fate, fortune, and destiny? about parent-child relationships? I stress that the aim of this assignment is not to write polished paragraphs, and I urge students to abbreviate their critical comments (as well as the names of characters and type of speech) wherever possible, as illustrated in the following examples. The first is in a study of the characterization of Edmund, the second one by a student writing on the question of justice.

Edm. in sol. (I.ii.127–29) "should have been that I am ... "
Edm. mocks his father's beliefs.

Glo. to O. Man (IV.i.36) "As flies to wanton boys . . ."
Blames injustice on gods; ignores humans' guilt.

Students must list several quotations related to their chosen questions from each act, and, where none occur, they need to speculate on the reason for this lack. An investigation involving the dramatization of Cordelia, for example, would have to state that she does not appear in acts II and III, having been banished by her father and gone to France. I also ask that students make occasional comments on the language: striking images, the way a "jingle-jangle" couplet may undercut what is being said, or the signal Shakespeare gives us in a switch from blank verse to prose. By a variety of means, then, analytical skills are sharpened.

Students conclude with a paragraph summarizing what they have learned. Occasionally a question (usually one not raised in the opening class) cannot be answered by the text, or a topic originally considered meaningful proves insignificant. I urge students, however, not to start over again (unless we are writing a finished paper) but only to write an honest conclusion. The purpose of the exercise may be fulfilled sufficiently without the kind of proof one needs for a paper. (When we do write a paper on *Lear*, however, an investigation becomes the best possible beginning; I return the exercise in time for the paper to be written.) Conclusions vary widely, but at least each student has come to an independent decision about an important facet of the play. A business major, for example, who began with questions of value (How can we judge character? What is the best measure of a person's true worth? riches? words? or deeds?) concluded her work as follows:

> The play begins with Lear's misjudgment of his daughters; he attempts to measure their love by the words they speak. Throughout the play, there are many references to worth: money, jewels, precious metals, and titles are some of the measures of value. Contrasts of rich with poor, noble with base, and fortune with misfortune illustrate kinds of evaluation. Tragedy also strips away noble façades and exposes base characters.

Another student, dealing with sight and blindness, wrote this conclusion:

> Light and darkness and sight and blindness represent falseness and truth in *Lear*. Light, such as the sun, moonbeams, stars, etc., often symbolizes a reliance on the physical world to provide obvious noninterpretive truth (which it never does). At other times, sight in general, and eyes in particular, have positive connotations, represent-

ing the illumination of truth found in the darkness of despair. There are two types of sight as well as of blindness: physical and spiritual. Each is capable of creating its inverse.

One virtue of this method is that students come to class prepared—and sometimes eager—to argue a point of view. During the class period, all participate, and they learn a good deal from one another rather than from my lecturing (although I still guide the discussion by questions or comments). They argue coherently about whether Lear learns anything and, if so, what; whether Edmund repents; and why Edgar acts as he does toward his father. According to other teachers, some students continue arguing as they walk down the hall: their involvement, then, is evident. Students also recommend the assignment (even though some complain about the time necessary to write one) because they claim that they understand the play and, consequently, enjoy the classes more than they would with straight lecture or unstructured discussion. They also feel confident about writing a paper on the play during the second week of our study.

The investigations also tell me much more about the thinking of individuals than I could learn in a class period. Sometimes, for example, I see that they do not understand important lines like Lear's "O reason not the need! Our basest beggars / Are in the poorest thing superfluous" when they write comments such as "Is man a beast if he cannot prove himself otherwise?" or "Contrasts rich with poor." We then explore such a speech in the next class. Having encouraged students also to write—in addition to critical comments—whatever they wish to write in response to the text, I respond to their jottings when appropriate. Sometimes, for example, they ask, "Is this too farfetched?" or "Is this what the word means?" Besides answering these kinds of questions, I often raise a few others, such as the following: "But do you believe him?" or "Loyal, yes, but wise?" or "But what does the Fool say about this?" or "Could this be satiric?" Usually their notes are predictable but at other times they seem to learn as they write: one, for example, wrote, "Isn't it ironic that Lear describes homeless wretches in terms of dwelling in places: 'houseless,' 'sides,' 'window'd'? Oh, but now Lear has no home either." Another, responding to Cordelia's prayer in IV.vii, wrote (albeit in a mixed metaphor), "Give Dad back *whatever* he had so that his mind/body can be in harmony again. But then, gods didn't take away his harmony. He punctured it with his own vain needle." Occasionally a student also recalls parallels from other plays. One, for example, commented that when Edmund criticizes "the excellent foppery of the world," we recall Iago's "Virtue, a fig! 'Tis in ourselves that we are thus or thus" (*Othello* I.iii.319). Before they reduce all independence to villainy, however, I point out an enigmatically similar kind of statement from a heroine such as Helena of *All's Well*: "Our remedies oft in ourselves do lie, /

Which we ascribe to heaven" (I.i.208–09). One semester this quotation sparked a discussion of existentialism from students who had just explored it in another class. The idea of self-reliance never fails to interest them.

Certain problems do arise in using this method. The major one concerns the time required to do the work. I insist that students find only a few quotations from each act, but the overreachers consistently spend hours exploring and writing about the issues and often produce ten-page studies. I urge them not to attempt completion and emphasize that we share results. Nevertheless, the overreachers almost always exceed the assignment. Grading is not an issue because I write only "Satisfactory" (or, if it is incomplete, "Unsatisfactory") on the average study. If the work seems minimal or problematic, however, I write "Satisfactory –"; if it is both thorough and perceptive, a "Satisfactory +." I collect them at the end of the semester, mainly to keep them out of circulation. But I also like to glance at the kind of consistent work a student has done when I am giving the final grade for the course. If students ask for their investigations after the course, however, I do return them.

Although the class discussions constitute an immediate reward of this method, other benefits also appear as students develop into better readers, writers, and speakers. A few even produce additional creative pieces, such as poems (like the cobra-shaped one written by a Cleopatra hater who investigated phallic imagery in *Antony and Cleopatra*), simulated newspaper articles, and even whole plays. Although I have more misgivings about the teaching of *King Lear* than I do about any other play, the thoughtful efforts of many students keep me experimenting with these and other methods. After exploring the play together, we have at least achieved a greater sense of our dependence on one another.

King Lear in a Course on Shakespeare and Film

Hugh M. Richmond

King Lear provides an effective climax for a course on Shakespeare and film, since there are four substantial productions readily available: those of Peter Brook, Grigori Kozintsev, Jonathan Miller (BBC Shakespeare series), and Michael Elliott (with Laurence Olivier). Television versions such as Miller's and Elliott's can now be projected inexpensively on large video-screens, satisfactory for big audiences. The course Shakespeare and Film in the English Department at the University of California at Berkeley enrolls about two hundred undergraduates from all levels, of whom one-third are non-English majors. This size helps to justify the costs of film rental and projection, but a similar if more modest program stressing the use of performance (it uses more televised versions, such as those of the BBC series and those locally produced in the Shakespeare Program) has proved successful and economical in a class of twenty-five students.

The larger course at Berkeley evolved from a conventional lecture series covering twelve of Shakespeare's major plays. To heighten awareness of the text as script and to enrich and diversify the course format, the instructor, colleagues, and students began to give readings, with extremely positive results in student interest, involvement, and understanding, reflected in improved interpretive skill and more vigorous essay writing. Typical readings or performances included such scenes from *Lear* as the love test, Edmund's "Thou, Nature, art my goddess," and the beach scene between Gloucester and Lear. With cooperation from our campus Educational Television Office, these scenes were videotaped for closer analysis; some were even shot on location, such as the storm scenes of *Lear*, which were videotaped in a storm-ravaged park near the campus. The use of excerpts soon expanded to performances of modest playlets, such as *Edgar and Edmund*, an adaptation by students from *Lear*'s subplot. After such a variety of performances, student writing by both participants and observers, which remains the primary concern of the course, reflected a heightened textual awareness that is at least as precise and sophisticated as any New Critic could wish. This encouraged further development of performance approaches, including the use of slides illustrating the structure of the original Elizabethan theaters and of reconstructions such as that at Ashland, as well as of historical and modern productions. Now full-length productions, both live and televised, derive from the course in a year-round Shakespeare Program—though *Lear* has so far proved too challenging to attempt.

In view of the difficulty of synchronizing courses with predictable professional Shakespeare productions on local stages, we decided to lease several sixteen-millimeter prints of major Shakespeare films, of which twelve are now available to University of California campuses, with a similar number of videotapes. These are shown to the class in addition to the regularly scheduled sessions, and this series is supplemented by coordinated Shakespeare film showings at the campus Pacific Film Archive and at local cinemas. It is thus possible to ensure repeat showings, often in different formats (35 mm.), or to show different versions of the same play. We also avoid the cost of repeated showings by increasing the availability of videocassette versions of such films as Zeffirelli's *Taming of the Shrew* for individual student review at campus media centers.

The Berkeley course is not specialized in approach or recruitment. It merely requires students to have studied two Shakespeare plays before admission and to have some interest in such filmmaking techniques as camera work and editing. These prerequisites are met by most students in the humanities, and indeed by most Berkeley students: the course recruits many students for the English major. The course begins with a discussion of various comedies and histories, plays that permit the illustration of Renaissance culture, English history, and the nature of Elizabethan theaters. A good example is Olivier's *Henry V*. By the time students reach *Lear* they are well attuned to Shakespeare's language, to Elizabethan stage conventions, and to the counterpoint of literary values with the aesthetics of performance, whether on the modern or Elizabethan stage or for film and television. Such multidimensional awareness of the text is a major gain over traditional approaches, but it demonstrably also enhances the understanding, involvement, and enjoyment generated by even an adequate performance—with consequent improvement in recall of detail. The use of multiple versions ensures that none appears definitive, and the obvious discrepancies with the printed text foster concern to recognize the superiority of the latter to any given reading.

In the film class, students are required to complete their reading of the text before the first lecture, on a Tuesday afternoon of a week we may call week A. The lecture covers classic literary interpretations, beginning with Charles Lamb's notorious attack, in his essay "On the Tragedies of Shakspeare," on the staging of Shakespeare in general and *Lear* in particular. Lamb's Romantic revulsion from the constraints of staging is balanced against Wilson Knight's insistence, in "*King Lear* and the Comedy of the Grotesque," from *The Wheel of Fire*, on the functional nature of Lear's grotesqueness and almost comic humiliation. This leads naturally to a scrutiny of Jan Kott's absurdist reading of the play as a precursor of Beckett's in *Shakespeare Our Contemporary*. Such pessimistic readings are linked to W. R. Elton's skeptical interpretation in King Lear *and the Gods*. The alternative, more balanced judgments of A. C. Bradley in *Shakespearean Tragedy* and Maynard Mack in King Lear *in Our Time* offset these views. Thus the lecture outlines the broad range of current interpretations and evaluations as a prelude to seeing performances illustrating them. It is followed by a discussion period, principally consisting of questions and answers. Student responses and views serve to clarify issues compressed in the lecture presentation.

The class then adjourns to a nearby auditorium where Brook's *King Lear* is projected. After the lecture's careful exploration of negative readings of the play, students readily perceive Brook's relentless distortion of the text, starting from the omission of the comic opening dialogue between Kent and Gloucester (an omission intended to heighten the interest of Lear's ambiguous first word in the film: "Know"). The cutting of much of the play's poetry and humor is painfully apparent, as is the extreme suppression of the subtler and more positive aspects of the characterization. Despite an iconographic identification of Edgar with a thorn-crowned, martyred Christ in the storm scenes, Edgar's increasingly effective role in the play's later scenes is deliberately edited out. Brook shows him isolated on the beach, pushed around contemptuously by Kent at the very end. The passages that display his redemptive skills with his father and brother are minimized or cut (just as in the 1982 production at Stratford-upon-Avon, which followed the film's reading).

Nevertheless, the effect of this film on students is powerful. Its discontinuous, hectic, harsh, and violent texture (reflecting its debts to Antonin Artaud's idea of the Theater of Cruelty) communicates the play to them in modern cinematic terms that make its worldview seem intensely contemporary and intelligible. The film uses the full range of visual conventions and devices to which two decades of film and television viewing have sensitized them. Having previously seen such more traditionally picturesque color films as Zeffirelli's *Romeo and Juliet* and Olivier's *Henry V*, they find that Brook's violent, wintry, jarring realism in grainy black and white convinces them overwhelmingly of Shakespeare's tragic intensity and unsentimental insight. Hardly anyone remains indifferent or contemptuous, though some are shocked.

Brook's deliberately radical challenge to audience expectations about a classic play provides a useful starting point from which to explore more traditional interpretations. These readings in turn lead naturally to the illustration of a more positive view of the play reflected in Kozintsev's film, which I show after class on Tuesday of week B, having lectured on conflicting interpretations both on Thursday of week A (mostly about Brook) and on Tuesday of week B (mostly about Kozintsev). Indeed, before my Thursday lecture in week A, I meet students for informal discussion of

Brook's film at what is usually a very crowded coffee hour. In my lecture that day, I begin with Kozintsev's review of Brook's interpretation, leading to his own treatment of the text, as outlined in his book on the making of his own film: King Lear: *The Space of Tragedy.* This excellent survey of both stage and film productions of *Lear* provides a contemporary complement to Marvin Rosenberg's stage history in *The Masks of* King Lear. I also draw on the filmmaking data in Roger Manvell's *Shakespeare and the Film,* which has useful details regarding Brook's treatment of the script, and on the dexterous film criticism in Jack Jorgens's *Shakespeare on Film.*

Jorgens's book provides the basis for a broader lecture on Thursday of week B (following the Tuesday showing of Kozintsev's version) on performance as a critical tool for interpretation of the play. Jorgens's perceptive juxtapositions of film and text have rightly been hailed as the vindication of film studies' power to generate authentic mainline Shakespeare criticism. In particular he demonstrates how contrasting yet complementary the Kozintsev version is to Brook's. Despite its icy Danish landscape, the Brook film is often claustrophobic, exploiting grotesque close-ups in which the framing cuts across conventional human perspectives, reducing Lear's face, for example, to bulbous, apelike inhumanity as he curses Goneril and Regan. By contrast, Kozintsev sees a smaller Lear from a distance, in broad spatial terms appropriate to historical perspectives of Russian Marxism. This vast visual scale offsets the limitations of the oversolemn Russian script. The landscapes shown are sweeping and un-English, and the exceptional broad-screen format (70 mm.) intensifies this superhuman vision. The camera favors long rising or panning craneshots that afford exhilarating open views, often revealing an individual's place in the environment, and surveying the whole of society, as in the opening shots. Later, Lear and Cordelia are swept along in a flowing river of refugees that runs alongside a broad natural stream—readily interpreted as the impersonal tide of nature and time. This broad perspective gives depth and richness to Kozintsev's view of the play. His film favors positive factors as much as Brook has minimized them: the Fool is not killed; Gloucester's grotesque fall at Dover is cut; and Edgar's evolution as a hero of the people gives him that commanding role at the end of the film that is implied by Shakespeare's deliberate anachronism in inserting the name of this Anglo-Saxon hero, the first high king of England, into the play's pre-Roman setting.

The juxtaposition of these two films opens up for students the extreme range of meanings and options compressed within Shakespeare's text. Most perceive that neither film is "wrong": each vividly illustrates one reading, or element, of the play. However, this perception provides only the starting point for further discussion of the text, including questions of editing and cutting it for performance; scholars such as Steven Urkowitz remind us that in Shakespeare's day such adjustments were already occurring, perhaps with Shakespeare's own participation (*Shakespeare's Revision*). The whole question of use and adaptation of sources extends from Bullough's account of Shakespeare's use of them in adjusting narrative plot and characterization to the stage, through the happy ending of Nahum Tate's *Lear*, which Norman Rabkin finds so illuminating in *Shakespeare and the Problem of Meaning*, to the issue of transposing the text to a film script, which needs far less of its kinetic imagery and descriptions of storms and landscapes, as we see in Manvell's account of how Ted Hughes tried to revise *Lear* for Brook. More ominously, the miniaturization of the play for television may reduce it to static, close-in shots that eliminate most of the play's physical sweep and rhetorical vigor, as Urkowitz plausibly asserts in his critical review of the BBC production ("*King Lear* without Tears"). Perhaps only Olivier's virtuosity permits *Lear* to transcend the limitations of the television format; certainly we empathize more with Michael Hordern as the pathetic father Baptista, in Zeffirelli's *Taming of the Shrew*, than as Lear.

By comparing Shakespeare's text with its sources and with such modern adaptations, we perceive the richness of the play, which fosters critical theories and judgments that only performance allows us to test on our pulses. For example, it is one thing to study the role of the Fool in the light of Enid Welsford's *Fool*, but quite another, and no less illuminating, to compare Brook's wryly skeptical philosopher-wit with Kozintsev's picturesque primitive, with his plaintive music, too charming to kill off. And both of these should be contrasted in turn to the stage effects of, say, Adrian Noble's professional music-hall clown (in the tradition of Grock, Chaplin, and Keaton) who ends up stabbed to death by the unwitting Lear in the 1982 production by the Royal Shakespeare Company. In all these versions, *Lear* achieves a unique blend of compulsive concern for justice with a drastic demonstration of the vicissitudes of human experience—a blend that leads to unpredictable developments of human potential for both good and evil. This radicalism fits it for even the most provocative modes of reinterpretation in our own time, without loss of its intrinsic character as an antiestablishment play. Its grotesqueries, brutality, sardonic humor, and wry survey of human psychology and institutions show how far Shakespeare shares, anticipates, and perhaps even preconditions our modern awareness in deeper and wiser ways than even Kott perceives or Artaud would tolerate.

The exploration of the costly restructuring of a play for film also clarifies student awareness of the original motives of Shakespeare's script in terms of audience response. Even a film projection provides group responses offering a fresh context for evaluating such episodes as the blinding of Gloucester or the killing of Edmund, as well as the pathos of Cordelia's death. The convulsive, even traumatic responses generated by these passages prove that performance affords fresh critical material not available to the reader. More charmingly, the lyric beauty of Kozintsev's images of Lear's "flower child" phase reminds us of the play's more positive and delightful aspects: as Lear crouches among the wild flowers, his white hair blends into the bleached grass in a Wordsworthian synthesis with the landscape surely true to Shakespeare's awareness (and Lear's) of heroic rediscovery of humanity's deep interdependence with nature. Even Brook's crueller, overexposed images in the beach scene still generate a philosophic sense of a Shelleyan "white radiance of eternity." These calmer long shots clarify and transcend the selfish, dogmatic narrowness of Lear's earlier, theatrical sense of justice, as in the trial scene (III.vi), when he is hallucinating and momentarily mad in truth. All versions necessarily demonstrate the remarkable potentiality for human growth validated by the aged Lear's discovery of new values.

The difficulties of teaching *Lear* through film usually prove fewer than one anticipates. Film prints can be readily rented and projected at moderate cost. The techniques of film analysis are well displayed in the paperback editions of Manvell and Jorgens, in Charles Eckert's anthology *Focus on Shakespearean Films*, and in Andrew McLean's filmographies in *Shakespeare: Annotated Bibliographies and Media Guide*. The frequently asserted defects of Shakespearean films are not a negative factor pedagogically—my students regularly say that they learn almost as much from the defects of a specific performance as from its virtues. The reconciliation of any performed version of *Lear* to one's own interpretation becomes a normal part of critical experience, though it is wise not to force students to become too technical. Even students who prefer to write traditional critical studies seem to gain in empathy and insight when exposed to several performances. My surveys of postgraduates show that the films, instead of diminishing interest in other versions of the text, encourage appreciation of further productions of Shakespeare—surely every teacher's goal.

"Is This the Promis'd End?"
Teaching the Play's Conclusion

David L. Kranz

When King Lear enters with the dead Cordelia in his arms near the end of the play (V.iii.256 in the Muir edition), three surviving characters comment in shocked, quizzical, and emotionally charged phrases on what they and the theater audience see:

> KENT.   Is this the promis'd end?
> EDGAR.   Or image of that horror?
> ALBANY.   Fall and cease. (262–63)

The loyal Kent asks whether he is witnessing the Apocalypse, Edgar wonders if he sees but a representation of that catastrophic end of the world, and Albany, who moments earlier prayed that the gods defend Cordelia from harm, now resignedly wishes that all structures fall and all life cease. In the shared responses of these on-stage commentators at least three points are clear: (1) they are not sure of what Lear's minidrama represents and thus ask questions of it; (2) they are shocked by the severity of what they see and deeply moved by the suffering Lear endures; and (3) they resort to cosmological religious interpretation in order to make sense of Lear's plight but are aware that what they see may be a fiction, an "image" of cosmic catastrophe.

If Shakespeare intended these points as metadramatic guides for the audience, twentieth-century Shakespearean scholars and critics have, in interpreting the end of *King Lear*, reflected them in various ways. Uncertainty about precisely what the last seventy or so lines of the play mean has, in fact, led to a long-standing critical debate. On the one hand, numerous scholars since A. C. Bradley have suggested that, however painful the suffering of Lear, the end of the play contains some kind of affirmation, most often one related to Christian moral or cosmological schemes. For these interpreters, Lear's last moments are sources of optimism, or at least suggestive of heavenly silver linings. On the other hand, several critics treat *King Lear*, partly on account of its ending, as Shakespeare's most pessimistic statement of the human condition. These interpreters dwell on the shocking severity of the tragedy's end and scorn the optimists' resort to religious myth as a mere convenient fictional anesthetic that comfortably blinds its advocates to the nihilistic truth Shakespeare intended to dramatize. A third group of Shakespeareans, moreover, has recently argued that Shakespeare intended the ending and the entire play to be ambiguous and unresolved, however dark in action or light in suggestion.

Because the bitter end of the tragedy is so richly problematical and has inspired such a heated critical debate, I try to create a pedagogical event around it—namely, a class debate. Critical concentration on the end of the play in this form seems to provide students with a degree of the emotional urgency that they miss by not experiencing *King Lear* in a theater. But I use a class debate not simply to take advantage of a critical curiosity in order to engage student minds; student disputation is not a gimmick merely tacked on to a conventional examination of the drama. Rather, in juxtaposing optimistic, perhaps redemptive views of the ending with pessimistic, perhaps nihilistic perspectives, the debate is wholly consistent with the dialectical design of *King Lear*.

One reading of this dialectical design is John Danby's *Shakespeare's Doctrine of Nature*. The dialectic throughout the play, at times overt and at times implied, involves a worldview that asserts the existence of divine justice and order and a worldview that does not assume such justice and order. From the very beginning, Lear's cursing banishment of Cordelia (I.i.107–19) and his later disparaging comments about her (208–12) reveal his assumption that he acts in accordance with the "operation of the orbs / From whom we do exist and cease to be," with some design in nature that functions in a just manner. Gloucester too believes in this ordered universe, as his remarks on global disruption make clear (I.ii.100–11), but Edmund's sarcastic remarks on his father's astrological superstition (115–30), as well as his earlier obeisance to a nature of material-oriented "lusty stealth" (11), disclose quite different assumptions about the world. For Edmund, belief in an order within nature is merely a convenient and pleasant fiction, an insubstantial thing, a "nothing." This continuing dichotomy of worldviews persists to its final appearance in the play: the demise of evil in the form of Edmund and the sisters appears consistent with a providential moral order in nature, but the death of good in the form of Cordelia does not. For some critics, the latter's hanging mocks all belief in an invisible moral order and thus, in Kent's words, "All's cheerless, dark, and deadly" (V.iii.289). Others take comfort in the just destruction of the evil trio and, like Lear, try to see something meaningful in the corpse of Cordelia. These critics see, optimistically, life beyond death in Lear's "Look there, look there" (V.iii.310); the first group of critics, however, pessimistically sees the mere delusion of a madman. The two critical camps thereby mirror the dialectic within the play that concerns skepticism about or faith in an invisible moral order.

The play's dialectic and the debate among critics are readily transferred to a classroom debate. Both the debate format and the plentiful, highly debatable criticism enable me to introduce students to Shakespearean scholarship in a way that forestalls simple, slavish adoption of the insights of secondary sources. And having students debate the meaning of the end of *King Lear* gives me a good index of how effectively I have taught the play. The mechanics of the student debate are quite simple. I ask eight volunteers to argue about the meaning of the play from V.iii.256 to the end. Is the ending optimistic, perhaps redemptive, or pessimistic, perhaps nihilistic? The debaters divide into two groups, each with two presenters and two rebutters, and are given several days to prepare. I demand that each presentation (about 15 minutes) consist of an exegesis of the play's end (including some close analyses of the lines), an argument about the rest of the play that supports the exegesis, some evidence that attempts to disprove the opposing view of the end, and some reference to published critical research, most of which I have placed on reserve in the library. Each rebuttal (also 15 minutes in duration) must refer specifically to arguments presented by the other side, and anticipation of those arguments is encouraged. Students not debating are required to be judges. I ask them to take notes during the debate and to have something to say about it or about their sense of the ending in a free discussion period (the last 20–30 minutes of the class) after the debate. The judges must also turn in written reports several days later, arguing for the side they determine to have won and outlining their own views of the end of *King Lear*. Having set up the event, I advise the debaters, referee the debate, clarify points that are badly articulated, moderate the free discussion period, report the judges' decision in a later class, and offer my own interpretation.

Though no two debates are the same, I can offer a sample summary of the main points student debaters have made. In doing so, moreover, I shall endeavor to name secondary critical sources that amplify the arguments and evidence summarized.

In explicating the conclusion, the pessimistic side stresses the pain and desolation of what can be seen and verified, drawing nihilistic implications from the evidence. They point out that Cordelia, the play's most clearly ideal figure, is as dead as her sisters: Lear asserts her death with certainty three times (258–60, 269, and 304–07), and others say nothing to the contrary. If so, she cannot "redeem" either Lear's sorrows or the general curse under which the world of Lear labors. Her death, moreover, demonstrates the lack of a hidden moral order in nature and thus the hopelessness of faith in invisible "nothings." Additionally, Lear's triple attempt to find life in his daughter's corpse is the result of mere deluded hope. As with Gloucester at the nonexistent cliff, despair is only prevented by delusion, this time self-induced. Finally, the on-stage commentators, men whose moral and psychological health is usually unquestioned, see only desolation (e.g., the quotations above of Kent, Albany, and Edgar), note Lear's deluded perspective (292–93), or make hopeful statements that are immediately undercut by all-too-visible truths. Albany, for example, says, "The Gods defend her!" (254) just before Lear's entrance with Cordelia in his arms, and then says, "All friends shall taste / The wages of their virtue, and all foes / The cup of their deservings" (301–03), before exclaiming "O! see, see!" as he watches Lear's pitiful questioning of the injustice of Cordelia's death. Provocative readings along these lines can be found in J. Stampfer, "The Catharsis of *King Lear*"; Nicholas Brooke, "The Ending of *King Lear*"; John D. Rosenberg, "King Lear and His Comforters"; and John Shaw, "*King Lear*: The Final Lines."

The optimistic, sometimes redemptive point of view usually acknowledges the desolation at the end of the play but emphasizes, taking advantage of several ambiguities, lines that intimate suprarational possibilities. Lear's final words, "Look on her, look, her lips, / Look there, look there!" (309–10), may suggest, by their repetition and vagueness, an insight beyond the worldly "see, see" of Albany and others, perhaps a vision of Cordelia alive in heaven. This possibility is enhanced by other language in the scene, most notably the spiritual intimations of a new heaven and earth in talk of the Apocalypse, which ends, in Revelation at least, with the revealed New Jerusalem. Kent's oblique "I have a journey, sir, shortly to go; / My master calls me, I must not say no" (320–21) may also be relevant here, since the journey may be to follow Lear to heaven. Interpretations in this vein may be found in Harold Goddard's *Meaning of Shakespeare*, Paul N. Siegel's *Shakespearean Tragedy and the Elizabethan Compromise*, and Roy W. Battenhouse's *Shakespearean Tragedy: Its Art and Its Christian Premises*. Furthermore, the sense of order and progression symbolized in the fact that Lear is king again at his death and is survived by a good ruler (whether Edgar in the First Folio version or Albany in the quarto version) may be reinforcing. Finally, whatever Lear's visionary capabilities, his obvious love for the ideal "nothing" that Cordelia may now purely represent makes clear his progress from the self-loving Lear at the beginning of the play. Statements of this kind, unsupported (I must acknowledge) by much explication, may be found in G. Wilson Knight's *Wheel of Fire*, Harold S. Wilson's *On the Design of Shakespearian Tragedy*, and L. C. Knights's *Some Shakespearean Themes*.

Students arguing for Lear's redemption often use the idea of positive progression mentioned above in arguments showing how the whole of the play supports an optimistic reading of the ending. Some, highlighting the conventional and symbolic nature of the characters, demonstrate that, as the evil figures get their just deserts, the good at the end must, by force of consistent design, be rewarded. Irving Ribner in *Patterns in Shakespearian Tragedy* and H. S. Wilson, among others, dwell on this structural argument, adding that Lear endures a purgatorial experience that must be given an appropriately elevated ending. Other optimists claim, perhaps following Paul Jorgensen's *Lear's Self-Discovery*, that the king learns humility through his ordeal and that this shows his progress from the blind pride with which he began. Another progressive argument may be found in Hugh L. Hennedy's "*King Lear*: Recognizing the Ending"; Hennedy claims that act V is a series of missed, then accomplished recognitions and thus that Lear's cryptic "look there, " part of the progress of recognitions, represents his knowledge that Cordelia lives in death. But the pessimists often counter with the view, outlined in J. K. Walton's "Lear's Last Speech," that Lear learns only the cruel realities of worldly injustice and the fact of death. The argument for a pattern of progress, furthermore, is countered by finding less positive schemes in the experience of the play. *King Lear* in its entire process, as opposed to the play selectively edited, exhibits a pattern in which hopeful moral and providential patterns are continually undercut and crushed. Brooke, as well as Stephen Booth in "On the Greatness of *King Lear*" and its later expansion in his book on *Lear* and *Macbeth*, may be consulted here.

Elements outside the play also impinge on the debate. The pessimists show that Shakespeare clearly excluded Christian elements explicit in his sources, but this fact could be countered, as Thomas P. Roche does in "'Nothing Almost Sees Miracles': Tragic Knowledge in *King Lear*," with the view that the play is a Christian exposure of the futility of paganism. In general, the optimists claim that Shakespeare and his audience, being Christian, would clearly see the pagan tragedy and the hidden Christian insights more easily than we do. But the pessimistic side may contend, in rebuttal, that the Renaissance included men who were quite positively disposed toward purely pagan ideas and attitudes. William R. Elton in King Lear *and the Gods* could be cited in support.

After the debate subsides (and much more raging occurs than my sample can indicate) and after the judges have spoken in discussion and written their verdicts, I give the class my views. Following critics such as John Rosenberg, S. L. Goldberg in *An Essay on* King Lear, and Derek Peat in "'And that's true too': *King Lear* and the Tension of Uncertainty," I believe that the play's ending is ultimately ambiguous, and purposely so. Yet some things are clear: Cordelia is dead, and the world of Lear is bleak and unjust, at least in human terms. But if the universe of *King Lear* is clearly indiscriminate and dark, the tragedy is not, by virtue of its ultimate ambiguity, empty of redeeming possibilities. Indeed, as Lear, recognizing his daughter's death, must search for her life, so the audience, faced with the "promis'd end," cannot but look for something more, even if it might be illusory. Geoffrey Bush in *Shakespeare and the Natural Condition* asserts that *King Lear* is a play of belief and that the audience sustains that airy "nothing" despite the sense that faith may be a pretense. In my opinion, the human capacity for belief is rarefied to its essence in *King Lear* precisely because the play leaves so few grounds for simple visual, experiential, and rational means from which to infer a metaphysical view. René Fortin in

"Hermeneutical Circularity and Christian Interpretations of *King Lear*" argues this point in Christian terms, showing that the essence of Christianity, which is mystery and hope (not justice and reward), is consistent with the play's inexorable pessimism. Moreover, along with Phyllis Rackin in "Delusion as Resolution in *King Lear*," I find Lear's struggle for insight at the end to be a heroical, creative act in the face of nihilism. Lear's mad hope, as Maynard Mack in King Lear *in Our Time* points out, is a delusory godsend, an illusion that is good. Finally, the "nothing" of belief is supported somewhat more palpably, but still ambiguously, by the tragedy's fullness of feeling. At the end of *King Lear*, both the onstage and the theater audience "see feelingly," thereby reinforcing the hope that Lear sees something when we all "look there." Thus, the debate is resolved for me in the paradoxical realization that the pessimism of things seen is at one with the optimism of "nothings" believed in.

EPILOGUE

A Course Devoted Exclusively to *King Lear*

J. W. Robinson

Students of average ability often appear mystified by much of Shakespeare's language. They will respond to the psychology and morality in (for example) *King Lear*; but when they have only a general (and sometimes erroneous) sense of what is being said, their responses can be halfhearted, even if they are enthusiastic about the play in general and interested in the culture of Renaissance England or the problems of the elderly. For this reason I wondered, several years ago, if I could get some undergraduates to go through *King Lear* line by line with me and, as a result, see as fully as possible the life and art in it.

Dubious of my ability to keep a whole class working together on a single play for the entire fifteen weeks of the semester (for three credit hours), I planned a ten-week course (for two credit hours), to be followed by an optional five weeks of independent study (for one credit hour). Students were to read aloud from the play at length, putting themselves into the characters, and the readings were to be interrupted by comments and questions from the class and me. Since the normal fifty-minute class is short for this purpose, I planned that the class would meet once a week for two and a half hours. Eighteen students, ten men and eight women, took the course. Except for a senior English major, a junior elementary education major, and a junior speech major, they were sophomores, five majoring in English and the others in civil engineering, dentistry, economics, elementary education, political science, "pre-law," and speech. Only two (English majors) had taken a course in Shakespeare before—our usual sophomore-level course, which covers about twelve plays.

For our text I inevitably chose the new Arden *King Lear*, edited by Kenneth Muir. This edition, of course, contains as much information about the language of the play as is available anywhere in one place, and it goes into far more detail than, for example, the Signet and Pelican editions frequently used for undergraduate courses. To prepare for the course, I absorbed as much of Muir's edition as I could, and I also tried to spark myself by reading a recent critical work, choosing Marvin Rosenberg's *Masks of King Lear* which not only concentrates in detail on how *Lear* has been acted (particularly useful for my purposes) but is also full of ideas about the play in general. I had earlier read some of Harley Granville-Barker's famous prefaces and J. L. Styan's *Shakespeare's Stagecraft;* and G. L. Brook's *Language of Shakespeare* helped me put some order into my linguistic knowledge, which had earlier been much increased by Hilda Hulme's *Explorations in Shakespeare's Language.* (S. S. Hussey's *Literary Language of Shakespeare* is now also available.)

At the first class meeting I explained that together we were going to try to find as fully as possible the meaning of the play; I fortunately hit the right note, and the class soon developed a useful sense that we were embarked on a joint enterprise likely to demand our full powers. I also demonstrated exactly what kind of information Muir's edition provides. (The students proved undaunted by the scholarly apparatus of this book; in fact, they liked it.) I went on to give short accounts of early modern English, of Shakespeare's language, and of his theater (I took to class a 3' x 2' reproduction, borrowed from our theater department, of the cut-open drawing by C. W. Hodges of his reconstruction of the Globe, from *The Globe Restored*). I also explained the concept of the subtext. I cast the first act (which has sixteen speaking parts) at random, necessarily ignoring the sex of the students. I told them to rehearse their parts, to be prepared to answer questions about their characters, and to read the whole play and Muir's introduction by the following week.

The twenty-five hours of class time proved insufficient for a reading of the entire play, even though we stuck to the plan and doggedly read and discussed. The only exceptions were a few short spells spent early on listening to a recording of the play with Paul Scofield as Lear (dir. Howard Sackler), which I introduced to help the students make their own readings more energetic, and seeing a film of the Joseph Papp production, directed by Edwin Sherwin, with James Earl Jones as a very moving Lear. After the second class meeting, when we had reached only the end of the first scene (307 lines), I selected the scenes for our reading: I.ii, iv; II.iii, iv; III.iv, vii; IV.i, vi, vii; V.iii. All the students liked reading. Neither expecting nor discouraging great acting, I taught (by example) the good readers to be patient with the poor readers; our reading became bolder and more accomplished as the course progressed. We changed parts each week. I only sparingly corrected pronunciation. We would read for ten or fifteen minutes, then go back over what we had read, often for thirty or forty minutes. Once the class was under way, we rather freely commented on one anothers' interpretations. If speculation or New Criticism began to run wild, I came up with short comments on the Elizabethan "world picture" and on Jacobean political and social life, and Muir's notes kept us in touch with the realities of contemporary language and literature. In the end we had read about half the play.

What occurred in class was not different in kind from what happens (I assume) in many undergraduate Shakespeare classes, only we had the time to explore one play more thoroughly than usual. Readings, followed by discussions of the subtext, context, and staging, led to discussions about meaning. An example from the first scene will give some idea of how we discussed the meaning of the lines just read. *Darker*, in "Meantime, we shall express our darker purpose" (I.i.35), is glossed as "more secret" (Harbage, Pelican ed.; Kittredge-Ribner) or "hidden" (Fraser). Muir glosses the line with a suggestion by William Empson that Lear's renunciation "in the eyes of the world . . . would be a gloomy one." Students add (surely correctly) that *darker* also has the sense of "murkier" and shades of the unholy in it. I then ask the students such questions as the following: "In what tone of voice does Lear speak this line? Is he ashamed? Proud? Defensive? Daring? Tricky? Mysterious?" I have the student reading Lear's part read the line again: *darker* comes out aggressively, sounds more right than before, and also produces merriment. This and similar questions (*crawl*, I.i.40, proves fruitful, given Lear's fondness for hunting) provoke much comment, based squarely on what is said and what is meant in the first scene, about Lear's kingdom, his rule, his personality, his relations with his daughters, and his plans, as well as on the gerontology, "Freudian family romance," and aggression in the play.

As the reading progresses, the more legitimate and challenging become questions about the contexts and echoes of the scenes. "Darker purpose," for example, comes up again when we reach Edgar's rich and "mad" line, "The Prince of Darkness is a gentleman" (III.iv.140). When we come to IV.vi, I invite the students to work on the broken chains of meaning in Lear's "mad" speeches (IV.vi.81–200)—Muir's notes are helpful but not exhaustive—and to relate them to preceding events in the play. Why does his mind run or wander in these particular channels? This scene of Lear's madness reverses the ceremony and formality with which the play begins, and students spend much time making the connections between Lear now and Lear earlier. Some, despite Lear's advanced age, diagnose him as having Alzheimer's disease (the affliction that causes early senility) since they have seen it in family friends or in relatives. Others raise the broader thematic questions of sense and madness, wisdom and folly.

A detailed reading of the play leads to insights through attention to even such matters as stage directions (or the lack thereof). For example, Muir tells us that *"Enter Lear, fantastically dressed with wild flowers"* (IV.vi.80) was invented by an eighteenth-century editor as a substitute for the quarto's blunt *"Enter Lear mad."* I ask the students to find some justification for this stage direction (see IV.iv.3-6) and also for other such directions and indications of place in the scene headings. The students then become detectives and begin to supply their own stage directions. "Give me the map there" (I.i.36) does not, of course, lead to discussion, but "Is not this your son, my Lord?" (I.i.7) leads to much comment about whether Edmund hears, or overhears, or does not hear the conversation, largely and embarrassingly about himself, between his father and the Earl of Kent in I.i.1-23.

The study of Lear's awakening (IV.vii.21-84) leads to a discussion of how meaning is distilled into style—in word and deed—and also of Shakespeare's dramatic tact. The new simplicity in Lear's diction and coherence in his thoughts—"For, as I am a man, I think this lady / To be my child Cordelia" (IV.vii.69-70)—invite comparison with his earlier ravings. Muir's note on "lady" and "child" is provocative, and Lear's "man," who now has "fresh garments on him" (IV.vii.22), stands comparison with his earlier and desperate notion of "man," pronounced as he rips his clothes off (III.iv.103-07). Cordelia's emotion-filled (but with what emotions?) brevity seems more acceptable now than in I.i. In contrast to his earlier scornful and vigorous kneeling in the face of rejection and disrespect (II.iv.143-54), Lear kneels (or tries to), humble and wobbly, even while those around him are lovingly and therapeutically respectful. At my suggestion, two students act out this same reconciliation scene from the old *King Leir* (Muir's edition contains selections from the major sources of the play): this is the only occasion when we desert our large seminar tables. Not only do Leir and Cordella go up and down, like buckets in a well, in their kneeling (I make the students do this), but their conversation runs for altogether too long on the very question of knees and kneeling. Questions of aesthetics arise, amid the hilarity.

The students write two long papers, describing the context, subtext, and staging of two short (very short, for thoroughness is needed) scenes of their own choosing that we have not read in class. The results are thoughtful, honest, and often accomplished, and they are more satisfactory, in my experience, than papers written on more general subjects, such as the purpose of the Fool in the play. Large issues—folly and wisdom, parents and children, plainness and hypocrisy—naturally emerge from our close study of the text, and they are more fruitfully taken up in class when they arise than written about in papers.

After the ten-week course, six students chose to pursue the optional five weeks of independent study. I asked each to write a thorough account of one source of *King Lear* and Shakespeare's use of it. The results were not particularly good, and I no longer give this kind of assignment because it is very hard for undergraduates not to paraphrase Geoffrey Bullough's essay on *King Lear* in volume 7 of *Narrative and Dramatic Sources of Shakespeare*. A much better assignment, I now realize, would have been to ask these six students to write long analyses of *Hamlet*, or parts of it, on the model of our approach to *King Lear*, although the new Arden *Hamlet* was not then available.

I encourage other teachers to try change-of-pace courses where major works are concerned. One may profitably devote a class period a week to readings by students, spend several weeks on one play (even at the expense of curtailing the consideration of other plays), and require undergraduate nonmajors to use new Arden editions or, now that they are becoming available, new Cambridge or Oxford editions, although not for more than one play.

Some assessments of this course on *King Lear* have come from my students, as well as from my personal sense of what was accomplished. In their "evaluations," three students expressed a wish that the course had gone on for the entire fifteen weeks, but the others declared ten weeks to be sufficient, one remarking on "the psychological uplift" thus blessedly available two-thirds of the way through the semester. Only one admitted to any boredom. All claimed to have learned an enormous amount about Shakespeare and his times, as well as about *King Lear*. Gratifying, even though ultimately not encouraging to English teachers, was the following comment: "This method of reviewing a Shakespearean play is the only one that makes sense—How can one possibly do a play justice in two or three class meetings? They can't." Throughout the course I made few references to other plays by Shakespeare, although I not infrequently hinted that our method of reading and studying *King Lear* was applicable to all plays. The students certainly did come to a good understanding of this one play and of the elements of drama, and this understanding is surely of primary importance. Class time was well spent, even though I gave no information about the development or scope of Shakespearean or Renaissance drama, made little effort to take up all the aspects of *King Lear* that I feel are important, and had no well-ordered list of points to make. At the end of our marathon (which was tiring) we all had the valuable sense that we did not, after all, manage to grasp every inch of meaning in the play.

PARTICIPANTS IN SURVEY OF SHAKESPEARE INSTRUCTORS

The following teachers of Shakespeare generously responded to the survey on the teaching of *King Lear* that preceded preparation of this volume. Without the invaluable information and insights so provided, the book would not have been possible.

John B. Alphonso-Karkala, New York State Univ. Coll., New Paltz; John C. Bean, Montana State Univ.; R. Mark Benbow, Colby Coll.; John Bligh, Univ. of Guelph, Ontario; Lynda E. Boose, Univ. of California, Los Angeles; Robert E. Burkhart, Eastern Kentucky Univ.; Ruth A. Cameron, Eastern Nazarene Coll.; Larry S. Champion, North Carolina State Univ.; Doris A. Clatanoff, Concordia Coll., Nebraska; Lance Cohen, Lawrence High School, Cedarhurst, New York; Robert G. Collmer, Baylor Univ.; Joan F. Dean, Univ. of Missouri, Kansas City; Trudy Drucker, Bergen Community Coll.; Thomas F. Dunn, emeritus, Drake Univ.; Richard D. Erlich, Miami Univ.; Michael Flachmann, California State Coll., Bakersfield; C. R. Forker, Indiana Univ., Bloomington; F. Richard Friedman, Central Oregon Community Coll.; Ruth Ann Gerrard, Austintown-Fitch High School, Youngstown, Ohio; E. Bruce Glenn, Academy of the New Church Coll.; Beth Goldring, Cowell Coll., Univ. of California, Santa Cruz; John K. Hale, Univ. of Otago, New Zealand; John B. Harcourt, Ithaca Coll.; Harriett Hawkins, Linacre Coll., Oxford, England; Eugene Hill, Mt. Holyoke Coll.; James E. Hirsh, Univ. of Hawaii, Manoa; Delmar C. Homan, Bethany Coll.; Maurice Hunt, Baylor Univ.; J. Dennis Huston, Rice Univ.; Ann E. Imbrie, Vassar Coll.; Lowell E. Johnson, St. Olaf Coll.; Robert Johnson, Miami Univ.; George Burke Johnston, emeritus, Virginia Polytechnic Inst. and State Univ.; William Kemp, Mary Washington Coll.; Arthur F. Kinney, Univ. of Massachusetts, Amherst; Jean Klene, CSC, St. Mary's Coll., Indiana; Peggy A. Knapp, Carnegie-Mellon Univ.; David L. Kranz, Dickinson Coll.; Anne Lancashire, University Coll., Univ. of Toronto; Gordon Lell, Concordia Coll., Minnesota; Mark Lidman, Univ. of South Carolina, Sumter; Robert Lynch, New Jersey Inst. of Technology; Fred R. MacFadden, Coppin State Coll.; Toni McNaron, Univ. of Minnesota; Anthony Merzlak, Suffolk Univ.; John J. Murray, Univ. of Scranton; Paralee Norman, Northwestern State Univ. of Louisiana; Ann Paton, Geneva Coll.; Vincent F. Petronella, Univ. of Massachusetts, Boston; Robert B. Pierce, Oberlin Coll.; Phyllis Rackin, Univ. of Pennsylvania; Hugh M. Richmond, Univ. of California, Berkeley; J. W. Robinson, Univ. of Nebraska; Judith Rosenthal, California State Univ., Fresno; Kenneth S. Rothwell, Univ. of Vermont; Brownell Salomon, Bowling Green State Univ.; Hanna Scolnicov, Hebrew Univ. of Jerusalem; Sara Jayne Steen, Montana State Univ.; J. L. Styan, Northwestern Univ.; Mark Taylor, Manhattan Coll., City Univ. of New York; Sally Taylor, Brigham Young Univ.; Frances Teague, Univ. of Georgia; Michael Warren, Cowell Coll., Univ. of California, Santa Cruz; George W. Williams, Duke Univ.; Bruce W. Young, Harvard Univ.; Robert Zaslavsky, Bryn Mawr Coll.; Georgianna Ziegler, Univ. of Pennsylvania; Virginia Zúñiga-Tristán, Universidad de Costa Rica.

WORKS CITED

Books and Articles

Abrams, M. H., gen. ed. *The Norton Anthology of English Literature.* 4th ed. 2 vols. New York: Norton, 1979.

Adams, John Cranford. *The Globe Playhouse: Its Design and Equipment.* Cambridge: Harvard UP, 1942.

Adee, Alvey Augustus, ed. *King Lear (The Players' Text of 1608, with the Heminges and Condell Text of 1623).* Bankside Shakespeare 10. New York: Shakespeare Soc. of New York, 1890.

Adelman, Janet, ed. *Twentieth Century Interpretations of* King Lear. Englewood Cliffs: Prentice, 1978.

Aers, David, and Gunther Kress. "The Language of Social Order: Individual, Society, and Historical Process in *King Lear.*" *Literature, Language and Society in England: 1580-1680.* Ed. David Aers, Bob Hodge, and Gunther Kress. Dublin: Gill, 1981. 75-99.

Akrigg, G. P. V. *Jacobean Pageant: Or, The Court of King James I.* 1962. New York: Atheneum, 1974.

Allen, Michael J. B., and Kenneth Muir, eds. *Shakespeare's Plays in Quarto: A Facsimile Edition of Copies Primarily from the Henry E. Huntington Library.* Berkeley: U of California P, 1982.

Alpers, Paul J. "*King Lear* and the Theory of the 'Sight Pattern.'" *In Defense of Reading: A Reader's Approach to Literary Criticism.* Ed. Reuben A. Brower and Richard Poirier. New York: Dutton, 1962. 133-52.

Altman, Joel B. *The Tudor Play of Mind: Rhetorical Inquiry and the Development of Elizabethan Drama.* Berkeley: U of California P, 1978.

Aristotle. *Poetics.* Trans. S. H. Butcher. *Criticism: The Foundations of Modern Literary Judgment.* Ed. Mark Schorer, Josephine Miles, and Gordon McKenzie. New York: Harcourt, 1958. 199-217.

Bamber, Linda. *Comic Women, Tragic Men: A Study of Gender and Genre in Shakespeare.* Stanford: Stanford UP, 1982.

Barber, C. L. "The Family in Shakespeare's Development: Tragedy and Sacredness." *Representing Shakespeare: New Psychoanalytic Essays.* Ed. Murray M. Schwartz and Coppélia Kahn. Baltimore: Johns Hopkins UP, 1980. 188-202.

Barnet, Sylvan, gen. ed. *The Complete Signet Classic Shakespeare.* New York: Harcourt, 1972.

———. "Some Limitations of a Christian Approach to Shakespeare." *ELH* 22 (1955): 81-92.

Barnet, Sylvan, Morton Berman, and William Burto. *The Study of Literature: A Handbook of Critical Essays and Terms.* Boston: Little, 1960.

Battenhouse, Roy W. *Shakespearean Tragedy: Its Art and Its Christian Premises.* Bloomington: Indiana UP, 1969.

Beckerman, Bernard. *Shakespeare at the Globe, 1599-1609.* New York: Macmillan, 1962.

Bergeron, David M. *Shakespeare: A Study and Research Guide.* New York: St. Martin's, 1975.

Berman, Ronald. *A Reader's Guide to Shakespeare's Plays: A Discursive Bibliography.* Rev. ed. Glenview: Scott, 1973.

Bettelheim, Bruno. *The Uses of Enchantment: The Meaning and Importance of Fairy Tales.* New York: Knopf, 1976.

Bevington, David, ed. *The Complete Works of Shakespeare.* 3rd ed. Glenview: Scott, 1980.

———. *Shakespeare.* Goldentree Bibliographies. Arlington Heights: AHM, 1978.

Bindoff, S. T. *Tudor England.* 1950. Baltimore: Penguin, 1963.

Black, James. "*King Lear:* Art Upside-Down." *Shakespeare Survey* 33 (1980): 35–42.

Blayney, Peter W. M. *Nicholas Okes and the First Quarto.* Vol. 1 of *The Texts of* King Lear *and Their Origins.* 2 vols. Cambridge: Cambridge UP, 1982– (vol. 2 forthcoming).

Bodkin, Maud. *Archetypal Patterns in Poetry: Psychological Studies of Imagination.* London: Oxford UP, 1934.

Boose, Lynda E. "The Father and the Bride in Shakespeare." *PMLA* 97 (1982): 325-47.

Booth, Stephen. King Lear, Macbeth, *Indefinition, and Tragedy.* New Haven: Yale UP, 1983.

———. "On the Greatness of *King Lear.*" Adelman 98-111.

Booty, John E., ed. *The Book of Common Prayer, 1559.* Charlottesville: UP of Virginia, 1976.

Bowers, Fredson. *On Editing Shakespeare.* Charlottesville: UP of Virginia, 1966.

Bradbrook, M. C. *Themes and Conventions of Elizabethan Tragedy.* Cambridge: Cambridge UP, 1935.

Bradley, A. C. *Shakespearean Tragedy.* 1904. New York: Meridian, 1960.

Brook, G. L. *The Language of Shakespeare.* London: Deutsch, 1976.

Brooke, Nicholas. "The Ending of *King Lear.*" *Shakespeare 1564-1964.* Ed. Edward A. Bloom. Providence: Brown UP, 1964. 71-87.

Brown, John Russell, ed. *Shakespeare in Performance: An Introduction through Six Major Plays.* New York: Harcourt, 1976.

———. *Shakespeare's Plays in Performance.* 1966. New York: St. Martin's, 1967.

Bullough, Geoffrey, ed. *Narrative and Dramatic Sources of Shakespeare.* 8 vols. London: Routledge, 1957-75. Vol. 7.

Burckhardt, Sigurd. *Shakespearean Meanings.* Princeton: Princeton UP, 1968.

Bush, Geoffrey. *Shakespeare and the Natural Condition.* Cambridge: Harvard UP, 1956.

Byrne, Muriel St. Clare. *Elizabethan Life in Town and Country.* 1925. London: Methuen, 1970.

Campbell, Lily B. *Shakespeare's Tragic Heroes: Slaves of Passion.* Cambridge: Cambridge UP, 1930.

Campbell, Oscar James, and Edward G. Quinn, eds. *The Reader's Encyclopedia of Shakespeare.* New York: Crowell, 1966.

Cavell, Stanley. "The Avoidance of Love: A Reading of *King Lear.*" *Must We Mean What We Say?* 1969. Cambridge: Cambridge UP, 1976. 267–353.

Chambers, E. K. *The Elizabethan Stage.* 4 vols. Oxford: Clarendon, 1923.

———. *William Shakespeare: A Study of Facts and Problems.* 2 vols. Oxford: Clarendon, 1930.

Champion, Larry S. King Lear: *An Annotated Bibliography.* 2 vols. New York: Garland, 1980.

Charney, Maurice. *How to Read Shakespeare.* New York: McGraw, 1971.

———. "'We Put Fresh Garments on Him': Nakedness and Clothes in *King Lear.*" Colie and Flahiff 77–88.

Chaudhuri, Sukanta. *Infirm Glory: Shakespeare and the Renaissance Image of Man.* Oxford: Clarendon, 1981.

Clemen, W. H. *The Development of Shakespeare's Imagery.* Cambridge: Harvard UP, 1951.

Colie, Rosalie L. *Shakespeare's Living Art.* Princeton: Princeton UP, 1974.

Colie, Rosalie L., and F. T. Flahiff, eds. *Some Facets of* King Lear: *Essays in Prismatic Criticism.* Toronto: U of Toronto P, 1974.

Cook, Ann Jennalie. *The Privileged Playgoers of Shakespeare's London, 1576–1642.* Princeton: Princeton UP, 1981.

Craig, Hardin. *The Enchanted Glass: The Elizabethan Mind in Literature.* New York: Oxford UP, 1936.

Creeth, Edmund. *Mankynde in Shakespeare.* Athens: U of Georgia P, 1976.

Danby, John F. *Shakespeare's Doctrine of Nature: A Study of* King Lear. London: Faber, 1949.

Danson, Lawrence, ed. *On* King Lear. Princeton: Princeton UP, 1981.

Dean, Leonard F., ed. *Shakespeare: Modern Essays in Criticism.* Rev. ed. 1967. New York: Oxford UP, 1982.

Dent, R. W. *Shakespeare's Proverbial Language: An Index.* Berkeley: U of California P, 1981.

Doran, Madeleine. *Endeavors of Art: A Study of Form in Elizabethan Drama.* 1954. Madison: U of Wisconsin P, 1972.

Duthie, George Ian, ed. *Shakespeare's* King Lear: *A Critical Edition.* Oxford: Blackwell, 1949.

Duthie, George Ian, and John Dover Wilson, eds. *King Lear.* Cambridge Shakespeare. Cambridge: Cambridge UP, 1960.

Ebisch, Walther, in collaboration with Levin L. Schücking. *A Shakespeare Bibliography*. 1930. New York: Blom, 1968.

――――. *Supplement for the Years 1930–1935 to* A Shakespeare Bibliography. 1936. New York: Blom, 1968.

Eckert, Charles W., ed. *Focus on Shakespearean Films*. Englewood Cliffs: Prentice, 1972.

Edwards, Philip. "Shakespeare and the Healing Power of Deceit." *Shakespeare Survey* 31 (1978): 115–25.

Elton, G. R. *England under the Tudors*. 1955. London: Methuen, 1962.

Elton, William R. *King Lear and the Gods*. San Marino: Huntington Library, 1966.

Evans, G. Blakemore, textual ed. *The Riverside Shakespeare*. Boston: Houghton, 1974.

Everett, Barbara. "The New *King Lear*." *Critical Quarterly* 2 (1960): 325–39.

Faber, M. D., ed. *The Design Within: Psychoanalytic Approaches to Shakespeare*. New York: Science House, 1970.

Farnham, Willard. *The Medieval Heritage of Elizabethan Tragedy*. Berkeley: U of California P, 1936.

――――. *The Shakespearean Grotesque: Its Genesis and Transformations*. Oxford: Clarendon, 1971.

――――. *Shakespeare's Tragic Frontier: The World of His Final Tragedies*. 1950. New York: Barnes, 1973.

Fly, Richard. *Shakespeare's Mediated World*. Amherst: U of Massachusetts P, 1976.

Fortin, René E. "Hermeneutical Circularity and Christian Interpretations of *King Lear*." *Shakespeare Studies* 12 (1979): 113–25.

Fraser, Russell A. *Shakespeare's Poetics in Relation to* King Lear. London: Routledge, 1962.

――――, ed. *The Tragedy of King Lear*. Signet Classic Shakespeare. New York: NAL, 1963.

Fraser, Russell A., and Norman Rabkin, eds. *Drama of the English Renaissance*. 2 vols. New York: Macmillan, 1976.

French, Carolyn S. "Shakespeare's 'Folly': *King Lear*." *Shakespeare Quarterly* 10 (1959): 523–29.

French, Marilyn. *Shakespeare's Division of Experience*. New York: Summit, 1981.

Frye, Northrop. *Anatomy of Criticism: Four Essays*. Princeton: Princeton UP, 1957.

Frye, Roland Mushat. *Shakespeare and Christian Doctrine*. Princeton: Princeton UP, 1963.

――――. *Shakespeare: The Art of the Dramatist*. Rev. ed. London: Allen, 1982.

Furness, Horace Howard, ed. *King Lear*. New Variorum Ed. of Shakespeare. 1880. New York: Dover, 1963.

Gaskell, Philip. *A New Introduction to Bibliography*. New York: Oxford UP, 1972.

The Geneva Bible: A Facsimile of the 1560 Edition. Introd. Lloyd E. Berry. Madison: U of Wisconsin P, 1969.

Goddard, Harold. *The Meaning of Shakespeare*. Chicago: U of Chicago P, 1951.

Goldberg, Jonathan. *James I and the Politics of Literature: Jonson, Shakespeare, Donne, and Their Contemporaries*. Baltimore: Johns Hopkins UP, 1983.

———. " 'Upon a publike stage': The Royal Gaze and Jacobean Theater." *Research Opportunities in Renaissance Drama* 24 (1981): 17–21.

Goldberg, S. L. *An Essay on* King Lear. London: Cambridge UP, 1974.

Goldman, Michael. *Shakespeare and the Energies of Drama*. Princeton: Princeton UP, 1972.

Goldsmith, Robert Hillis. *Wise Fools in Shakespeare*. East Lansing: Michigan State UP, 1955.

Granville-Barker, Harley. *Prefaces to Shakespeare*. 1927. Princeton: Princeton UP, 1952.

Greenblatt, Stephen. *Renaissance Self-Fashioning: From More to Shakespeare*. Chicago: U of Chicago P, 1980.

Greenfield, Thelma Nelson. "The Clothing Motif in *King Lear*." *Shakespeare Quarterly* 5 (1954): 281–86.

Greg, W. W. "The Date of *King Lear* and Shakespeare's Use of Earlier Versions of the Story." *Library* 4th ser. 20 (1939–40): 377–400.

———. *The Editorial Problem in Shakespeare: A Survey of the Foundations of the Text*. 3rd. ed. Oxford: Clarendon, 1954.

———, ed. *King Lear 1608 (Pied Bull Quarto)*. Shakespeare Quarto Facsimiles 1. London: Oxford UP, 1939.

Gurr, Andrew. *The Shakespearean Stage, 1574–1642*. 2nd ed. Cambridge: Cambridge UP, 1980.

Halio, Jay L., ed. *King Lear*. Fountainwell Drama Texts. Edinburgh: Oliver, 1973.

Halliday, F. E. *A Shakespeare Companion*. Rev. ed. 1964. Baltimore: Penguin, 1969.

Hankins, John Erskine. *Backgrounds of Shakespeare's Thought*. Hamden: Archon, 1978.

Harbage, Alfred. *As They Liked It: An Essay on Shakespeare and Morality*. New York: Macmillan, 1947.

———, ed. *King Lear*. Pelican Text. Baltimore: Penguin, 1959.

———. *Shakespeare's Audience*. 1941. New York: Columbia UP, 1969.

———, gen. ed. *William Shakespeare: The Complete Works*. Baltimore: Penguin, 1969.

Hattaway, Michael. *Elizabethan Popular Theatre: Plays in Performance*. London: Routledge, 1982.

Haydn, Hiram. *The Counter-Renaissance*. New York: Scribner's, 1950.

Heilman, Robert Bechtold. *This Great Stage: Image and Structure in* King Lear. 1948. Seattle: U of Washington P, 1963.

Hennedy, Hugh L. "*King Lear*: Recognizing the Ending." *Studies in Philology* 71 (1974): 371–84.

Hetherington, Robert A. "The *Lears* of Peter Brook." *Shakespeare on Film Newsletter* 6.1 (1982): 7.

Hinman, Charlton, ed. *The First Folio of Shakespeare: The Norton Facsimile*. New York: Norton, 1968.

———. *The Printing and Proof-Reading of the First Folio of Shakespeare*. 2 vols. Oxford: Clarendon, 1963.

Hirsh, James E. *The Structure of Shakespearean Scenes*. New Haven: Yale UP, 1981.

Hodges, C. Walter. *The Globe Restored: A Study of the Elizabethan Theatre*. 2nd ed. New York: Coward, 1968.

Holland, Norman N. *Psychoanalysis and Shakespeare*. New York: McGraw, 1964.

Holloway, John. *The Story of the Night: Studies in Shakespeare's Major Tragedies*. 1961. Lincoln: U of Nebraska P, 1966.

Holman, C. Hugh. *A Handbook to Literature*. 3rd ed. Indianapolis: Odyssey, 1972. (Based on the original by William Flint Thrall and Addison Hibbard, 1936.)

Honigmann, E. A. J. *Shakespeare: Seven Tragedies: The Dramatist's Manipulation of Response*. London: Macmillan, 1976.

Hornstein, Lillian Herlands. "King Robert of Sicily: Analogues and Origins." *PMLA* 79 (1964): 13–21.

Hosley, Richard. "The Playhouses and the Stage." Muir and Schoenbaum 15–34.

Hulme, Hilda M. *Explorations in Shakespeare's Language*. London: Longmans, 1962.

Hunter, G. K., ed. *King Lear*. New Penguin Shakespeare. 1972. Baltimore: Penguin, 1981.

———. "Shakespeare's Reading." Muir and Schoenbaum 55–66.

Hussey, S. S. *The Literary Language of Shakespeare*. London: Longman, 1982.

Johnson, Samuel. *Johnson on Shakespeare*. Ed. Arthur Sherbo. New Haven: Yale UP, 1968. Vols. 7 and 8 of *The Yale Edition of the Works of Samuel Johnson*. Ed. A. T. Hazen and J. H. Middendorf. 11 vols. to date. 1958–. (Contains preface and notes to Johnson's 1765 edition of Shakespeare.)

Jonson, Ben. *Ben Jonson's Sejanus*. Ed. Jonas A. Barish. 1965. Vol. 3 of *The Yale Ben Jonson*. Ed. Alvin B. Kernan and Richard B. Young. 7 vols. New Haven: Yale UP, 1962–74.

Jorgens, Jack J. *Shakespeare on Film*. Bloomington: Indiana UP, 1977.

Jorgensen, Paul A. *Lear's Self-Discovery*. Berkeley: U of California P, 1967.

Joseph, Bertram. *Acting Shakespeare*. London: Routledge, 1960.

———. *Elizabethan Acting.* London: Oxford UP, 1951.

———. *Shakespeare's Eden: The Commonwealth of England 1558-1629.* London: Blandford, 1971.

Joseph, Miriam. *Shakespeare's Use of the Arts of Language.* New York: Columbia UP, 1947.

Jung, C. G. *Two Essays on Analytical Psychology.* Trans. R. F. C. Hull. New York: Meridian, 1956.

Kahn, Coppélia. "The Absent Mother in *King Lear.*" *Rewriting the Renaissance: The Discourses of Sexual Difference.* Ed. Margaret Ferguson, Maureen Quilligan, and Nancy Vickers. Chicago: U of Chicago P, 1986.

Keast, W. R. "Imagery and Meaning in the Interpretation of *King Lear.*" *Modern Philology* 47 (1949): 45-64.

———. "The 'New Criticism' and *King Lear.*" *Critics and Criticism.* Ed. R. S. Crane. Chicago: U of Chicago P, 1952. 108-37.

Keats, John. *The Poems of John Keats.* Ed. Jack Stillinger. Cambridge: Harvard UP, 1978.

Kelly, Henry Ansgar. *Divine Providence in the England of Shakespeare's Histories.* Cambridge: Harvard UP, 1970.

Kelso, Ruth. *Doctrine for the Lady of the Renaissance.* 1956. Urbana: U of Illinois P, 1978.

———. *The Doctrine of the English Gentleman in the Sixteenth Century.* [Urbana: U of Illinois P, 1929].

Kernan, Alvin. "Formalism and Realism in Elizabethan Drama: The Miracles in *King Lear.*" *Renaissance Drama* 9 (1966): 59-66.

———, ed. *Modern Shakespearean Criticism: Essays on Style, Dramaturgy, and the Major Plays.* New York: Harcourt, 1970.

Kernodle, George R. "The Symphonic Form of *King Lear.*" *Elizabethan Studies and Other Essays.* Ed. E. J. West. Boulder: U of Colorado, 1945. 185-91.

King, T. J. *Shakespearean Staging, 1599-1642.* Cambridge: Harvard UP, 1971.

Kirschbaum, Leo. "Albany." *Shakespeare Survey* 13 (1960): 20-29.

Kittredge, George Lyman, ed. *Sixteen Plays of Shakespeare.* Boston: Ginn, 1946.

———, ed. *The Tragedy of King Lear.* By William Shakespeare. Rev. Irving Ribner. Waltham: Blaisdell, [1967].

Knight, G. Wilson. *The Wheel of Fire: Interpretations of Shakespearian Tragedy.* Rev. ed. 1949. London: Methuen, 1972.

Knights, L. C. *Some Shakespearean Themes.* London: Chatto, 1959.

Kökeritz, Helge. *Shakespeare's Names: A Pronouncing Dictionary.* 1959. New Haven: Yale UP, 1972.

———. *Shakespeare's Pronunciation.* New Haven: Yale UP, 1953.

Kott, Jan. *Szkice o Szekspirze.* Warsaw: Państwowy Instytut Wydawniczy, 1961. Trans. Boleslaw Taborski as *Shakespeare Our Contemporary.* Garden City: Doubleday, 1964.

Kozintsev, Grigori. King Lear: *The Space of Tragedy*. Trans. Mary Mackintosh. Berkeley: U of California P, 1977.

Lamb, Charles. "On the Tragedies of Shakspeare Considered with Reference to Their Fitness for Stage Representation." 1811. *Charles Lamb on Shakespeare*. Ed. Joan Coldwell. New York: Harper, 1978. 24–49.

Levin, Richard. *The Multiple Plot in English Renaissance Drama*. Chicago: U of Chicago P, 1971.

Lewis, C. S. *The Discarded Image: An Introduction to Medieval and Renaissance Literature*. Cambridge: Cambridge UP, 1964.

Lovejoy, Arthur O. *The Great Chain of Being: A Study of the History of an Idea*. 1936. Cambridge: Harvard UP, 1957.

Lyons, Bridget Gellert. "The Subplot as Simplification in *King Lear*." Colie and Flahiff 23–38.

Mack, Maynard. King Lear *in Our Time*. Berkeley: U of California P, 1965.

Mahood, M. M. *Shakespeare's Wordplay*. 1957. London: Methuen, 1979.

Manvell, Roger. *Shakespeare and the Film*. New York: Praeger, 1971.

Marlowe, Christopher. *Tamburlaine the Great, Parts I and II*. Fraser and Rabkin 1: 205–61.

Matchett, William H. "Some Dramatic Techniques in *King Lear*." McGuire and Samuelson 185–208.

McFarland, Thomas. *Tragic Meanings in Shakespeare*. New York: Random, 1966.

McGuire, Philip C., and David A. Samuelson, eds. *Shakespeare: The Theatrical Dimension*. New York: AMS, 1979.

McLean, Andrew M. *Shakespeare: Annotated Bibliographies and Media Guide for Teachers*. Urbana: NCTE, 1980.

McManaway, James G., and Jeanne Addison Roberts. *A Selective Bibliography of Shakespeare: Editions, Textual Studies, Commentary*. Charlottesville: UP of Virginia, for the Folger Shakespeare Library, 1975.

McNeir, Waldo F. "The Role of Edmund in *King Lear*." *Studies in English Literature* 8 (1968): 187–216.

Miller, Jonathan. Comments in publicity releases for BBC-TV/Time-Life, Inc., *King Lear*. Issued by Stone Associates, Los Angeles, and WNET, New York, 1982.

Milward, Peter. *Biblical Themes in Shakespeare: Centring on* King Lear. Tokyo: Sambi, 1975.

———. *Shakespeare's Religious Background*. Bloomington: Indiana UP, 1973.

Montrose, Louis Adrian. "The Purpose of Playing: Reflections on a Shakespearean Anthropology." *Helios* 7.2 (1979–80): 51–74.

Muir, Kenneth, ed. *King Lear*. Arden Shakespeare. 1952. Rev. ed. London: Methuen, 1980.

———. "Samuel Harsnett and *King Lear*." *Review of English Studies* ns 2 (1951): 11–21.

——. "Shakespeare's Imagery—Then and Now." *Shakespeare Survey* 18 (1965): 46-57.

——. *Shakespeare's Sources: Comedies and Tragedies*. London: Methuen, 1957.

——. *The Sources of Shakespeare's Plays*. New Haven: Yale UP, 1978.

Muir, Kenneth, and S. Schoenbaum, eds. *A New Companion to Shakespeare Studies*. Cambridge: Cambridge UP, 1971.

Nims, John Frederick. *Western Wind: An Introduction To Poetry*. 2nd ed. New York: Random, 1983.

Novy, Marianne. "Patriarchy, Mutuality, and Forgiveness in *King Lear*." *Southern Humanities Review* 13 (1979): 281-92.

Nowottny, Winifred M. T. "Some Aspects of the Style of *King Lear*." *Shakespeare Survey* 13 (1960): 49-57.

Onions, C. T. *A Shakespeare Glossary*. 2nd rev. ed. Oxford: Clarendon, 1949.

Ornstein, Robert. *The Moral Vision of Jacobean Tragedy*. Madison: U of Wisconsin P, 1960.

Parker, Barry M. *The Folger Shakespeare Filmography*. Washington, DC: Folger Shakespeare Lib., 1979.

Partridge, Eric. *Shakespeare's Bawdy*. Rev. ed. New York: Dutton, 1969.

Peat, Derek. "'And that's true too': *King Lear* and the Tension of Uncertainty." *Shakespeare Survey* 33 (1980): 43-53.

Pechter, Edward. "On the Blinding of Gloucester." *ELH* 45 (1978): 181-200.

Peckham, Morse. *Man's Rage for Chaos: Biology, Behavior, and the Arts*. Philadelphia: Chilton, 1965.

Perret, Marion. "The Making of *King Lear*." *Shakespeare on Film Newsletter* 8.2 (1984): 1, 7.

Perrett, Wilfrid. *The Story of King Lear from Geoffrey of Monmouth to Shakespeare*. 1904. New York: Johnson, 1970.

Rabkin, Norman. *Shakespeare and the Problem of Meaning*. Chicago: U of Chicago P, 1981.

Rackin, Phyllis. "Delusion as Resolution in *King Lear*." *Shakespeare Quarterly* 21 (1970): 29-34.

Reiss, Timothy J. *Tragedy and Truth: Studies in the Development of a Renaissance and Neoclassical Discourse*. New Haven: Yale UP, 1980.

Ribner, Irving. *Patterns in Shakespearian Tragedy*. 1960. London: Methuen, 1971.

Ridley, M. R., ed. *King Lear*. New Temple Shakespeare. London: Dent, 1935.

Roberts, Preston Thomas, Jr. "The Redemption of King Lear." *Renascence* 26 (1973-74): 189-206.

Roche, Thomas P., Jr. " 'Nothing Almost Sees Miracles': Tragic Knowledge in *King Lear*." Danson 136-62.

Rosen, William. *Shakespeare and the Craft of Tragedy*. Cambridge: Harvard UP, 1960.

Rosenberg, John D. "King Lear and His Comforters." *Essays in Criticism* 16 (1966): 135–46.

Rosenberg, Marvin. *The Masks of* King Lear. Berkeley: U of California P, 1972.

Rothwell, Kenneth S. "Mediating between Student and Shakespeare: Finding a 'Frame of Discourse.' " *Teaching Notes* 4.4 (1980): 1–2.

———. *A Mirror for Shakespeare: A Study Guide for [27 of] the Plays.* 1980. Burlington: IDC, 1982.

———. "Programs for Invention: Themes, Topics, and Shakespeare." *Leaflet* (Journal of the New England Association of Teachers of English) 80.1 (1981): 3–7.

Rowse, A. L. *The England of Elizabeth: The Structure of Society.* New York: Macmillan, 1951.

Sackville, Thomas, and Thomas Norton. *Gorboduc.* Fraser and Rabkin 1: 81–100.

Satin, Joseph, ed. *Shakespeare and His Sources.* Boston: Houghton, 1966.

Schmidt, Alexander. *Shakespeare-Lexicon.* Ed. Gregor I. Sarrazin. 6th ed. 2 vols. Berlin: de Gruyter, 1971.

Schoenbaum, S. *Shakespeare's Lives.* Oxford: Oxford UP, 1970.

———. *William Shakespeare: A Documentary Life.* New York: Oxford UP, 1975.

———. *William Shakespeare: Records and Images.* New York: Oxford UP, 1981.

Sewall, Richard B. *The Vision of Tragedy.* New Haven: Yale UP, 1959.

Shaw, John. "*King Lear*: The Final Lines." *Essays in Criticism* 16 (1966): 261–67.

Siegel, Paul N. *Shakespearean Tragedy and the Elizabethan Compromise.* New York: New York UP, 1957.

Skulsky, Harold. "*King Lear* and the Meaning of Chaos." *Shakespeare Quarterly* 17 (1966): 3–17.

Smith, Gordon Ross. *A Classified Shakespeare Bibliography, 1936-1958.* University Park: Pennsylvania State UP, 1963.

Smith, Irwin. *Shakespeare's Blackfriars Playhouse: Its History and Its Design.* New York: New York UP, 1964.

———. *Shakespeare's Globe Playhouse: A Modern Reconstruction in Text and Scale Drawings.* New York: Scribner's, 1956.

Smith, Lacey Baldwin. *The Elizabethan World.* 1966. Rpt. (with profuse illustrations) as *The Horizon Book of the Elizabethan World.* New York: American Heritage, 1967.

Soellner, Rolf. *Shakespeare's Patterns of Self-Knowledge.* Columbus: Ohio State UP, 1972.

Sophocles. *Oedipus the King.* Trans. Thomas Gould. Prentice-Hall Greek Drama Series. Englewood Cliffs: Prentice, 1970.

Spencer, Theodore. *Shakespeare and the Nature of Man.* 2nd ed. New York: Macmillan, 1949.

Spevack, Marvin. *The Harvard Concordance to Shakespeare.* Cambridge: Belknap–Harvard UP, 1973.

Spivack, Bernard. *Shakespeare and the Allegory of Evil: The History of a Metaphor in Relation to His Major Villains.* New York: Columbia UP, 1958.

Sprague, Arthur Colby. *Shakespeare and the Actors: The Stage Business in His Plays (1660-1905).* Cambridge: Harvard UP, 1944.

Spurgeon, Caroline F. E. *Shakespeare's Imagery and What It Tells Us.* 1935. Cambridge: Cambridge UP, 1965.

Stampfer, J. "The Catharsis of *King Lear.*" *Shakespeare Survey* 13 (1960): 1-10.

Stauffer, Donald A. *Shakespeare's World of Images: The Development of His Moral Ideas.* 1949. Bloomington: Indiana UP, 1973.

Steel, Flora Annie, ed. *English Fairy Tales.* New York: Mayflower, 1979.

Stoll, Elmer Edgar. *Art and Artifice in Shakespeare: A Study in Dramatic Contrast and Illusion.* Cambridge: Cambridge UP, 1933.

Stone, Lawrence. *The Crisis of the Aristocracy: 1558-1641.* Oxford: Clarendon, 1965.

———. *The Family, Sex and Marriage in England, 1500-1800.* New York: Harper, 1977.

Stone, P. W. K. *The Textual History of* King Lear. London: Scolar, 1980.

Styan, J. L. *The Shakespeare Revolution: Criticism and Performance in the Twentieth Century.* Cambridge: Cambridge UP, 1977.

———. *Shakespeare's Stagecraft.* Cambridge: Cambridge UP, 1967.

Sypher, Wylie. *Four Stages of Renaissance Style: Transformations in Art and Literature, 1400-1700.* Garden City: Anchor-Doubleday, 1956.

Talbert, Ernest William. *The Problem of Order: Elizabethan Political Commonplaces and an Example of Shakespeare's Art.* Chapel Hill: U of North Carolina P, 1962.

Tate, Nahum. *The History of King Lear.* 1681. *Five Restoration Adaptations of Shakespeare.* Ed. Christopher Spencer. Urbana: U of Illinois P, 1965. 201-74.

Taylor, Gary. "The War in *King Lear.*" *Shakespeare Survey* 33 (1980): 27-34.

Taylor, Gary, and Michael Warren, eds. *The Division of the Kingdoms: Shakespeare's Two Versions of* King Lear. Oxford: Oxford UP, 1983.

Tilley, Morris Palmer. *A Dictionary of the Proverbs in England in the Sixteenth and Seventeenth Centuries: A Collection of the Proverbs Found in English Literature and the Dictionaries of the Period.* Ann Arbor: U of Michigan P, 1950.

Tillyard, E. M. W. *The Elizabethan World Picture.* London: Chatto, 1943.

Tobin, John J. M. "Apuleius and the Bradleian Tragedies." *Shakespeare Survey* 31 (1978): 33-43.

Traversi, D. A. *An Approach to Shakespeare.* 3rd ed. Garden City: Doubleday, 1969.

Turner, Victor W. *The Ritual Process: Structure and Anti-Structure.* Chicago: Aldine, 1969.

Urkowitz, Steven. "*King Lear* without Tears." *Shakespeare on Film Newsletter* 7.2 (1983): 2.

———. "Lord Olivier's *King Lear.*" *Shakespeare on Film Newsletter* 8.1 (1983): 1, 3.

———. *Shakespeare's Revision of* King Lear. Princeton: Princeton UP, 1980.

Van Doren, Mark. *Shakespeare.* 1939. Garden City: Doubleday, 1953.

van Gennep, Arnold. *The Rites of Passage.* Trans. Monika B. Vizedom and Gabrielle L. Caffee. 1908. London: Routledge, 1960.

Van Laan, Thomas F. "Acting as Action in *King Lear.*" Colie and Flahiff 59–75.

———. *Role-Playing in Shakespeare.* Toronto: U of Toronto P, 1978.

Vickers, Brian, ed. *Shakespeare: The Critical Heritage.* 6 vols. London: Routledge, 1974–81.

Viëtor, Wilhelm, ed. *King Lear: Parallel Texts of the First Quarto and the First Folio.* Shakespeare Reprints 1. Marburg: Elwert'sche, 1892.

Walker, Alice. *Textual Problems of the First Folio.* Cambridge: Cambridge UP, 1953.

Walton, J. K. "Lear's Last Speech." *Shakespeare Survey* 13 (1960): 11–19.

Warren, Michael J. "Quarto and Folio *King Lear* and the Interpretation of Albany and Edgar." *Shakespeare: Pattern of Excelling Nature.* Ed. David Bevington and Jay L. Halio. Newark: U of Delaware P, 1978. 95–107.

Weidhorn, Manfred. "Lear's Schoolmasters." *Shakespeare Quarterly* 13 (1962): 305–16.

Wells, Stanley, ed. *Shakespeare: Select Bibliographical Guides.* London: Oxford UP, 1973.

Welsford, Enid. *The Fool: His Social and Literary History.* London: Faber, 1935.

West, Robert H. *Shakespeare and the Outer Mystery.* Lexington: U of Kentucky P, 1968.

Wheelwright, Philip. *The Burning Fountain: A Study in the Language of Symbolism.* Bloomington: Indiana UP, 1954.

———. *Metaphor and Reality.* Bloomington: Indiana UP, 1962.

Whitaker, Virgil K. *Shakespeare's Use of Learning: An Inquiry into the Growth of His Mind and Art.* San Marino: Huntington Library, 1953.

Wickham, Glynne. *Early English Stages, 1300–1660.* 3 vols. London: Routledge, 1959–81.

Willbern, David. "Shakespeare's Nothing." *Representing Shakespeare: New Psychoanalytic Essays.* Ed. Murray M. Schwartz and Coppélia Kahn. Baltimore: Johns Hopkins UP, 1980. 244–63.

Wilson, Harold S. *On the Design of Shakespearian Tragedy.* Toronto: U of Toronto P, 1957.

Wilson, John Dover, ed. *Life in Shakespeare's England: A Book of Elizabethan Prose.* 2nd ed. 1913. Cambridge: Cambridge UP, 1949.

Wittreich, Joseph. *"Image of that horror": History, Prophecy, and Apocalypse in King Lear.* San Marino: Huntington Library, 1984.

Wright, Louis B. *Middle-Class Culture in Elizabethan England.* Chapel Hill: U of North Carolina P, 1935.

Wright, Louis B., and Virginia A. Lamar, eds. *The Tragedy of King Lear.* Folger Library General Reader's Shakespeare. 1957. New York: Washington Square, 1967.

Zesmer, David M. *Guide to Shakespeare.* New York: Barnes, 1976.

Zitner, Sheldon P. *"King Lear and Its Language."* Colie and Flahiff 3–22.

Films, Video Productions, Slides, and Recordings

Brook, Peter, dir. *King Lear.* Film. With Paul Scofield and Irene Worth. Athena-Laterna Films, 1971. B & w. 134 min. Available from Films Inc., 440 Park Ave. S., New York, NY 10016.

Elliott, Michael, dir. *King Lear.* Video production. With Laurence Olivier and Colin Blakely. Granada Television International, 1983. Col. videocassette. 158 min. Available for rental or purchase on ½" videocassettes (¾" U-Matic) from Films for the Humanities, Inc., Box 2053, Princeton, NJ 08540.

Folger Library Slide Sets. SS-202 (*Costumes in the Age of Shakespeare*), SS-203 (*The Life of Shakespeare*), and SS-212 (*The Globe Theatre*). Each set includes 20 slides, with narrative description of each slide and a Folger booklet. Folger Shakespeare Library, 201 E. Capitol St., SE, Washington, DC 20003.

Kozintsev, Grigori, dir. *King Lear.* Film. With Yuri Jarvet and Elza Radzins. Lenfilm, 1971. B & w. 140 min. Russian, with English subtitles. Available on 16 mm film from Audio Brandon Films, Inc., 34 MacQuesten Parkway St., Mt. Vernon, NY 10550; or on VHS or Beta videocassette from Tamarelle's French Film House, 110 Cohasset Stage Rd., Chico, CA 95926.

Miller, Jonathan, dir. *King Lear.* Video production. With Michael Hordern and Frank Middlemass. BBC-TV/Time-Life, Inc., 1982. Col. videocassette. 180 min. Available for rental or purchase on ½" videocassettes from Time-Life, Inc., Video, Box 666, Radio City Sta., New York, NY 10101.

Rylands, George, dir. *King Lear.* Recording. The Marlowe Society and Professional Players. 4 records. Argo, RG 280–283, 1961.

Sackler, Howard, dir. *King Lear.* Recording. With Paul Scofield. Shakespeare Recording Society. 4 records. Caedmon, SRS-S-233, 1965.

Shakespeare: New Productions (1975-80). Slides. Photography by Thomas F. Holte, commentary by Jean Klene. KaiDib Films International, PO Box 271, Glendale, CA 91209. Also see *Set One (1958-70)* and *Set Two (1970-74)*.

Sherwin, Edwin, dir. *King Lear*. Video production. With James Earl Jones. Prod. Joseph Papp. New York Shakespeare Festival, Central Park, New York, NY. Live performance taped by Public Broadcasting System, 1973.

INDEX